P9-CDH-140

LOSING
IRAQ

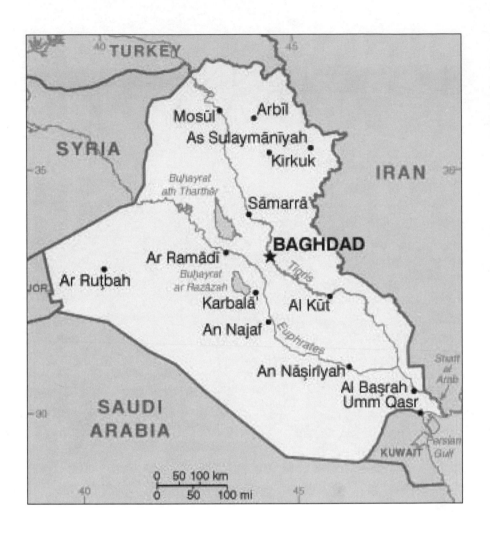

LOSING IRAQ

—◆—

INSIDE THE POSTWAR RECONSTRUCTION FIASCO

DAVID L. PHILLIPS

Former Senior Adviser to the
U.S. Department of State

Westview Press
A Member of the Perseus Books Group

Published by Westview Press,
A Member of the Perseus Books Group

Designed by Brent Wilcox
Text set in 10.5-point Berling Roman

Library of Congress Cataloging-in-Publication Data
Phillips, David L.
   Losing Iraq : inside the postwar reconstruction fiasco / David L. Phillips.
      p.   cm.
   Includes bibliographical references and index.
   ISBN 0-8133-4304-6 (hardcover : alk. paper)
   1. Postwar reconstruction—Iraq.   2. Iraq War, 2003.   I. Title.
DS79.769.P55   2005
956.7044'31—dc22
                                          2005003069

05 06 07 08 / 10 9 8 7 6 5 4 3 2 1

To
SARAH
and our newborn daughters,
TARA *and* MAYA.
May future generations live in a world
free from tyranny and war.

CONTENTS

ACKNOWLEDGMENTS

This book is about the Iraqi people's struggle for freedom. Despite the difficulties faced in Iraq, we owe Iraqis our continued support so that their dream of democracy can be realized.

Iraqis participating in the Democratic Principles Working Group deserve special commendation. So do the Iraqi Kurds with whom I have worked closely for many years. Their sacrifice and the sacrifice of other Iraqis must not be in vain.

INTRODUCTION

The Tigris River swept us downstream until the boatman started the outboard engine and we turned into the current and headed upriver. The wooden fishing boat labored against the swirling brown waters as we slowly made our way across the Tigris from Syria to Iraqi Kurdistan. A complex of military bunkers was visible on a hillside just a couple of kilometers away, and I could make out human figures manning the watchtower. Though we were well within range of skilled marksmen, I was assured that the boat's crossing was a routine occurrence. The Iraqi soldiers in the tower were drinking tea, not readying their weapons.

As we approached the boat landing, a sign came into view: "Welcome to Iraqi Kurdistan." I could see a fleet of Toyota land cruisers waiting in the car park under a Kurdish flag that listed in the hot summer sky. An official from the Kurdistan Democratic Party (KDP) got out of the lead car to greet me. He was accompanied by a group of Kurdish fighters called peshmerga ("those who face death"). The peshmerga are revered in Kurdish society for their martyrdom in the struggle against Saddam Hussein.

The commander of our security detail wore traditional baggy pants, a colorful cummerbund and safari style shirt typical of peshmerga. Despite the dust, his high-laced army boots were perfectly polished. With military precision, he saluted smartly and barked orders as the peshmerga jumped into the back of their vehicles and our convoy got under way.

— —

My involvement in Iraq started in 1988. A Kurdish doctor named Najmaldin Karim visited my office at the Congressional Human Rights Foundation and showed me gruesome photos of Kurdish civilians killed in Halabja, a Kurdish city near the Iraq-Iran border. The photos depicted

1

the twisted corpses of old men in turbans and small girls in colorful garb scattered like rag dolls on the street. Victims hugged their children in silent embraces, anguish frozen on their faces.

On March 16, 1988, an aircraft with Iraqi air force markings circled over Halabja before discharging a deadly yellow cloud containing mustard and sarin nerve gasses. The lethal chemical cocktail burned the skin, eyes, and lungs, and caused cancer, deformities, and neurological damage in its victims. During Saddam's genocidal campaign against the Kurds, thousands of tons of chemical and biological weapons were used to attack as many as two hundred villages and towns in Iraqi Kurdistan.[1] Up to 5,000 people died in Halabja that day.

Soon after the Gulf War, I traveled with Karim to Iraq. The journey started in southeastern Turkey, where we boarded a minibus with other guests traveling from Diyarbakir to Suleimania for a meeting of the Patriotic Union of Kurdistan (PUK). The scene in Habur on the Iraq-Turkey border was absolute chaos. Habur was a remote truck stop, but when the UN imposed sanctions on Iraq after the Gulf War, it became a major transit point for food and other commodities that were being illegally transported into Iraq. Smuggling oil to Turkey, Iraqi trucks strapped canisters under the lorry bed, causing a thick oil slick on the road for miles on either side of the border. Iraq felt like no-man's land. Everyone was armed with an AK–47 or Kalashnikov. We stopped at a roadside eatery that served lamb kabobs before encamping at a private home partly collapsed from an artillery shell.

Though Karim worried that the roads would be impassable, there was no snow and we were able to make our way to Dohuk for lunch with Sami Abdul Rahman. Sami had served as governor of the Northern Territories in the early 1970s, but rejoined the peshmerga when Saddam failed to fulfill his promise of autonomy for Iraqi Kurdistan. Over the years, I would have many pleasant visits with Sami, including a meeting in July 2002 when we spent hours on his patio discussing Iraq's draft constitution.

After Dohuk, Karim and I went to Erbil for an emotional reunion. Karim had not seen his family since fleeing Iraq in 1972. When we walked in the door, it seemed as though they had been waiting for their son all these years. Karim recalled, "It was exciting being with them again. The last time I had seen my brothers they were little boys. Everyone had aged so much." The Karim family told stories about their life in Iraq under Saddam. The father was dignified, the brothers excited. The mother wept and described the family's joy at hearing her son on the Voice of America; Karim reminisced, "My father was proud of what I had done for our people."[2]

We finally arrived in Suleimania. There was no electricity or heat, so I wore my coat and boots to bed. Though Suleimania was under Kurdish control, the city is south of the 36th parallel and did not receive protection from Western aircraft patrolling the no-fly zone. The Kurds lived with insecurity born of the knowledge that Saddam's forces could attack at any time. It had been just three months since Suleimania had been liberated. If Saddam wanted to send a message, there would be no better time than during the PUK Congress the next day.

Because I came from Washington, D.C., the Kurds assumed I was an official emissary of President George H. W. Bush. When I offered support from the American people for freedom, democracy, and human rights (*Azadi, Democraci, Buji*), the conference plenary erupted into wild applause. Barham Salih, a PUK official who would become Iraq's deputy prime minister in 2004, translated my remarks. Covering the microphone, he leaned over and said with a grin, "You should run for president of Kurdistan."

My focus, however, was on humanitarian issues. In Halabja, I spoke with traumatized victims hideously transformed from exposure to chemical weapons. I visited a clinic and saw young children with terrible deformities and brain defects. They recounted tales of torture.

One Kurdish boy described being led at gunpoint onto an army truck. There were thirty large vehicles in the convoy, each crammed with Kurdish women and children. After traveling overnight to an unknown destination in the desert, they were unloaded near a 100-foot-long trench. The Kurds were lined up and executed, their bodies toppling into the trench. The boy told me he was only wounded but feigned death as he lay in the pit filled with bodies and blood. He was able to sneak away before earth-moving equipment came to bury the corpses. A man described his detention by an agency of the intelligence services. His hands were tied behind his back and he was attached to a meat hook in the ceiling; electrodes were then hung from various parts of his body to increase the pain during interrogations.

At a refugee camp outside Suleimania, I met four Shi'a women dressed in black from head to toe. I remember their bright blue eyes filling with tears as they described the atrocities committed against them and their families. After the 1991 uprising, Saddam's security forces had come to their village near Hilla. Their husbands, fathers, and sons were forced to perform sexual acts on each other. Glass bottles were inserted into their rectums and then shattered. Before being executed, the men watched as soldiers raped each of the women. I wanted to cry with them, to reach out and comfort them. However, I knew they were not seeking my comfort or consolation. They wanted me to go home and tell their stories so that the world would know of their suffering and take action against Saddam Hussein.

During the uprising of March 1991, Kurds captured millions of Iraqi secret police documents. The documents were compulsively detailed and unambiguously self-incriminating. In addition to written accounts, evidence included video and audiocassettes of executions and torture sessions. Meetings planning the use of poison gas were also recorded.

The PUK agreed to transport the materials to a secret location in North America. With logistical help from the Defense Intelligence Agency, fourteen tons—more than 4 million pages in 857 cartons—were stored in the U.S. National Security Archives. Jalal Talabani gave me a stack of documents to carry out. As one of the first couriers, I distributed the documents to policymakers and the media as soon as I arrived back in the United States.

During my return to Iraqi Kurdistan in August 1993, Ahmad Chalabi gave me a tour of the Iraqi National Congress (INC) headquarters. The facility was a beehive of activity. It bristled with state-of-the-art computer, communications, and spy equipment. Chalabi described the INC's activities to overthrow Saddam. Over the next decade, Chalabi would emerge as a polarizing figure, not only with Iraqis but also with Americans.

In 1995, Chalabi had a falling out with the Central Intelligence Agency over a botched coup attempt that was infiltrated by Saddam's agents. To make matters worse, conflict broke out between the KDP and PUK. When Talabani invited cooperation with Iranian forces, the KDP sought assistance from Saddam's Republican Guard to drive the PUK out of their Suleimania stronghold and across the Iranian border. During the debacle, Iraqi Republican Guard units overran the INC headquarters in Salahuddin and executed scores of dissidents.

Saddam emerged stronger and in greater control. A perverse paradox came to pass. Saddam had become the guarantor of Kurdish autonomy. As long as he remained in power, the U.S. and Britain would protect the

Kurds. In the event of Saddam's removal, the Kurds' future would be uncertain.

— —

During my visits to Iraq, I came to appreciate how Saddam's authoritarian rule had suppressed simmering hostilities between Iraq's ethnic and religious groups. Kurds were wary of Arab Shi'a, whom they thought would transform Iraq into an Islamist state on the model of Iran; Arab Sunnis feared domination by Iraq's Shi'a majority; Iraqis and Arabs in neighboring countries were suspicious of Kurds for their secular ways and pro-Western positions. Alliances are always shifting in a part of the world where "the enemy of my enemy is my friend."

I learned several important lessons from working with Iraqis over the years. Iraq's problems always arose because of abuses by the central government; therefore, decentralizing authority was the best way to harmonize competing claims between Iraq's factions. Many Iraqis, especially Iraqi exiles and Kurds, see federalism as the most effective system for power sharing. By preserving a meaningful role for Baghdad, federalism can fulfill democratic aspirations while strengthening territorial integrity.

Historically, Iraq's internal affairs had been influenced by meddlesome neighbors who seek a stake in Iraq's future. The Gulf War was a victory for multilateralism; George H. W. Bush established an international coalition, including many Arab states that not only gave political and logistical support but also helped finance the military campaign. Establishing an international coalition helped foster international cooperation after the war.

Although George W. Bush is often criticized for not having had a postwar plan for Iraq, these charges are baseless. Through the Future of Iraq Project, extensive planning involved seventeen federal agencies and hundreds of Iraqis. It spent $5 million and produced detailed recommendations for running Iraq. Because I had hands-on experience working with Iraqis, the State Department asked me to facilitate the Democratic Principles Working Group, which the Iraqis called "The Mother of all Working Groups."

The problem was not the absence of a plan. Iraq was thrown into crisis when Bush administration officials, especially Pentagon political appointees, rushed to war and decided to ignore the planning that was underway.

That the Bush administration attacked Iraq without a strategy to win the peace was a personal disappointment. Upon realizing that the Future of Iraq Project was being ignored, I resigned as a senior adviser from the State Department on September 11, 2003.

— —

Losing Iraq is necessarily a selective work, combining insider information with knowledgeable observation garnered from my position at the Council on Foreign Relations and as an analyst for NBC News. The book describes the extent of planning, what went wrong, and why. It also asserts that, after a year of failed occupation, the Bush administration came full circle in adopting many recommendations of the Future of Iraq Project. But by then, the well was poisoned. What would have been hard had been made even harder.

The book considers the context in which the United States decided on military action in Iraq. The September 11, 2001, terrorist attacks had a profound effect on President Bush and the American people. To confront terrorism, Bush abandoned the Cold War emphasis on deterrence and embraced a Doctrine of Preemption affirming the right of the United States to attack potential foes before they could harm the United States. By the time Bush gave his "axis of evil" speech in January 2002, preemption had become a core principle of U.S. foreign policy. The link between terrorist organizations and state sponsors of terrorism had emerged as the strategic cornerstone of the administration's war against terrorism.

The 1998 Iraqi Liberation Act made regime change official U.S. policy, but efforts to organize the Iraqi opposition floundered until Bush's election. Bush's closest advisers turned their attention to Iraq immediately after 9/11. Vice President Dick Cheney was the chief proponent of toppling Saddam Hussein. Defense Secretary Donald H. Rumsfeld saw Iraq as an opportunity to demonstrate America's unparalleled military might while transforming the military into a faster and more mechanized force. Pentagon political appointees, such as Deputy Defense Secretary Paul D. Wolfowitz, and other neo-conservatives such as Richard N. Perle, who chaired the Defense Policy Board, envisioned Iraq as a prototype for democratizing the Middle East. The "new Iraq" would be a launch point for undermining the Ba'athists in Syria; it would pressure the mullahs in Iran, enhance Israel's security, and transform rogue states into democracies serving U.S. energy and security interests.

I believe that Bush decided to remove Saddam through force if necessary when his national security team met in Crawford, Texas, on August 21, 2002. Bush had already proved his willingness to forego multilateral institutions and agreements that, in his view, impeded the pursuit of national interests. Cheney believed the UN was irrelevant and wanted to move immediately; however, Bush sided with Secretary of State Colin L. Powell in agreeing to give diplomacy a last chance.

When Bush addressed the UN General Assembly on September 12, 2002, he invoked the memory of terror attacks against the United States and challenged the world body to enforce its resolutions requiring Iraq's disarmament. If the United Nations was not able or willing to disarm Saddam, Bush made it clear that the United States would act alone to eliminate a gathering threat and liberate the Iraqi people.

— —

How could such noble intentions go so wrong? The White House and Pentagon political appointees thought they could liberate a country without talking to those they were liberating. Of course, military victory was never in doubt. The problem occurred in the execution of postwar plans to stabilize and democratize Iraq.

When it came to nation-building, the Bush administration did not have a detailed program. All it had was one person—Ahmad Chalabi—whom neo-conservatives wanted to anoint as Iraq's future leader. Chalabi provided bogus intelligence on Iraq's weapons of mass destruction (WMD). He convinced the Pentagon that Iraqis would welcome coalition forces "with flowers." When concerns were raised about chaos after Saddam's removal, Chalabi claimed to control an underground security structure with tens of thousands of Iraqis, which he would activate as soon as coalition forces entered Baghdad.

Relations between the Office of the Secretary of Defense (OSD) and the State Department became intensely acrimonious. U.S. officials vied for control over the Iraq policy. In the process, Pentagon political appointees ran roughshod over the State Department. Powell took the brunt for advocating multilateralism and a UN role.

To foster partnership and enhance legitimacy, the Future of Iraq Project tried to engage Iraqis representing the country's diverse ethnic and religious groups. However, it was clear from the beginning that empowering Iraqis was antithetical to the Pentagon's goal of pushing

Chalabi into power. Advocates of military action grew increasingly concerned that further planning would reveal difficulties and weaken the case for war.

A pattern was established during the planning for war, which kept recurring at key moments during Iraq's postwar transition. U.S. officials either ignored the advice of Iraqis or listened only to Iraqis who told them what they wanted to hear. The OSD believed that after a brief transition period, authority could be handed over to an interim government dominated by Iraqi exiles. It thought that, after dismantling the Ba'ath Party, Iraq's technocrats would transfer their loyalties to a new administration and Iraq would continue to function more or less as before. It assumed that the costs of reconstruction would be paid almost entirely from oil revenues.

The Future of Iraq Project was no silver bullet for Iraq's problems. To be sure, its reports were not definitive blueprints. Pentagon officials thought the endeavor was too theoretical and academic. But their outright dismissal—and even undermining—of the project was a serious mistake. No formal directive was issued terminating the Future of Iraq Project; it just ceased to function after the White House assigned postwar responsibility to the OSD in January 2003.

— —

As the successor to the Future of Iraq Project, General Jay M. Garner's Office for Reconstruction and Humanitarian Assistance (ORHA) focused its planning on a humanitarian emergency involving the displacement of more than a million Iraqis, including the possible use of WMD. ORHA also anticipated oil-well fires and Iraq's neighbors sending in troops. None of these contingencies came to pass. After just a few months on the job, Garner was dismissed and replaced by Ambassador L. Paul Bremer III.

After the statue of Saddam was toppled in Firdos Square on April 9, 2003, Iraqis could not believe that the formidable U.S. military was able to vanquish Saddam's Republican Guard yet lacked the capabilities to prevent looting and control civil strife. More than any other factor, the coalition's inability to curtail the escalating violence poisoned Iraqis against the United States. Worsening security conditions eroded America's standing with Iraqis and transformed the "liberation" into what U.S. officials described as "occupation."

Bremer made a series of catastrophic decisions that compounded problems. While the Future of Iraq Project anticipated that war criminals in the Iraqi armed forces and intelligence services would be prosecuted, it envisioned untainted elements in the security structure working in partnership with coalition forces. When Bremer's Coalition Provisional Authority (CPA) issued a decree disbanding the army and then failed to pay the salaries and pensions of army personnel, Bremer transformed 400,000 Iraqis and their extended families from potential partners into antagonists.

Instead of targeting individuals, Bremer's de-Ba'athification plan emphasized guilt through association. Though the Ba'ath leadership was responsible for terrible atrocities, including genocide, not all Ba'ath members were war criminals. Many Iraqis joined because they had no choice. Even doctors and teachers were required to join the party if they wanted a job.

The United States limited the UN's postwar role by scorning the world body at the outset. Charged with irrelevance, the UN was wary of involvement. Though UN Secretary General Kofi Annan believed the war was illegal, he sent Sergio Vieira de Mello, his special representative, to Baghdad. The United Nations suspended operations when Sergio and twenty-one others were killed during a terrorist attack on UN headquarters in Baghdad on August 19, 2003.

After decades of suffering Saddam's tyranny, Iraqis wanted to assume responsibility for self-government immediately after liberation. When Bremer appointed the Iraqi Governing Council, it was rejected by Iraqis as a puppet of the United States. He named a committee to develop plans for drafting Iraq's constitution, but Ayatollah Ali al-Sistani, Iraq's most respected Shi'a cleric, insisted that the constitution could be drafted only by a democratically elected body. Sistani also rejected Bremer's plan for indirect elections.

One of Bremer's last decrees concerned national elections. Determining there was not enough time to conduct a census or draw district lines, he instructed block voting for nationwide elections to select a national assembly. The decision undermined the representation of minorities. It also precluded the possibility of postponing elections in parts of Iraq gripped by violence.

The Transitional Administrative Law (TAL)—Iraq's interim constitution—was objectively the CPA's greatest achievement. When it was adopted on March 8, 2003, the interim constitution was heralded as a breakthrough in Iraqi governance. It enshrined democracy, a bill of rights, and federalism. Drafted by some of the same Iraqis who participated in the Future of Iraq Project, the TAL bore a striking resemblance to documents produced by the Democratic Principles Working Group.

Many Iraqis, especially Arab Shi'a, rejected the interim constitution because of the CPA's involvement. They complained that it was negotiated in a secret process and approved without hearings or public debate. In particular, Sistani objected to preferences for Iraqi Kurds and the limited role of Islam. Sponsored by the United States, UN Security Council Resolution 1453 recognized the interim government but failed even to mention the Transitional Administrative Law. The decision to abrogate the TAL turned it into a relic of the Bush administration's failed efforts to reshape Iraq.

— —

The Bush administration will ultimately be judged for the reasons it went to war—and what it leaves behind in Iraq.

It is now known that U.S. officials exaggerated the imminent threat of Iraq's WMD; Wolfowitz admitted, "For reasons that have a lot to do with the U.S. government bureaucracy, we settled on the one reason that everyone could agree on which was weapons of mass destruction."[4] Charles A. Deulfer, the chief U.S. weapons inspector, concluded in his report that, at the time of the U.S. invasion, Iraq did not possess chemical or biological weapons and was not seeking to develop nuclear weapons. The 9/11 Commission found no collaborative relationship between Iraq and al-Qaeda. Revelations that U.S. soldiers tortured detainees at Abu Ghraib eroded the virtuous claim that the United States went to war to end the era of torture chambers and mass graves.

— —

It is still too early to assess the final outcome of developments in Iraq. However, the notion of establishing a liberal democracy has been lost. Despite the cost of troops and treasure, idealism was overwhelmed by a brutal insurgency and the halting process of restoring sovereignty to Iraqis.

After 9/11, the nexus between a rogue state, as Iraq was, and a terror organization, such as al-Qaeda, was a truly frightening prospect. Having seen firsthand the impact of chemical weapons in Halabja, I believed the president when he insisted that Iraq had WMD and maintained that Saddam was an imminent threat. As the drums of war beat louder, I reconnected with the Kurds and other Iraqis. If war was inevitable, I wanted Iraqis to have the best chance of realizing their democratic aspirations.

— —

The Iraq war will not be the last time the United States uses its military to eliminate a rogue regime or preempt an adversary from acquiring weapons of mass destruction. Though events in Iraq are still unfolding, I hope that applying lessons from Iraq can help inform the transition from authoritarianism to democracy in other countries.

The Future of Iraq Project did not have all the answers. However, its findings, had they been heeded, could have provided useful guidance enabling the U.S. to fulfill its promise of liberation. Ignoring it was just the first in a series of mistakes. The resulting postwar fiasco undermined U.S. interests and tragically betrayed the hopes of the Iraqi people.

David L. Phillips
New York City
July 1, 2004

CHAPTER 1

THE DRUMS OF WAR

G EORGE W. BUSH DID NOT IMAGINE THAT PREEMPTION and nation-building would preoccupy his presidency. However, the 9/11 terror attacks gave Bush a defining mission. To defend the American homeland and U.S. global interests, the United States would retaliate against failed states, such as Afghanistan, that provided sanctuary to al-Qaeda or other shadowy terrorist networks. It would also act preemptively, targeting rogue regimes to prevent them from developing weapons of mass destruction (WMD), which could be used against the United States or given to terror groups.

Having traveled overseas only a couple of times, it is clear that Bush lacked knowledge about international issues before he won the White House. His farthest trip away from home was to China, when his father was ambassador. During that visit, the younger Bush never left the embassy compound.

Bush's lack of international experience did not, however, make him an isolationist. During the 2000 campaign, he professed support for U.S. engagement in world affairs, insisting that "to build a proud tower of protectionism and isolation would invite challenges to our power."[1]

George W. Bush embraces the use of U.S. diplomatic, economic, and military might to build a better world and to promote global freedom. Consistent with America's tradition and heritage, Bush maintains that the United States would never use its unparalleled military strength for national advantage. Speaking for the president, national security adviser Condoleezza Rice extolled the purity of America's mission: "We may be the only great power in history that prefers greatness to power and justice to glory."[2]

Bush's global goals are consistent with those of his predecessors dating back to President Harry Truman. According to Truman, "It must be the policy of the United States to support free peoples who are resisting attempted subjugation."[3] To this end, Truman made a strategic decision that U.S. power could be effectively projected via international organizations. He sponsored the Marshall Plan to rebuild Europe; NATO's (the North Atlantic Treaty Organisation) creation in 1949 also affirmed the link between U.S. security interests and those of Western Europe. Regarding the means to achieve objectives, Truman's successors all affirmed the view that America's extensive overseas interests could best be defended through international organizations and alliances— until George W. Bush.

Bush differs from his predecessors, including his father, on the instrumentalities for exercising power. He is wary of working with international organizations lest those entanglements impede U.S. interests. He is prepared to engage multilaterally, but only on his terms. Bush believes that leadership means the courage to do what he thinks is right and in the national interest. Even if other countries object at first, Bush is convinced that they will eventually come around to the U.S. point of view.

Bush's antipathy towards internationalism and his willingness to go it alone stand in marked contrast to the views of President Bill Clinton, who championed globalization and relied extensively on a web of interconnected interests. However, Bush reflexively rejected Clinton's initiatives, accusing him of tainting America's image and squandering its prestige internationally.

Decrying the principle of humanitarian intervention, Bush and his advisers criticized Clinton's deployment of U.S. forces to Haiti, Somalia, Bosnia, and even Kosovo. Using troops for nation building was anathema. As Rice flatly stated, "The 82nd airborne should not escort kids to kindergarten."[4] Bush was just as emphatic: "We should not send our troops to stop ethnic cleansing and genocide outside of our strategic interest. I don't like genocide and I don't like ethnic cleansing, but the president must set clear parameters as to where troops ought to be used and when they ought to be used."[5]

During the first months of Bush's presidency, U.S. allies realized that Bush was serious about foregoing multilateral institutions and agreements. Though fifty-four countries ratified the Kyoto Protocol, Rice proclaimed that the climate-control treaty was "dead."[6] The administration withdrew from the Comprehensive Test Ban Treaty; balked at a new protocol to the Biological Weapons Convention; opposed a pact to control small-arms trafficking; and launched a determined and heavy-handed campaign to undermine the International Criminal Court.

But when it came to Iraq, Bush was initially content to continue his predecessor's policy of exerting pressure on Saddam Hussein through multilateral sanctions and support for groups in exile. Bush endorsed the 1998 Iraq Liberation Act, which allocated $97 million in U.S. government goods and services to support Iraqi oppositionists trying to overthrow Saddam. In 2001, Bush sought to strengthen the UN's role by replacing existing sanctions with so-called smart sanctions targeting dual use and military goods. Colin Powell stated, "We have kept [Saddam] contained, kept him in his box."[7]

Though Bush's national security team focused on traditional threats and big power politics, Bush bore a personal grudge against Saddam. Indeed, Bush came into office with the idea of addressing unfinished business from the Gulf War and avenging Saddam's attempted assassination of his father in 1993. To George W. Bush, Saddam was more than a tyrant bent on developing weapons of mass destruction. He was the "guy that wanted to kill my dad."[8]

IF George W. Bush had ever been inclined to find false security behind America's borders, 9/11 changed all that. The terror strikes had a huge impact on Bush personally, as they did upon every American: The continental United States was attacked for the first time since the War of 1812. The American people felt an unprecedented sense of vulnerability.

Within a few days, the U.S. Congress unanimously gave Bush permission to use "all necessary and appropriate force against those nations, organizations, or persons he determines planned, authorized, committed, or aided the terrorist attacks that occurred on September 11, 2001."[9] Reflecting the international community's united support, France's *Le Monde* bore the headline, "We Are All Americans."[10] A few days later, the UN Security Council adopted Resolution 1368, which condemned the attacks and authorized all necessary steps in response; NATO invoked Article 5, affirming that the attack on the United States represented an attack on the Alliance.

Bush concluded that the United States should aggressively prosecute a global war on terror and destroy its enemies. He warned, "We will not wait for the authors of mass murder to gain weapons of mass destruction. We must act now, because we must lift this dark threat from our age and save generations to come."[11]

The 9/11 attacks also prompted a reevaluation of the overall U.S. security strategy that had existed since the beginning of the Cold War. Bush came to believe that

> deterrence—the promise of massive retaliation against nations means nothing against shadowy terrorist networks with no nation or citizen to defend. Containment is not possible when unbalanced dictators with weapons of mass destruction can deliver those weapons or missiles or secretly provide them to terrorist allies. The war on terror will not be won on the defensive. We must take the battle to the enemy, disrupt his plans, and confront the worst threats before they emerge. In the world we have entered, the only path to safety is the oath of action. And this nation will act.[12]

The internation community grew increasingly alarmed by Bush's penchant for unilateral action. Fears were compounded by his moral invocations concerning the conduct of U.S. foreign policy. In jihadist vocabulary similar to Osama bin Laden's, Bush discarded nuance by dividing the world into good and evil. With deep conviction, he proclaimed that "our responsibility to history is already clear: to answer these attacks and rid the world of evil."[13] He also threatened: "We will pursue nations that provide aid or safe haven to terrorism. Every nation in every region now has a decision to make. Either you are with us or you are with the terrorists."[14] Bush pronounced U.S. intervention in Afghanistan a "crusade" and declared that "liberty is not America's gift to the world. Liberty is God's gift to every human being in the world."[15]

The United States was at war, but it was not clear who the enemy was. The Defense Policy Board, a standing group of defense and national security experts that advises the secretary of defense, met in the Pentagon on September 19, 2001. The former Pentagon adviser Richard Perle was accompanied by Ahmad Chalabi, the leader of the Iraqi National Congress. Chalabi proceeded to make a strong argument for skipping Afghanistan and attacking Iraq. Though al-Qaeda was harbored by the Taliban in Afghanistan, Chalabi argued that Iraq was more threatening in a dangerous world where, according to the seventeenth-century English philosopher Thomas Hobbes, "Life is war of all against all."

Richard A. Clarke, Bush's antiterrorism chief, was amazed when, days after 9/11, Donald Rumsfeld broached the idea of bombing Iraq. Clarke pointed out that there was no evidence linking al-Qaeda and Iraq. According to Clarke, Rumsfeld complained about the poor selection of high-value targets in Afghanistan. "I don't want to put a million-dollar missile on a five-dollar tent."[16] "No, no. Al-Qaeda is in Afghanistan," Clarke responded, "We need to bomb Afghanistan."[17]

Bush instructed Clarke to find a link between Iraq and the al-Qaeda terrorist attacks. According to Clarke, "The president dragged me into a room with a couple of other people, shut the door, and said, 'I want you to find whether Iraq did this.' The entire conversation left me in absolutely no doubt that George Bush wanted me to come back with a report that said, 'Iraq did this.'"[18]

Treasury Secretary Paul O'Neill said that regime change in Iraq was on the agenda at Bush's first National Security Council meeting on January 30, 2001. Instead of focusing on Osama bin Laden and a strategy for securing and stabilizing Afghanistan, Bush and his advisers seized on 9/11 to make the case for overthrowing Saddam Hussein.

B USH insisted: "I'm tired of swatting flies. I'm tired of playing defense. I want to play offense. I want to take the fight to the terrorists."[19] Recalibrating America's approach to terrorism, Bush also wanted to send an unambiguous warning to countries that sponsor terrorism: "We want to cause them to change their views."[20]

The administration saw Afghanistan as the first stage in an open-ended global war against terrorism. Bush wanted action. One week after the terrorist attacks, George J. Tenet, the CIA director, presented Bush with a "Worldwide Attack Matrix" detailing ongoing or planned covert antiterrorism activities in eighty countries. Anxieties were fueled by anthrax mailings. Americans felt a sense of imminent risk when it was reported that a "dirty bomb" had been smuggled into the United States.

After 9/11, the administration focused on failed states that provided haven to terrorists. The administration was also concerned about states that aided or provided safe harbor to terror groups such as Afghanistan, Iran, Syria, Yemen, and Sudan. In addition, U.S. troops were deployed and military assistance significantly expanded to weak states such as Georgia, Nepal, and in the Philippines. By the time President Bush delivered his "axis of evil" speech on January 29, 2002, the link between terrorist organizations and state sponsors of terrorism had become the cornerstone of the administration's national security strategy.

Bush addressed the nation: "States like Iran, Iraq, and North Korea, constitute an axis of evil. By seeking weapons of mass destruction, these regimes pose a grave and growing danger. They could provide these arms to terrorists, giving them the means to match their hatred. They could attack our allies or attempt to blackmail the United States. In any of these cases the price of indifference would be catastrophic." Presaging the "Doctrine of Preemption," Bush fired a verbal shot at those who might conspire to harm the United States. "I will not wait on events, while dangers gather. I will not stand by, as peril draws closer and closer. The United States of America will not permit the world's most dangerous regimes to threaten us with the world's most destructive weapons."[21]

The preference for unilateral action reflected a growing aversion to diplomacy, which is inherently about negotiation and compromise. Some senior officials disdained diplomacy and believed there should be no negotiation with states that support terror groups. They also argued that force is the only appropriate response to terrorist threats.

Administration hawks were mostly concerned about Iraq, which had defied sixteen UN Security Council resolutions demanding its disarmament. "The leader of Iraq is an evil man," he proclaimed in ratcheted-up rhetoric. "We are watching him carefully."[22] Bush underscored the danger posed by terrorists possessing weapons of mass destruction, demanding that Saddam surrender his WMD and allow enforcement by international monitors. When asked what he would do if Saddam refused, Bush replied, "He'll find out."[23]

Public statements about Iraq coincided with private instructions laying the groundwork for war. Within days of the Taliban's fall, Bush began accelerating plans to topple Saddam. In December 2001, he told General Tommy R. Franks that the Defense Department's Central Command (CENTCOM) should start preparing war plans for Iraq, to include lines of attack, specific targets for U.S. missiles and warplanes, and the composition of highly mechanized ground forces. From $100 to $200 million in additional funds was given to the CIA for covert operations. Clarke also asserted that the White House diverted $700 million from Afghanistan to pay for infrastructure that could be used for military operations in Iraq.

"**F**UCK Saddam. We're taking him out,"[24] Bush told Rice in March 2002. Abandoning disarmament in lieu of regime change represented a sea change in America's approach to Iraq. On *Face the Nation*, Rice left no room for doubt: "The world will be much safer when the Iraqi people have a regime that they deserve, instead of the regime they have."[25]

The case for war included intelligence reports on the existence of mobile biological weapons labs, stockpiles of anthrax, and aerial drones designed to deliver WMD. The administration also believed there was a link between Iraq and al-Qaeda, the insinuation being that Saddam was behind the World Trade Center bombing of 1993. Press reports indicated that Mohammed Atta had met with an Iraqi agent in Prague just months before 9/11.

Bush was convinced that "Iraq was involved."[26] Dick Cheney was the administration's most vehement and persuasive advocate of regime change. In 2002, he made approximately ten visits to the CIA headquarters at Langley Field to discuss information that could be used to support the administration's war plans in Iraq. Cheney threw down the gauntlet in an address to the Veterans of Foreign Wars Association:

> Armed with an arsenal of these weapons of terror, and seated atop 10 percent of the world's oil reserves, Saddam Hussein could then be expected to seek domination of the entire Middle East, take control of a great portion of the world's energy supplies, directly threaten America's friends throughout the region, and subject the United States or any other nation to nuclear blackmail. . . . Simply stated, there is no doubt that Saddam Hussein now has weapons of mass destruction. There is no doubt he is amassing them to use against our friends, against our allies, and against us. And there is no doubt that his aggressive regional ambitions will lead him into future confrontations with his neighbors—confrontations that will involve both the weapons he has today, and the ones he will continue to develop with his oil wealth.[27]

As it became clear that the administration wanted to attack Iraq, Powell accepted the inevitability of a confrontation with Saddam. He testified to the Senate: "It has long been, for several years now, a policy of the United States government that regime change would be in the best interests of the region, the best interests of the Iraqi people. And we are

looking into a variety of options that would bring that about."[28] The former allegation was later dismissed, the latter went unverified.

B Y the time I traveled to northern Iraq to discuss constitutional
power-sharing arrangements in the summer of 2002, the United
States had already telegraphed plans to broaden the war on terror beyond Afghanistan.

Though North Korea boasted about its nuclear weapons program,
Bush depicted Iraq as the most dangerous country in the axis of evil. He
asserted that Saddam intended to use his weapons of mass destruction to
attack the United States, or that he would provide WMD to terrorists in-
tent on attacking America.

"America must not ignore the threat gathering against us," Bush said.
"Facing clear evidence of peril, we cannot wait for the final proof—the
smoking gun—that could come in the form of a mushroom cloud."[31] In
graphic terms, Bush also invoked Saddam's torture chambers and rape
rooms; I needed no persuading about the brutality of the Iraqi regime.

In the years between 2002 and my previous visit to Iraqi Kurdistan, the
Kurds had made the most of their de facto independence to realize
progress and prosperity. They had a lot to gain by getting rid of Saddam
and establishing a democratic Iraq, but they also had a lot to lose. I wanted
to hear directly from the Kurds what they thought about U.S. military action, so I contacted them to arrange my passage to Iraqi Kurdistan.

CHAPTER 2

— ◆ —

IRAQI KURDISTAN

AFTER THE U.S. HAD ESTABLISHED A NO-FLY ZONE FOR Iraqi Kurdistan, Saddam Hussein tried to squeeze the Kurds by withdrawing his troops and imposing a total embargo of food and fuel. The plan backfired. Instead of returning to the fold, Kurds established self-rule, transforming the Kurdish area into a laboratory for Iraq's future democratic development. During my visits to Iraqi Kurdistan in 1992 and 1993, I was impressed by how the Kurds had made the most of their isolation to recover from Saddam's genocide and start rebuilding their homeland.

As a special government employee, I had the latitude to initiate projects so long as they were consistent with U.S. objectives. When I told Under-secretary of State Marc Grossman of my plan to return to Iraqi Kurdistan, he arranged for his colleagues in the Bureau of Near Eastern Affairs (NEA) to brief me; Grossman asked that I report back after my trip.

Qubad Talabani, who represented the Patriotic Union of Kurdistan (PUK) in Washington, D.C., offered to arrange my transit through Syria to Iraqi Kurdistan with Syria's Interior Ministry. Turkey had tightened its border with Iraq. The only way of entering, other than through Baghdad, was by way of Syria and then by boat across the Tigris River. Qubad assured me that Syrian intelligence would approve the application because it was endorsed by the "big guy." Qubad was referring to his father, Jalal Talabani, the long-standing PUK leader. After a delay of several weeks, Qubad called to tell me that the Syrians expected me at the border crossing on July 5, 2002.

When I asked for a letter confirming the arrangements, Qubad was amused. Instead of a letter, I was given a code number—3462—and told to appear at an outpost in the eastern desert of Syria, about an hour's journey from the city of Qamishle. There, in a cinderblock hut, an official would be waiting with a registry containing my name, passport information, and code number. He would certify my departure and provide a document permitting my return from Iraq back into Syria.

The PUK's Damascus representative was supposed to meet me at the airport and take care of loose ends. When my flight from Vienna arrived after midnight, the airport was chaotic with throngs waiting outside customs to greet friends and family. Though I had a sinking feeling when no one stepped forward to meet me, Muhammad finally approached after everyone else had left the terminal. We went to his flat for a couple hours of rest and, before dawn, returned to the airport just as the Syrian Airlines domestic counter opened. I paid $20 in cash for a ticket on the first flight to Qamishle.

Upon arrival, the Kurds gave me a breakfast of yogurt, cheese, and toast. We then drove through the desert, passing small oil-pumping stations that shimmered in the oppressive morning heat. After crossing the Tigris into Iraqi Kurdistan, I was greeted by officials from the Kurdistan Democratic Party (KDP). Our convoy sped off to the home of Massoud Barzani, son of the legendary Kurdish leader Mula Mustafa Barzani.

An old Kurdish adage goes: "The Kurds have no friend but the mountains." Kurds have a bitter history of betrayal and disappointment.

When the United States helped broker the Algiers Accord, which ended a border dispute between Iraq and Iran in 1974, Tehran withdrew its support for the Iraqi Kurds and so enabled Saddam to use brute force in putting down the Kurdish rebellion. When the Iraqi Kurds sided with Iran during the 1980–1988 Iran-Iraq War, Saddam Hussein feared a joint Iranian-Kurdish offensive. In 1988, he appointed his first cousin, Ali Hassan al-Majid ("Chemical Ali"), secretary general of the Ba'ath Party's Northern Bureau and gave him "special powers . . . to solve the Kurdish problem and slaughter the saboteurs."[1] Chemical Ali then banned "all human existence" in a thirty-kilometer swath of territory on the Iraq-Iran border and ordered "random bombardments using artillery, helicopters and aircraft in order to kill the largest number of persons present in these prohibited zones." He proclaimed: "All persons captured shall be detained and interrogated by the security services and those between fifteen and seventy shall be executed after useful information has been obtained."[2]

From February 23 to September 6, 1988, Ali led a systematic effort to exterminate the Kurds of northern Iraq. The campaign was called Anfal, which means literally "the spoils." The term is drawn from the Quran's eighth verse (*Sura*), which describes how the followers of Muhammad razed and pillaged the villages of nonbelievers. As many as 182,000 people perished during the Anfal campaign, which included the use of chemical weapons in an attack against Halabja on March 16, 1988.

Although human rights activists were outraged by Saddam's actions, the Reagan administration fought hard against the Prevention of Genocide Act of 1988 (S. 2763). In large part due to the efforts of Reagan's national security adviser, Colin Powell, the legislation never made it out of committee.

The Anfal campaign's scorched-earth policy had destroyed half of Iraq's farmland. Washington responded by expanding food assistance to Iraq through the U.S. Agricultural Commodities Export Credit Program. Legislators protested the U.S. coddling of Iraq. At a hearing of the Senate Foreign Relations Committee on June 15, 1989, Senator Alfonse D'Amato, a Republican from New York, called Saddam the "mad dog of the Middle East."[3] Senator Jesse Helms, a Republican from North Carolina, unfurled a chart that listed companies providing chemical weapons to Iraq. Senator Nancy Kassebaum, a Republican from Kansas, courageously advocated cutting ties, even though wheat farmers in her home state would be adversely affected. When Iraq invaded Kuwait, President George H. W. Bush reversed U.S. policy and started a massive military buildup, its mission being to oust Saddam.

After a six-week pounding by coalition armed forces, the Gulf War ended on February 28, 1991. At the urging of Dick Cheney, who was then the defense secretary, the United States decided not to march on Baghdad. Cheney forcefully argued that invading Iraq would cause the country's bloody breakup.

Iraq is a mosaic of ethnic and religious groups. Under Ottoman rule, which stretched from the Balkans to Basra and lasted for centuries, the territory of modern-day Iraq was divided into administrative regions called "villayets," their provincial capitals being Basra, Baghdad, and Mosul. Though Arab Sunnis represented less than 20 percent of the population, the Ottomans assigned them leading positions in Iraq's administration. When the state of Iraq was created after World War I, Britain preserved the dominant role of Iraq's Arab Sunnis. Severely marginalized by the Ottomans, the British, and the Ba'athists, Iraq's

Arab Shi'a majority launched an insurgency during the final days of the Gulf War.

By mid-March, 70 percent of Basra province in southern Iraq was in open rebellion. The Supreme Council for Islamic Revolution in Iraq (SCIRI), an Iranian-backed Shi'a group, reported that their militia had executed the provincial governor, the chief of police, the security chief, and the head of the local Ba'ath Party. They also captured the city of Hilla in the Euphrates River Valley, sixty miles south of Baghdad.

When the Kurds launched an uprising of their own, Saddam faced insurrections across the country. On March 19, Kirkuk fell to the Kurdish peshmerga, who fired celebratory shots in the air as they rolled into the city on pick-up trucks. Their jubilation was short-lived. Ceasefire terms denied Iraq the use of fixed-wing aircraft, but permitted helicopter gun ships. Using American-made Sikorsky helicopters, Saddam counterattacked agains Shi'a militia in the south and Kurdish peshmerga in the north.

The United States did nothing to prevent Saddam's deadly strikes. Calculating that neither the Kurds nor the Shi'a were strong enough to take over Iraq, George H. W. Bush decided to forsake the very people he had incited into rebellion. He was influenced by key coalition partners. The Saudis were concerned that a pro-Iranian Shi'a leadership would emerge in the south, giving Tehran a power base on Saudi Arabia's border. The Turkish government in Ankara, which was waging its own struggle against Kurdish separatists, worried that the emergence of an independent Iraqi Kurdistan would further incite Turkey's restive Kurdish population. To rid Iraq of Saddam, the United States was banking on a coup by one of the army's generals rather than a popular uprising. The Arab world concluded that, for all its talk about democracy in the Middle East, the United States preferred dictatorship to an unpredictable political process.

Saddam's reprisal was merciless—about 200,000 Arab Shi'a were killed. Near Hilla, a mass grave contained an estimated 30,000 victims. Saddam also caused an ecological disaster by draining the marshes of southern Iraq, which displaced half a million people.[4] In northern Iraq, 1.5 million Kurds fled over the mountains to Turkey and Iran. Television cameras showed Kurds shivering in the cold and dying from exposure.

Iraqi Kurds called on the United States to intervene and create conditions for the return of refugees. They asked the Bush administration to prevent Iraq's attacks, to deploy a special force that would create a safe haven, and to deliver emergency food rations for those encamped in the mountains. Najmaldin Karim also asked U.S. officials to establish direct contact with Kurdish leaders for the purpose of negotiating Iraq's future governance. However, U.S. officials remained noncommittal. They were concerned that involvement would delay the return of U.S. troops or draw the United States deeper into a quagmire in Iraq. Bush explained that the UN resolution had only authorized the U.S.-led coalition to drive Iraq out of Kuwait.

When Secretary of State James A. Baker visited Turkey, U.S. Ambassador Morton I. Abramowitz insisted that Baker see for himself the severity of the crisis. Baker was so appalled that he called Bush and Defense Secretary Dick Cheney from his plane and insisted that the United States undertake a humanitarian intervention. Bush was chastened by Turkey's President Turgut Ozal and other allies. By mid-April, the United States, Great Britain, and France announced a no-fly zone above the 36th parallel, thus creating a safe haven in Iraqi Kurdistan. Abramowitz worked closely with the Turks in arranging facilities to assist in delivering food and blankets. As part of "Operation Provide Comfort," the U.S. military set up and supplied refugee camps on the border between Iraq and Turkey. When more than 10,000 American soldiers established humanitarian enclaves in Iraqi Kurdistan, Kurds returned to their homes in a crescent-shaped slice of territory along the Turkish, Syrian, and Iranian borders. Though "Operation Northern Watch" was never approved by the UN Security Council, U.S. war planes used Incirlik Air Force Base in southeastern Turkey to secure the air space against reprisals by Saddam.

On April 25, 1991, Jalal Talabani and Massoud Barzani visited Baghdad to discuss arrangements for Kurdish administration of the northern territories. The world was shocked when they were photographed kissing Saddam. Their meeting was a reminder that no enmity is permanent in a region where alliances are expedient and constantly refashioned.

O N the day the Gulf War ended, the Congressional Human Rights Foundation, which I led from 1988–1995, convened a Capitol Hill conference on "The Future of Democracy in Iraq." Jalal Talabani, Hoshyar Zebari, and Sami Abdul-Rahman came from Iraqi Kurdistan. Arrangements were made for the Kurdish delegation to meet Richard Schifter, the assistant secretary of state for human rights, but the meeting was canceled at the last minute because the Bush administration was concerned that an official meeting would be interpreted as support for Kurdish independence. The Kurds were not even allowed inside the building. Instead, a low-level official met them at the Columbia coffee shop, around the corner from the State Department.

Though Iraqi Kurds were barred from federal offices in Washington, D.C., discreet contact was under way between Barzani, Talabani, and Marc Grossman, who was then deputy chief of mission at the U.S. Embassy in Ankara. Grossman was not allowed to meet the Kurdish leaders on the embassy's premises, but he invited them to his home, where they discussed the humanitarian crisis and Kurdish plans for stabilizing and governing Iraq after Saddam.

After Kurds and Arab Shi'a were slaughtered during the uprising, the world started to pay attention to their plight. In May 1991, I hosted a roundtable with members of the Kurdistan Front that included Kurds, Turkmen, and Assyrians. Previously, persuading people to attend meetings of Iraqi opposition figures had been a struggle, but this time the Capitol Hill conference room was flooded with legislators, staffers, and press representatives. A State Department notetaker was present, but U.S. officials were still reluctant to meet openly with Saddam's opponents.

IRAQI Kurds refer to the period between 1991 and 2003 as the "golden years." From my visit in 1992, I remembered Dohuk as a sleepy hamlet nestled in the mountains. Ten years later, it had become a teeming metropolis. Dohuk's streets were filled with traffic, including large trucks openly transporting oil and other goods from Iraq to Syria and Turkey. Dohuk's commercial outlets were stocked with Turkish consumer goods and Japanese electronics. A shopping mall had sprung up in the city center. The Mazi supermarket, built on the site of a former Republican Guard base, was fully stocked with staples and exotic foodstuffs. Dohuk University's modern campus occupied the former Ba'ath Party headquarters and prison. An Armani knock-off outlet sold Italian-style suits.

Iraqi Kurdistan is a remote, landlocked territory that straddles trade routes to Turkey, Syria, and Iran. In violation of UN sanctions and with full cognizance of U.S. authorities, the Kurds derived significant benefits from transit fees and smuggling operations, which generated up to $50 million a month.

Money also flowed into the local economy from the United Nations Oil for Food Program, which supervised the sale of Iraqi oil and used the proceeds for food and medicine and to repair infrastructure. Of the total revenues, 13 percent were earmarked for humanitarian activities in Iraqi Kurdistan. The Kurds complained about UN acquiescence in allowing Iraqi authorities to obstruct projects that could contribute to Kurdistan's becoming self-sufficient; they also resented UN officials who skimmed funds from their portion of the account. Despite the Kurds' grievances, corruption was less serious in Iraqi Kurdistan than in other parts of the country. For the first time in Iraq's history, the Kurds were benefiting from a share of the nation's oil wealth.

When I saw Massoud Barzani in July 2002, he welcomed without reservation George W. Bush's pledge to overthrow Saddam Hussein. I was surprised by Barzani's wholehearted support for regime change. Given Iraqi Kurdistan's progress, the Kurds had a lot to lose.

With the moment of liberation drawing near, Barzani suggested that the Kurds were developing their own plan for governance in Iraq. He believed that the Kurds' experience with democratic self-rule would inspire other Iraqis. According to Barzani, Iraqi Kurdistan was a model for the rest of Iraq. He was careful not to be too publicly outspoken in calling for Saddam's ouster lest Saddam vent his anger with the United States by launching a preemptive strike against the Kurds.

The Kurds' precarious position was apparent the next day during my drive to Suleimania. The road winds through beautiful and lush countryside along the Zab River before coming to a dead-end on the outskirts of the city. We turned left and drove up the hill a few hundred yards into Suleimania. A wrong turn would have been disastrous because a Republican Guard military checkpoint lies down the hill on the outskirts of Chamchamal. If Saddam ever decided to attack, his armored divisions could overrun major cities such as Suleimania and Erbil in a matter of hours. A humanitarian emergency would ensue, as UN stockpiles contained rations sufficient only for a few days.

When we reached Suleimania, I went immediately to see Barham Salih. He was receiving petitioners when I arrived at his office, and, although I do not speak Kurdish, I could see the skill with which he listened, asked questions, and made people feel that the PUK administration was responsive to their needs.

Barham was full of pride. He pointed out that in 1991 there were only 804 schools; but, during more than a decade of self-rule, the Kurdistan Regional Government had built another 2,700. In 1991, Kurdistan had only one university, but by 2002 there were three, in Erbil, Dohuk, and

Suleimania. In ten years of self-government, the Kurds had built twice as many hospitals for themselves as were built over the past seventy years. There were 1,870 doctors, as opposed to 548 in 1991. Civil society was vigorous; 138 media outlets operated in Suleimania alone. Barham and I drove by the former Ba'ath Party headquarters, which had been turned into a museum of atrocities. We strolled through Freedom Park, a former military garrison and mass gravesite now transformed into a recreational area. Children were flying kites and families gathered under the shade trees for summer picnics. Barham pointed out the fashionable ladies of Kurdistan, who wore high heels and make-up.

Barham took me to his home, which was surrounded by a cement and stone wall, and showed me the courtyard where he had narrowly escaped assassination by Ansar al-Islam, a radical Islamist group made up mainly of Kurds with ties to al-Qaeda. In April 2002, Barham was leaving home when the phone rang. As he ducked back into the house, a team of assassins opened fire, killing five of his bodyguards. Two of the assassins were killed in the ensuing shoot out. Another fled, but was later captured by Kurdish security services. After interrogation, the detainee confessed that he was a member of Ansar al-Islam.

When Ryan C. Crocker, the deputy assistant secretary in the State Department's Bureau of Near Eastern Affairs, briefed me before my departure for Iraq, he warned me not to visit Halabja. In the rugged mountains near Halabja along the Iran-Iraq border, about eight hundred Ansar al-Islam fighters were encamped; among them were a handful of Arab Afghans who, after the Taliban regime collapsed, had made their way from Herat in western Afghanistan across Iran and into Iraq. According to Barham, Saddam supported Ansar al-Islam as a force against the Kurds. Both Saddam and Ansar al-Islam hated the Kurds for their secular ways and ties to the United States.

The next day, Barham and I had dinner at a restaurant set high on a hill overlooking a green fertile plain north of Suleimania. We drank scotch and reminisced about the months he spent in my office back in 1993. Barham and the Kurds had come a long way since then.

Looking out over the valley below, Barham described the abundant natural resources of his homeland. The Tigris, Zab, Khaboor, Khazir, and tens of other smaller rivers, flow through Iraqi Kurdistan. He pointed to the horizon where, somewhere in the distance, the Dokan dam generates electricity for local use as well as for export. Kurdistan, the country's breadbasket, produces wheat, barley, rice, tobacco, cotton, and fruit.

Northeastern Iraq has about 5,000 square miles of mountain forest. In addition to iron, copper, zinc, and other minerals, Iraqi Kurdistan is rich in natural gas and oil, with an estimated reserve of 10 billion barrels; new energy fields, such as Tak Tak, may also have great potential.

I asked Barham how he felt about the possibility of war. He maintained that the Kurds were not embarking on anything new, as they have been fighting the Iraqi regime for decades. Barham explained that the Kurds had come to realize that it was in their interest to help shape Iraqi politics and bring about a representative federal government in Baghdad. He admitted that Kurds dream of an independent state, but, resigned to historical and geographic realities, they realized that their only real option was to remain a part of Iraq. Though Barham preferred that the Iraqis topple Saddam on their own, he doubted that a coup was in the cards. He believed that Iraqis looked with pride at what had been achieved in Iraqi Kurdistan and, in the struggle to build a democratic Iraq, Kurdistan should be seen as a model for remaking the rest of the country.

Barham genuinely believed that "Iraq's transformation would change the dynamics of Middle Eastern politics."[5] He was convinced that the new Iraq could become a pillar of stability in the Middle East and a catalyst for major change in the region's balance of power. "There are very few cases in history when moral and political arguments coincide," Barham added. "It is morally right to help the people of Iraq, to stop genocide or end these terrible abuses. It is politically right for stability in the Middle East to bring about a representative government that will be at peace with the region."[6]

He insisted that Iraqis were not afraid of war. Their biggest fear was that the United States would lose resolve and leave Saddam in power, thus allowing another Ba'athist general to take his place. Powell insisted that if Saddam launched a preemptive strike against Iraqi Kurdistan, the United States would respond at a time and place of its choosing. But the Kurds wanted a guarantee that the United States would defend them, and Talabani asked for gas masks in case chemical weapons were used.

THE next day I visited the commander of the KDP peshmerga. When the general invited me for a special tour of his "war room," I was expecting a state-of-the-art facility with computer simulations and sophisticated communications. Instead, there was a large table covered with mud structures that were meant to signify villages and wooden soldiers for peshmerga. A yellowing plastic-covered map was tacked to the wall. Pins identified the location of Iraqi troops.

Barham had boasted about the peshmerga's command and control system. But no matter how brave the peshmerga, they were clearly no match for Saddam's well-trained forces. The general acknowledged that Kurdish cities would be quickly overrun, but maintained that his men could mount an effective resistance from the mountains. He asked me to carry back to Washington a list of weapons the peshmerga would need if they were attacked or for use during the first phase of a military offensive against Saddam.

My last meeting in Iraqi Kurdistan was with Sami Abdul-Rahman, a respected elder statesman with vast experience in Kurdish and Iraqi politics. After the Kurdish rebellion of 1968, Saddam extolled "brotherhood" between Arabs and Kurds and amended Iraq's constitution to provide for Kurdish cultural autonomy. He appointed Sami as minister for Northern Affairs. When Saddam failed to carry out the autonomy agreement of March 11, 1970, Sami resigned and joined the peshmerga.

We sat on the patio of his office in Salahuddin and gazed out at the vast Mesopotamian plain; Sami reflected on the difficulties facing Iraq; indeed, many of the issues he raised that day would dominate the deliberations of the Future of Iraq Project. His views were also prescient of problems that affect Iraq today.

Religion and ethnicity matter to Iraqis who, as a people, lack a strong sense of national identity. Sami insisted that Iraq's problems were typically caused by the central government's efforts to suppress ethnicity. Governance was always characterized by a high degree of centralization, a situation dating back to the 1925 constitution. He emphasized that decentralization was critical to the development of democracy in Iraq. The best way to balance the competing demands for democracy and unity would be through a federal structure. Sami explained that Kurds prefer federalism because it offers a greater guarantee than simple autonomy, whose entrenchment can be more easily revoked. Federalism is a voluntary association between parties who decide it is in their common interest to form a unified state. It is a contract binding equal groups, whereas autonomy is bestowed by the central government to a lesser party.

The KDP's draft constitution emphasized checks and balances. Some sections seemed to have been written by America's Founding Fathers:[7]

Democracy requires democratic freedoms including that of expression, belief, organization, assembly and others. It assumes that power can be transferred peacefully through the holding of free elections at the ballot box; recognizes the principle of a multiparty system and the concept of an opposition; and consolidates the principles of the separation of powers and protects the independence of the judiciary by giving it the last word in the settlement of constitutional disagreements.

The draft enumerated specific functions of the central government such as national defense and the control of monetary policy. For the most part, however, it envisioned governance at the local level. It proposed a local executive, assembly, and judiciary. To provide security, the peshmerga would be transformed into a civilian defense corps comparable to the U.S. National Guard. The federal entity would collect taxes and levy customs to support public services such as health, education, and social welfare. It would regulate trade and land ownership, and it would own its natural resources, including oil and gas. The draft highlighted the importance of women's rights. Regarding cultural issues, Kurdistan would control language, education, and religious matters. Symbols of cultural identity, such as the flag and the seal, would be used. Sami envisioned two regions in Iraq: one Kurdish, the other Arab.

The KDP draft constitution had many shortcomings. I had no objection to the notion of "legitimate national interests." However, I was sure the assertion of "internal independence" would upset other Iraqis. In addition, the bifurcation of Iraq into Arab and Kurdish entities was too simplistic. Under Saddam, Iraq was made up of eighteen ethnically diverse provinces called "governorates." One million Kurds lived in Baghdad and large numbers resided in Mosul and Tikrit as well. But Sami's document defined a Kurdish federal entity based on ethnic rather than geographic considerations.

Over generations, Kirkuk's population flows made it a flash-point for ethnic conflict. After the first oil gusher in 1927, Kurds moved en masse to Kirkuk. To prevent the Kurds from controlling the region's oil wealth, the Ba'ath Party Revolutionary Command Council in 1974 issued a decree renaming Kirkuk province as Ta'amim province and dividing its territory. More than 100,000 Kurds fled the Kirkuk area during the Anfal campaign. Saddam's Arabization program resettled 279,000 Arab peasants and Arabs from the marshes outside of Basra, at the same time displacing

Kurds, Turkmen, and Assyrians from Iraqi Kurdistan. "Ethnic Correction" encouraged assimilation, offered rewards to Arabs who married Kurds, and renamed Kurdish places using Arabic. Arabs came to represent more than half the population of Mosul City and about a third of Kirkuk. Despite routine commercial contact, indigenous northerners resent Arabs, whom they see as tools of Saddam's Arabization program.

That afternoon and into the next day, Sami and I discussed power sharing between Iraq's ethnic and religious groups. We agreed that a priority for Kirkuk would be managing the return of refugees and displaced persons. An orderly return would mitigate conflict between Kurds and Turkmen and between rival Kurdish factions; it would also obviate widespread revenge taking against Arabs. Despite the regime's deliberate destruction of deeds and documentation, Sami envisioned a system of property claims and compensation that would include infrastructure rehabilitation, temporary shelter, and plans to generate employment.

I floated the idea of special status for Kirkuk. The arrangement would establish a free-standing municipality under international supervision. Its final status would be determined through international mediation, which might include a popular consultation.

Sami would have none of it. He insisted on Iraqi Kurdistan as one federal unit encompassing the provinces of Dohuk, Suleimania, Erbil, and Kirkuk, with Kirkuk as its capital. We agreed that all nationalities—Kurds, Arabs, Turkmen, and Assyrians—must have equal rights, and we discussed the feasibility of establishing cantons so that minority groups could control local government in areas where they represent a majority.

The KDP constitution also failed to address relations between Arab Sunnis and Arab Shi'a as well as the role of religion in governance. About 60 percent of Iraqis, 15 million people, are Shi'a. Many of the holiest Shi'a shrines are in Iraq. Najaf's exquisite gold-domed Imam Ali mosque commemorates the murder of the Prophet Mohammed's son-in-law in A.D. 661. The city of Karbala was built where Hussein, Mohammed's grandson, was slain by an army of the Sunni establishment. The schism in Islam occurred because Shi'a believe that only direct descendants should lead the faithful, whereas the Sunni assign leadership according to standing in the community. Black turbaned, Shi'a clerics (*Sayyeds*) are direct descendants of the Prophet Mohammed.

I suggested to Sami that the Kurds could best promote their interests by acting as a broker between Arab Sunni and Shi'a. Power sharing would require compromise and consent. If the Kurds took on board the views of other groups and tried to address their concerns, they could convince Arab Sunnis that federalism effectively promoted minority rights. Such an approach would also show the Shi'a that federalism could simultaneously promote democracy while strengthening Iraq's territorial integrity. Iraqis would face difficult decisions, but they agreed on one point: No one accepted domination by another group.

Sami asked me to convey his request that the U.S. government establish a forum to help plan the future of Iraq. Even as we spoke, the Future of Iraq Project was under way. Though Sami knew that he wanted regime change, he did not know that he would give his life for the cause. Sami and his son were killed by a suicide bomber in Erbil on February 1, 2004.

CHAPTER 3

——

THE FUTURE OF
IRAQ PROJECT

O N JULY 15, 2002, I WENT TO THE STATE DEPARTMENT
to report on my trip to Iraq. Ryan Crocker, the deputy assistant
secretary of state for Near Eastern affairs, joined my meeting with Undersecretary Marc Grossman. Crocker is a career diplomat who had held
positions as U.S. ambassador to Syria, Lebanon, Kuwait, and Afghanistan.
He represented the State Department at working-level interagency meetings on Iraq. Grossman frequently sat in for Deputy Secretary of State
Richard L. Armitage at meetings of the "deputies."

I described the Kurds' pro-U.S. position, as well as their anxiety about
the future. The Kurds worried that if they openly supported regime
change, Saddam might launch a preemptive strike to punish them and,
in the process, throw U.S. war plans out of sync. I relayed Sami's request.
I also told Grossman and Crocker that the Kurds wanted security guarantees and equipment to protect against chemical weapons.

Relations were tense between the Kurdish parties despite the veneer of
collegiality. I proposed that the State Department convene a "Washington
Agreement Implementation Review Conference" on the anniversary of
the accord, to reinvigorate rapprochement between the Kurds. While in
Iraqi Kurdistan, I had conveyed messages between Massoud Barzani and
Jalal Talabani regarding the Kurdistan National Assembly, which had not
met in six years. Without a push from the United States, Kurdish institutions would not function and overall progress was unlikely.

Barzani bitterly accused Turkey of undermining peace and progress in
Iraqi Kurdistan. Since 1988, Turkey has been fighting the Kurdistan

Worker's Party (PKK), a militant group demanding democratic rights for Turkey's 15–20 million Kurds. The U.S. government considers the PKK a terrorist organization and supports Turkey's efforts to attack them in the mountains on the Iraq-Turkey border. Each spring, the Turkish army launches search-and-destroy missions from its bases in southeastern Turkey as well as Iraqi Kurdistan. Barzani bitterly opposed Turkey's military operations; he maintained that Turkey's real interest was to acquire access to the rich oil fields of Erbil, Mosul, and Kirkuk. He also accused Ankara of fomenting discord between the Kurds and the Iraqi Turkmen Front (ITF), and of trying to undermine cooperation between Iraqi opposition groups.

I told Grossman and Crocker that tensions between the Kurdistan Democratic Party (KDP) and the ITF were reaching a tipping point. Barzani showed me a hidden-camera videotape catching a Turkish official from Ankara's Erbil liaison office paying an assassin to kill a Turkmen minister aligned with the KDP. Barzani was right to be incensed, but I urged him to avoid confrontation. If the United States had to choose between Turkey and the Kurds, it would side with Turkey every time.

Grossman wanted to know Barzani's views of the Iraqi opposition. In addition to the Iraqi National Congress (INC), the United States focused on the "Gang of Four"—the Kurdistan Democratic Party, the Patriotic Union of Kurdistan, the Iraqi National Accord, and the Supreme Council for Islamic Revolution in Iraq (SCIRI). I strongly urged Crocker, the State Department's point man with the Iraqi opposition, to include a reputable Sunni organization.

Rather than a center-out approach that focused on Baghdad, I suggested democracy-building start in the regions. Beginning in liberated parts of the country such as Iraqi Kurdistan, I proposed that constituencies select community leaders to serve in local government. In the event that the United States went to war, I envisioned liberated regions organizing local conferences and selecting delegates to a larger national conference that would evolve into a constituent assembly. In turn, the assembly would be responsible for organizing elections and drafting a constitution. Crocker remarked to Grossman, "Sound familiar? He got there himself."[1] The State Department's thinking was the same as mine.

A month later, Crocker invited me to assist the Future of Iraq Project's Democratic Principles Working Group. To accommodate the new assignment, my consulting agreement was moved from the State Department's Bureau for European and Canadian Affairs to the Bureau for

Near Eastern Affairs (NEA). My contract indicated that I was hired because of my expertise in working with the Iraqi opposition.

T HE Future of Iraq Project was a broad, voluntary effort to meld the talents, experience, and expertise of Iraqis in the service of a new Iraq. It was inspired by a conference at Columbia University in the fall of 2001, where, for the first time, several former Iraqi military officers met to discuss scenarios for reforming Iraq's military.

The State Department had originally planned to award a $5 million grant to the Middle East Institute to carry the work forward. However, when Ned Walker, the institute's director, made some off-color comments about Bush, the grant was cancelled.[2] Ahmad Chalabi wanted the grant to go to the INC and pulled strings with his backers in the U.S. Congress.[3] Grant agreements require congressional notification so that relevant committees can authorize the disbursement. Given Chalabi's contacts on Capitol Hill, any grant that Chalabi opposed would be sure to face a long and complicated fight for approval. As a result, the State Department decided to do the Future of Iraq Project in-house.

The Future of Iraq Project was coordinated by NEA's Office of Northern Gulf Affairs (NGA). Warrick, a mid-level career Foreign Service Officer, served as project director. He reported to NGA's director, David Pearce, who, in turn, reported to Crocker. Meetings were run by the State Department, and outside experts were brought in to advise U.S. officials and assist Iraqi participants.

Though the Future of Iraq Project was led by the State Department, it was an interagency initiative that included seventeen federal agencies, among them the Agency for International Development, the Treasury Department, the Defense Department, and the CIA. Personnel from the Joint Chiefs of Staff, the National Security Council, and the Office of the Vice President participated. Launched in April 2002, the Future of Iraq Project assembled more than 240 Iraqis from across the political spectrum, and included representatives from every ethnic group and major political party. It cost $5 million and produced 2,000 pages in thirteen volumes. To develop recommendations, groups worked on technical topics ranging from education to health, sanitation, and agriculture. Some groups also tackled economic issues, infrastructure, energy, and public finance. Others focused on security, governance, rule of law, and transitional justice.

Most meetings were held in the United Kingdom because cumbersome visa procedures made it difficult for many Iraqis, especially exiles with Iranian passports, to visit the United States. Participants were drawn mostly from the Iraqi diaspora except for Kurds, Turkmen, and Assyrians who resided in northern Iraq and could travel out of the country.

The goal was not to achieve consensus but to build a sense of solidarity and common purpose between Iraqis who were coming together to plan their country's recovery. For many Iraqis, this was the first time they had ever talked to each other or cooperated across ethnic and sectarian lines. They were excited about participating in a forum to discuss rebuilding Iraq's institutions. According to Grossman, the Future of Iraq Project was established "to begin practical planning for what could be done between now and the date of a change of government in Baghdad, and in the immediate aftermath of a transition."[4] Iraqis would face the huge task of reconstructing their country politically and materially after decades of neglect and mismanagement.

Chalabi initially refused to participate because he thought that the INC, as the umbrella organization for the Iraqi opposition, should be in charge. When he was unable to control it, he complained that the Future of Iraq Project was useless and should be canceled.[5]

Chalabi eventually realized that he could not afford to stand aside while Iraqis discussed the details of Iraq's transition to democracy. When the Democratic Principles Working Group was established, the INC shifted tactics and Chalabi assigned his top surrogates to participate. The INC envisioned the Democratic Principles Working Group as a vehicle to formalize plans for a government-in-exile with Chalabi at its head. If the train was leaving the station, the INC not only wanted to be on board but Chalabi wanted to make sure that the INC was driving the process.

Administration hawks were wary of allowing consultation to occur between Iraqi factions. They would have preferred to make key decisions about Iraq's future governance themselves. Other officials argued that Iraqi exiles as well as Iraqis within Iraq should be involved; they warned that legitimacy would be compromised unless a broadly representative group of Iraqis participated.

Though Chalabi's backers in the administration wanted to establish a government-in-exile with Chalabi in charge, the State Department resisted efforts to have the Future of Iraq Project endorse their approach.

On February 11, 2003, Grossman testified to the Senate Foreign Relations Committee: "Iraqis on the outside will not control decisions that will, ultimately, have to be made by all Iraqis. The Iraqi diaspora is a great resource but not a substitute for what all Iraqis will need to do together to work towards democracy in their country. Both we and the free Iraqis look forward to the day when all Iraqis are able to talk freely and work together to build a free and democratic Iraq."[6] Grossman explained, "The working groups were not to have an academic discussion but to consider thoughts and plans for what can be done immediately."[7]

Iraqis called the Democratic Principles Working Group "The Mother of All Working Groups." It addressed some of the most difficult issues confronting Iraq, such as security and de-Ba'athification. But most contentious was the establishment of a transitional authority paving the way for elections and a new constitution.

CHAPTER 4

—

INTERAGENCY
RELATIONS

T HE BUSH ADMINISTRATION WAS DIVIDED. AS EARLY
as January 30, 2001, the National Security Council (NSC) had discussed the need for a revamped Iraq policy, but interagency squabbles bogged down the process of formulating a coherent strategy for regime change. Bush's advisers were divided by ideology, not by tactics. Gridlock and paralysis resulted. So did bad blood, and it would fester and worsen over time.

Neo-conservatives ("neo-cons") saw regime change in Iraq as the catalyst for reshaping the broader Middle East. The State Department was wary. So-called Arabists, career Foreign Service Officers experienced in the Middle East, appreciated the difficulties of governing Iraq as well as the challenges of fostering liberal democracy in the region. After more than a year of interagency debate, the NSC approved a National Security Directive endorsing efforts to bring about a coup by a friendly general or from within the Ba'ath Party. It also recommended support for a popular rebellion led by Arab Shi'a in the south.

During August 2002, George W. Bush suffered withering criticism from foreign policy patricians who had served in his father's administration. James Baker supported military action against Iraq, but only after securing international authority from the United Nations Security Council; Brent Scowcroft warned that a military campaign against Iraq would undermine the war on terror; and Henry Kissinger criticized the administration for not having a focused policy.

Iraqis assiduously advocated regime change. On August 8, Jalal Talabani, Hoshyar Zebari, Ahmad Chalabi, and Abdul-Aziz Hakim of the
Supreme Council for Islamic Revolution in Iraq (SCIRI) met with Donald Rumsfeld and the chairman of the Joint Chiefs of Staff, General
Richard B. Myers. Dick Cheney participated through a secure video conference. This kind of high-level attention was unprecedented. It represented a far cry from earlier years when U.S. officials would not even
meet publicly with the Iraqi opposition.

After the meeting, the Iraqis were glowing. They felt that the top U.S.
leadership was sincerely interested in their views and had taken their
recommendations seriously. The Iraqis had not only emphasized the importance of a legitimate transitional authority but also expressed concern about security: U.S. armed forces would have to work with
indigenous groups to prevent looting and random acts of violence.

During the summer of 2002, a series of "Regional Strategies Meetings"
provided the cover for Bush's senior advisers to conduct discreet discussions about Iraq.[1] On August 21, Bush met with his top national security
advisers in Crawford, Texas. Dick Cheney, Condoleezza Rice, General
Richard Myers, and White House Chief of Staff Andrew Card attended.
Why did the president's advisers travel all the way to Crawford on one
of the hottest days of the year? The White House insisted that the routine meeting was called to discuss military reforms and that Iraq was not
on the official agenda.

I believe that the decision was made to push for regime change in Iraq
at this Crawford meeting. Henceforth, the question was not whether to
rid Iraq of Saddam Hussein but how to do it. Pentagon hawks wanted to
pull the trigger in the fall. Cheney and Rumsfeld clashed with Colin
Powell, who argued that attacking Iraq without first going to the United
Nations would undermine international cooperation in the war on terror. He contended that if the United States had to act, it would need allies in the battlefield and a coalition to provide access, basing, and
overflight rights. Powell was confident that he had persuaded the president to seek support from the international community.

After the Crawford meeting, Bush decided to go back to the United
Nations and demand that it enforce existing resolutions requiring Iraq's
disarmament. If Saddam failed to accept a vigorous weapons-inspection
regime, the United States would seek a UN Security Council resolution
authorizing all necessary means to disarm Iraq.

Bush overruled Cheney and Rumsfeld out of consideration for Britain's Prime Minister Tony Blair who was facing enormous domestic opposition, including from within his Labour Party, to joining the United States in a war on Iraq. Blair needed the cover of a UN Security Council resolution. To Powell's satisfaction, Bush agreed to help him.

It was a significant victory for Powell. Powell's experience as a soldier in Vietnam had shown him both the horrors of wars as well as the limits of military power. According to the "Powell Doctrine," armed combat should always be a last resort, but if war is inevitable, it should be waged with overwhelming force. Clearly defined goals and an exit strategy are essential in avoiding open-ended commitments. Every war needs a plan for winning the peace.

The UN trap riled Cheney. Within days of the Crawford meeting, he was publicly questioning the usefulness of inspections and pushing for a preemptive strike. Painting the president into a corner, Cheney threw down the gauntlet during his speech at the Veterans of Foreign Wars event on August 26, 2002: "A person would be right to question any suggestion that we should just get inspectors back into Iraq, and then our worries will be over. Saddam has perfected the game of cheat and retreat, and is very skilled in the art of denial and deception. A return of inspectors would provide no assurance whatsoever of his compliance with UN resolutions. On the contrary, there is a great danger it would provide false comfort that Saddam was somehow 'back in his box.'" He continued with a call to arms: "What we must not do in the face of mortal threat is give in to wishful thinking or willful blindness. We will not simply look away, hope for the best, and leave the matter to some future administration to resolve. The risks of inaction are far greater than the risk of action."[2]

The longer inspections went on without finding a smoking gun the less justification and support the Bush administration would have for using force. Given Saddam's tendency to cheat and retreat, Cheney worried that it could take months or longer before inspectors uncovered weapons of mass destruction in Iraq. Going slowly would not only give Saddam more time to accelerate his weapons program but would also undermine the claim that Iraq was an imminent threat. By August 2002, Central Command (CENTCOM) was hard at work refining the invasion plans.

Cheney's remarks caused an international firestorm. Governments around the world, including those of China, France, and Germany, de-

manded that the issue be solved diplomatically. President Hosni
Mubarak of Egypt warned that a military campaign could cause chaos in
the region. Saudi officials admonished the administration about unilateral action, advocating an approach in line with international law, just
like the first Gulf War, which was endorsed by the United Nations.

Blair and Powell thought that avoiding a showdown with the United
Nations was critical. In Afghanistan, the United Nations played a key
role through the "Bonn process" and was working on the ground to assist
reconstruction and pave the way for elections. Blair and Powell understood that the United Nations would also be needed to help rebuild
Iraq. Laying the groundwork for international cooperation before the
war would be essential to fostering international cooperation during the
reconstruction phase.

CHAPTER 5

— • —

BREAKING THE ICE

AFTER THE CRAWFORD MEETING OF AUGUST 21, U.S. officials scrambled to start planning for postwar Iraq. David Pearce insisted that no decision had been made about military action, but if a U.S.-led military coalition had to intervene, the United States wanted to have a plan for Iraq's economic and political reconstruction when combat ceased. On September 3–5, 2002, a group of prominent Iraqis would meet at a location outside London to discuss many of the key issues facing Iraq's transition to democracy. Pearce asked me to facilitate the meeting so that Iraqis could move beyond generalities about democracy to addressing the specifics of how Iraq's future democracy might be structured.

Pearce sought my guidance in organizing the Democratic Principles Working Group, because I had experience in running conflict-resolution meetings and enjoyed Marc Grossman's confidence.

Pearce, a steady diplomat with an unassuming manner, masks toughness and determination—useful qualities for dealing with Iraqis and managing U.S. interagency matters. He was shadowed by Tom Warrick who was more deeply immersed in Iraqi politics than any other U.S. official. Having spent years working with the Iraqi opposition, Warrick not only knew the personalities but also understood their nuanced relations. He appreciated the dynamic between Iraqi exiles and Iraqis living in Iraq; the latter naturally resented the exiles for living the good life overseas while they suffered under the brutal rule of Saddam Hussein.

Warrick was well intentioned, but too protective of his ties with Iraqis and overly possessive of the Future of Iraq Project. His reluctance to communicate and share work products exacerbated interagency tensions. To demonstrate its seriousness about postwar planning, the U.S. government should have assigned a senior official to the project, a heavyweight who could command greater respect from the Iraqis and who would have kept the interagency work on track.

Threatened by my good working relations with Pearce and Ryan Crocker, I sensed that Warrick was unhappy with the State Department's decision to involve me in the Future of Iraq Project. He also knew that I had friends in the upper echelons of the State Department. As a consultant, I could operate outside the envelope that constrained career personnel. I showed Warrick respect, but I did not allow him to bulldoze decisions that I thought were detrimental to the Iraqis. Pearce was glad to have me on board; he and I worked closely together, preparing everything from the Working Group's agenda to the configuration of the meeting room.

JUST a few days before the meeting, Pearce informed me that more than a dozen U.S. officials planned to attend. I objected strenuously: Filling the room with observers was a bad idea and would result in grandstanding by Iraqis; such behavior could be prevented only if U.S. officials kept a low profile. To keep the number of U.S. officials seated at the table to a minimum, I advised that only Pearce and Warrick join the circle. If U.S. officials insisted on observing, it would be best to seat them in a second tier.

A State Department staffer, as well as representatives from the Office of the Vice President (OVP), the Department of Defense, and the Joint Chiefs of Staff ultimately attended. The composition of that group revealed a lot about which agencies of the U.S. government were interested in the process. Samantha Ravich, an adviser to Dick Cheney, was the most active representative. The Iraqis respected Ravich and sought her support when there was a disagreement or impasse.

Although most of the Iraqis had never participated in a facilitated dialogue, it would be important for them to assume ownership of the meeting. I therefore warned Pearce not to create the impression that the Iraqis were being talked down to or instructed by the U.S. government. At the outset, the Iraqis would act like negotiators and assert hard-line positions. Some would try to win his support and seek endorsement from the U.S. government. I told him to anticipate histrionics and to remind the Iraqis that the meeting was merely a forum for ideas. No one

had given the Democratic Principles Working Group a mandate to negotiate on behalf of all the Iraqi people.

I also shared some conflict resolution tricks of the trade. The meeting
table should be round. Name placards should be arranged alphabetically.
Always go clockwise around the room. Schedule frequent coffee breaks.
Allow ample time for mixing and mingling. Some of the most meaningful discussions would occur not during formal sessions but on the mar-
gins of the meeting and during break time, so the Iraqis needed a chance
to get to know each other and develop a constructive group dynamic.

It was also important to provide structure to the conversation. Pearce
asked American University's Professor Abdul Aziz Said, an erudite and
respected academic, to present a paper entitled "The Challenge of Democratization in the Middle East." My paper—"Promoting National
Unity through Federal Systems of Governance"—focused on power
sharing and constitutional arrangements. I was identified as an expert
with the Council on Foreign Relations.

A group of thirty-two Iraqis gathered in the Surrey countryside. The
Working Group was made up of an unusually diverse ethnic and sectarian mix including Shi'a, Sunnis, Kurds, Turkmen, and Assyrians. They
came from a variety of vocations and included academics, intellectuals,
activists, and political opposition figures. Of the participants, twelve
were residents of the United States, ten lived in the United Kingdom,
four were from Kurdistan, and the rest lived in the United Arab Emirates, Iran, Syria, and various countries in continental Europe. Sami
Abdul Rahman and Qubad Talabani were there; I also knew many of the
other participants.

In the reception area at Heathrow, I ran into Rend al-Rahim and we
shared a car ride to the meeting place in Surrey. Half Sunni and half Shi'a,
Rend was born to a wealthy family in Baghdad. She had graduated from
Cambridge and the Sorbonne in Paris and became a currency trader in
Lebanon, Bahrain, and England. As head of the Iraq Foundation in Washington, D.C., Rend was a vocal advocate for regime change. While she was
shuffling papers in the taxi, I saw that she had both a U.S. passport and an
old Iraqi passport. She explained that her Iraqi travel document had long
expired; she had not been home since college. Despite her tough exterior,
Rend flashed a girlish excitement at the thought of returning to Baghdad.

Rend and I have known each other for years, but riding together from
the airport gave us a chance to catch up and discuss her expectations for

the meeting. She was skeptical, but thought the Iraqis would treat the endeavor more seriously if they were sure that the Bush administration was really going to war. Even if the United States did overthrow Saddam, she was not convinced of the U.S. commitment to democracy in Iraq. The United States was used to the status quo and, she suspected, would prefer another Ba'athist general to run the country. She also worried that Iraq could be taken over by radical Islamists or disintegrate if the Kurds made excessive demands.

Laith Kubba was another participant whom I have known since the Gulf War. Laith is a proud and intelligent man with a long history in Iraqi politics. Starting as a youth activist in the Shi'a Da'wa Party ("The Call"), Laith has deep roots in Iraq through the Kubba tribe, one of the country's largest and most influential. Though he was a founding member of the Iraqi National Congress (INC), he caused some bad blood by leaving to set up his own organization. During the morning coffee break, Laith told me about a recent visit to the Pentagon by Ahmad Chalabi and a delegation of Iraqi opposition figures. When Rumsfeld's staff realized that Laith had also been invited, they pulled him out of the queue and barred him from the conference room.

Other participants included Faisal al-Istrabadi, a professor of constitutional law at DePaul University; Faisal comes from a mixed Shi'a-Farsi and Turkmen-Kurdish background. As legal adviser to Adnan Pachachi, who served as Iraq's foreign minister and ambassador to the UN before the Ba'athists seized power in 1968, Faisal would play a key role in drafting Iraq's Transitional Administrative Law. Salem Chalabi, Ahmad's nephew, also participated. So did the INC's Entifadh Qanbar.

The opening dinner provided everyone the opportunity to socialize. Given the importance of personal rapport, I made a point of going from table to table and spending time with every member of the Working Group. I was particularly impressed by Mowaffak al-Rubaie, a former Da'wa member who would later become Iraq's national security adviser. Mowaffak told me that in 1979, the Iraqi police took him to a dungeon, tied him from the ceiling, and rotated him on a meat hook for hours. The torture left him afflicted with back pain and kidney ailments from which he still suffers. Mowaffak was arrested and tortured three times before fleeing Iraq.

Despite their differences, the Iraqis all agreed on the need for regime change and, if necessary, supported U.S. military action to liberate Iraq.

Many had personal experience as victims of Saddam. Some had scores to settle. All agreed with the Bush administration's assertion that Iraq had stockpiles of chemical and biological weapons. Some suspected that Saddam had a nuclear weapons programs. They also believed that Iraq operated a terrorist infrastructure and had ties to Ansar al-Islam.

Kanan Makiya was one of the most vocal and articulate critics of Saddam Hussein. Kanan enrolled at the Massachusetts Institute of Technology just as the Ba'ath Party was coming to power in 1968 and had lived overseas ever since. Though his father was Iraq's leading architect and designed many monuments to Saddam, Kanan gained notoriety for writing *The Republic of Fear.* At first, the book received little attention. However, its graphic details of systematic brutality made it a must-read after the Gulf War. An active INC member, Kanan taught at Brandeis University and served as director of Harvard University's Iraq Research and Documentation Project.

Kanan may have started as an academic, but he had a penchant for politics. In the 1990s, Kanan was taken under the wing of Paul Wolfowitz, Richard Perle, and other neo-conservatives. They had finally found an Arab who not only spoke eloquently on behalf of liberal democracy in the Middle East but also supported Israel. In addition, Kanan befriended Cheney, to whom he remained a confidant during the run-up to war in Iraq.

I was informed about Kanan's ties to the Pentagon and his special relationship with the OVP. Consistent with the INC's boycott of the Future of Iraq Project, Kanan and other INC personnel initially refused to participate in the Democratic Principles Working Group. The INC believed that the State Department preferred stability in the Middle East to the region's democratic transformation. Kanan stated: "Some people in the government are talking about democratic change and there are other people who think it's all a pile of garbage." In joining the Working Group, Kanan had decided to "hoist them on their own petard."[1]

During their visit to Washington on August 8, Iraqi opposition leaders agreed to finalize plans for Iraq's transition at a broad and inclusive political conference. The INC anticipated that the conference would endorse a government-in-exile, presumably led by Ahmad Chalabi. Kanan was one of Chalabi's primary proxies on the Democratic Principles Working Group. Leading an interim government dominated by exiles, Chalabi and his cohorts planned to take power in Baghdad when Saddam's regime started to crumble.

I HAD worked with Pearce on the substance and tone of his opening remarks. To start the ball rolling, Pearce spelled out the Working Group's terms of reference and described what we hoped to accomplish. The meeting was to be informal, exploratory, and nonbinding, a bridge between the 1992 Salahuddin Iraqi opposition meeting and the broader political conference.

Pearce kept his remarks brief so that the Iraqi participants could introduce themselves. It was the first time the Iraqis had been given an opportunity to address each other and, instead of pithy self-introductions, they made long-winded speeches. Pearce then summarized the Salahuddin Declaration, a launch point for our discussions.

In June 1992, the Iraqi National Congress was established as the coordinating body of the Iraqi opposition. On October 31, 1992, the Salahuddin Declaration committed the Iraqi opposition "to work together to eliminate the dictatorial and oppressive regime." To eliminate sectarian and racial oppression, it "endorsed a democratic, constitutional parliamentary, federal, and pluralist structure for Iraq. The national assembly reaffirmed its unfailing commitment to the unity and territorial integrity of Iraq and stressed that the true threat to Iraq's unity came from the dictatorial regime's attempt to divide the people. The national assembly committed . . . to removing Saddam's regime and ending Iraq's national tragedy."[2]

After some discussion about the history of Iraqi opposition, we asked the Iraqis about their expectations and help setting the meeting's agenda. Some were wary of clashes over competing interests. Others were upset by the presence of old foes. All were skeptical and thought the process wouldn't amount to much.

We wanted to consider pragmatic ways to use their ideas. There followed heated debate about the way forward. After much discussion, we proposed subcommittees to develop more detailed recommendations focusing on when to hold elections, how a transitional authority should be structured, and how a constituent assembly would come into existence. Several participants emphasized that, more than majority rule, the rule of law would be critically important when Saddam was overthrown.

Despite the passionate argument, most Iraqis demurred when it came to making decisions on behalf of all Iraqis. They acknowledged that neither they nor Iraqi exiles in general were empowered to represent the larger community of Iraqis captive inside the country. Humbled by the enormity of the task, one person noted "the utterly remarkable nature of this meeting. History could be in the making."[3]

Before presenting his paper on democracy in the Middle East, Professor Said commended the participants for engaging in what he called sustainable dialogue. As a learned behavior, he explained that it would take time for democracy to take root after decades of totalitarian rule in Iraq. Iraqis nodded in agreement when Said asserted that democracy cannot be imposed from outside, that it must reflect the history, culture, and values of Iraqis. Mowaffak agreed: "In Algeria and Sudan, for example, we saw tyranny in the name of Islam. This is very dangerous—politicizing religion or religicizing politics. The diversity of Iraqi society should dictate democracy and decentralization. That's the alternative vision to Saddam's tyranny of fear."[4]

The Working Group discussed ways to enhance the effectiveness and legitimacy of the transitional authority. Iraqis pointed out that the transitional period would "make or break" democracy in Iraq. They insisted that the interim authority should not exist for long. The Iraqis discussed the importance of moving quickly to hold free and fair elections. They also discussed whether the constitution should be adopted before or after the elections. They agreed that, because Iraq's future was in the hands of Iraqis, a national referendum on the constitution should be held as soon as possible. The Iraqis insisted that the U.S. mandate, as well as the role of the international community, be limited and clearly defined.

When it came to the sequence of events, Iraqi exiles wanted to stand up a governance structure as soon as possible. Iraqis with stronger ties inside the country wanted to go more slowly; they emphasized the importance of legitimacy and the need for local participation and ownership of the transition. Sunni Arab participation would be critical. Iraq's democratization would surely shift the power balance away from Sunnis, who had historically enjoyed a privileged position.

I presented information on lessons learned from post-conflict transitions in Bosnia, Kosovo, East Timor, and Afghanistan. My paper on federalism emphasized the need to assign the central government a meaningful role while guaranteeing group rights and decentralizing power to regional entities that would manage local affairs. It also described international power-sharing models that successfully promoted political, economic, and cultural rights. Federalism is a moveable feast. Its definition is malleable to resolve competing claims and accommodate the interests of all parties.

Faisal emphasized the difficult challenge of sharing power while preserving enough central authority to keep the country from falling apart:

"Iraq is a country in which diversity is inherent in the social fabric, with a rich heritage of cultures languages and beliefs. Throughout recent Iraqi history, diversity has been seen as a liability and a divisive force and therefore every effort has been made to suppress it." He also gave a caution: "Efforts to suppress the differences that are so intrinsic to Iraqi society have had disastrous consequences for the well-being and prosperity of the country, including the death of many people, internal wars, expulsions and the exodus of millions of Iraqis."[5]

Not only the Kurds but almost all the other participants recognized that federalism—with proper checks and balances—was the best way to ensure individual and group rights. Kassim Daoud of the Iraqi Democratic Movement affirmed that "the vast majority of Iraqi people, regardless of their ethnic, religious, or political classifications, believe that the only way to govern Iraq is through the establishment of a democratic system which protects the rights of the entire Iraqi people. The democratic system must be based on the principle of a federal state."[6] Led by Sami Abdul-Rahman, there followed an in-depth discussion of the differences between federalism, autonomy, and the devolution of powers.

Wary of becoming minorities in a part of Iraq dominated by Kurds, the Turkmen and Assyrians argued for limits to prevent federalism from becoming a pit stop on the path to Kurdish independence. Sami assured them that the Kurds intended to reintegrate into Iraq. Emphasizing the need for a fair and objective process, he described a population census leading to the demarcation of federal boundaries. Special minority rights would be adopted to protect non-Kurds living in Iraqi Kurdistan. Albert Yelda, an Assyrian who later became Iraq's ambassador to the Vatican, underscored the "need to establish a process for the adoption of a comprehensive and permanent constitution that also serves to protect the rights of all minorities, namely the Assyrians, Turkmen, Armenians, Yezidi, Iraqi Jews, etc. Were a federal state of Kurdistan established, the administrative rights of the Assyrians and Turkmen must be respected and safeguarded."[7]

Several speakers suggested that under a federal system the central government should retain control over defense policy, foreign policy, monetary policy, and natural resources. We also discussed the view of Iraq's neighbors towards federalism. They warned that Iraq borders several authoritarian states that would be threatened by democratic trends and might be tempted to meddle.

On security, Iraqis warned that revenge-taking, vigilantism, and looting could be widespread after Saddam's demise. Although there would be no danger in the north, where Kurdish peshmerga maintain control, the group recommended that U.S. troops work with reformed elements of the Iraqi Army in the center and south, as well as militia associated with the Supreme Council for Islamic Revolution in Iraq.

AFTER we adjourned, Pearce huddled with the interagency group to review the day's developments. Everyone was surprised by how well the meeting had gone so far. Ravich spoke positively about the ability of Iraqis to set aside their differences, look over the horizon, and find common ground. The ice had been broken; the Iraqis were interacting constructively.

I observed, however, that feeling good was just a beginning. An Iraqi-led structure was needed to manage follow-up activities; without it, Iraqis would focus on their differences instead of working together. Though Pearce was nominally in charge, Ravich was the ultimate arbiter of discussions involving interagency representatives. Concerned that the process might lose momentum, she emphasized the need for a trusted Iraqi to lead the endeavor.

After discreetly exploring the idea with some of the key Iraqi participants, I suggested that the Working Group set up task forces mirroring issues discussed in the plenary. Instead of a single Iraqi, we agreed on the need for a coordinating committee made up of members from different factions and groups. Diffusing responsibility would encourage ownership of the process. It would also guard against domination by the INC. To this end, each task force selected two people to serve on the committee; two at-large members were also chosen to help develop a final report. Ravich made sure that Kanan had a position on the coordinating committee.

The next morning, the Iraqis reviewed discussions and talked about the way forward. They agreed to establish task forces on (i) Civil Society and Civil and Political Rights, (ii) Human Rights and the Rule of Law, (iii) Federalism, and (iv) Transitional Issues. Pearce started discussion on protocols for the task forces and the coordinating committee: Each Working Group member would select membership in a task force. Everyone would participate in at least one task force, and more if desired. Any member of the Working Group could contribute to any of the task forces even if not formally a member. The views of other Iraqis, including those outside the Democratic Principles Working Group, could also be solicited.

Given the range of opinions on potentially divisive issues, we agreed that task force papers should provide a menu of options and that the final report would require approval by the Working Group as a whole. Consensus was preferred but not necessary. Dissenting opinions would be included in the text or as an annex. The final report would be submitted to the political conference of the Iraqi opposition.

During the break, the Iraqis bantered good-naturedly as they selected their task force assignments. We reconvened in task force groups, and members of the coordinating committee were announced; Kanan and Ghassan al-Atiyyah, a secular Shi'a, were selected as at-large members.

After adjourning, the Iraqis took stock of their accomplishments and congratulated each other. They had been tentative and uncertain at first. However, they had managed to hear one another and taken steps to overcome differences. Not only had the Iraqis developed better mutual understanding, they had agreed on a collaborative structure to advance their goals. The very process of getting together was valuable. Naysayers about regime change would have been assured by the tone and substance of the meeting. To be sure, important issues divided the Iraqis, but they had managed to work together. Not only did they agree on many issues but they had also agreed to disagree while maintaining a level of civility. If the Democratic Principles Working Group was any indication of how the various factions in Iraq would get along, Iraq's future was beckoningly bright.

Pearce was pleased with the outcome. Even Warrick, who worries as much as he works, allowed himself a moment of satisfaction. Pearce was glad that Ravich approved: An unfavorable report would have caused serious problems for the Future of Iraq Project. Not only had the Iraqis risen to the occasion, but U.S. officials had managed to cooperate despite the intense rivalries brewing in Washington.

CHAPTER 6

THE PRINCIPALS COMMITTEE

O N SEPTEMBER 12, 2002, AFTER A CEREMONY AT GROUND Zero commemorating the victims of the World Trade Center attacks, President Bush addressed the UN General Assembly: "All the world now faces a test and the United Nations a difficult and defining moment. Are Security Council resolutions to be honored and enforced, or cast aside without consequence? Will the United Nations serve the purpose of its founding, or will it be irrelevant?"[1] And concerning war: "If Iraq's regime defies us again, the world must move deliberately, decisively to hold Iraq to account. We will work with the UN Security Council for the necessary resolutions."[2] Bush's remarks were received with polite applause. The speech was neither a declaration of war against Iraq nor an attack on the international system. It put the world body front and center in the struggle between George W. Bush and Saddam Hussein.

Bush turned to his secretary of state to seek the necessary resolutions from the UN. Resolution 1441, adopted unanimously by the Security Council on November 8, 2002, warned Iraq of "serious consequences" and required the Security Council to reconvene and "consider the situation."[3] The political scientists Ivo Daalder and James M. Lindsay praised Powell's efforts: "As for Powell, he had won important internal battles— on whether to go to the United Nations, to seek a new resolution, and to compromise on the authorization to use force. And he had worked hard to persuade his colleagues on the Security Council to back a much more robust approach to requiring Iraq's compliance."[4]

Many member states believed that Washington was just using the United Nations to gain legitimacy for its inevitable war with Iraq. Council members rejected automatic military action. "We will not associate ourselves with military intervention that is not supported by the international community," said France's foreign minister, Dominique de Villepin. "War is always the sanction of failure." Playing off Donald Rumsfeld's disparaging reference to France and Germany as "Old Europe," de Villepin then proclaimed: "This message comes to you from an old country, France, from a continent like mine, Europe, that has known wars, occupation, and brutality."[5] The gallery burst into applause.

Administration hawks were bitter about Bush's decision to involve the United Nations. They dislike the UN for constraining the exercise of U.S. power in the world. To Richard Perle, the UN was just a "chatterbox on the Hudson."[6] According to Undersecretary of State John Bolton, "If the UN secretariat building in New York lost ten stories, it wouldn't make a bit of difference."[7]

B USH'S national security advisers were divided into three camps: hegemonists, neo-conservatives, and pragmatic internationalists. The hegemonists, Dick Cheney and Rumsfeld, believe in unilateral action to project U.S. military power countering threats to U.S. national security. Both came of age during the Cold War, when antagonists were recognizable nation-states. But September 11, 2001, changed their risk assessment. Terror networks were now stateless adversaries that lurked everywhere, even in the homeland. Cheney and Rumsfeld advocated military action to defeat enemies of the United States. Rather than find refuge in a fortressed America, they believe in seeking out opponents and defeating them before they attack. Cheney and Rumsfeld were convinced that Iraq represented "the central front in the war on terrorism."[8]

Many of Bush's national security advisers are neo-conservatives, who served as mid-level officials in the administration of George H. W. Bush. Simply put, neo-cons see the fight against terrorism as a battle between good and evil. They believe in using the U.S. military, not only to enhance security, but to enforce measures that reshape the world in America's image and, in the process, ensure future access to Middle Eastern oil. What is good for America is good for everyone else—even if they don't know it yet. Intelligent and persuasive, the neo-cons rejected stability as the primary objective of U.S. policy in the Middle East. They also rejected alliances with autocrats friendly to U.S. interests because, they argued, real stability is achieved only when the United States pressures regimes to adopt standards of good governance. The neo-cons greatly influenced Bush's view of the world and his approach to Iraq.

Led by Colin Powell, pragmatic internationalists believe that new global threats could best be met through international cooperation. Powell was not against using the military to protect the United States. He firmly believed, however, in working with allies and making sure that enough troops were deployed to accomplish the mission. Powell never tolerated the tethering of the United States by multilateral institutions; but he felt that selective application of multilateralism could effectively advance U.S. interests. Powell was an optimist who saw diplomacy as a tool for harnessing U.S. power and prestige to fashion a better world.

Powell was the only one of Bush's senior national security advisers who served in Vietnam. While Bush secured a place in the Texas Air National Guard, Cheney sought and won five deferments from the draft. Though none had ever seen combat, Cheney and the neo-cons blamed Powell for being too cautious and wary of war.

Cheney and Powell had worked well together in several previous administrations. For example, they cooperated effectively during the 1990 Gulf War when Cheney was secretary of defense and Powell chaired the Joint Chiefs of Staff. After 9/11, though, Cheney, Rumsfeld, and the neo-cons organized a concerted effort to marginalize Powell's influence within the administration. Their attacks on the UN were also indirect criticisms of Powell.

I N 1992, Cheney and Paul Wolfowitz helped draft a national security strategy that institutionalized preemptive action, while lamenting the restrictions of multilateralism and international law. Five years later, during the Clinton administration, Cheney, Rumsfeld, Wolfowitz, Perle, Bolton, and Scooter Libby, among others, established a sort of government-in-exile called the Project for the New American Century (PNAC). The PNAC called on the United States to take advantage of the unipolar moment to consolidate its hegemony in the world. It criticized Clinton for short-changing America's interests through his reluctance to back diplomacy with force.

The PNAC believed that regime change in Iraq would be the fulcrum for transforming the broader Middle East. Moreover, "While the unresolved conflict with Iraq provides the immediate justification, the need for substantial American force presence in the Gulf transcends the issue of the regime of Saddam Hussein." The PNAC wanted to "shape a new century favorable to American principles and interests" and advocated "America's unique role in preserving and extending an international order friendly to our security, our prosperity and our principles."[9] After getting rid of Saddam, they envisioned the U.S. dominating oil supplies through a proxy in Baghdad.

In 1998, fifteen PNAC members sent an open letter to Bill Clinton urging regime change in Iraq and calling on the United States to "recognize a provisional government of Iraq based on the principles and leaders of the Iraqi National Congress (INC) that is representative of all the peoples of Iraq."[10] The letter helped mobilize bipartisan support for the 1998 Iraq Liberation Act. The law stated that "it should be the policy of the United States to support efforts to remove the regime from power."[11] The PNAC envisioned America's invasion of Iraq sending shock waves through the Arab world. Invading Iraq would be a big blow against theocracies and state sponsors of terrorism. With Iraq transformed, Arab youth would become enamored with democracy, causing radical Islam to lose its appeal.

George W. Bush's worldview is shaped by his belief that the great struggles of the twentieth century ended in a victory for the forces of freedom. At the twentieth anniversary of the National Endowment for Democracy, Bush quoted the 2001 Arab Development Report of the United Nations Development Programme. The global wave of democracy had "barely reached the Arab states," he noted. "This freedom deficit undermines human development and is one of the most painful manifestations of lagging political development."[12] He continued in his own words: "The freedom deficit has terrible consequences. In many Middle Eastern countries, poverty is deep and is spreading; women lack rights and are denied schooling. Whole societies remain stagnant while the world moves ahead. These are not a failure of culture or a religion. These are the failures of political and economic doctrines. Military dictatorship and theocratic rule are on a straight smooth highway to nowhere."[13]

There is nothing wrong with promoting freedom and development around the world, of course. The question is, What methods are most effective in advancing those goals? Bush's plan envisioned Iraq as the opening phase of a regime change agenda that would also overthrow the Ba'athists in Syria and the mullahs in Iran. The interests of both the United States and Israel, America's most reliable ally in the region, would be advanced.

When Bush was elected in 2000, PNAC leaders left their positions in business and academia to join the administration, where they continued to advocate a forward freedom strategy for the Middle East. After 9/11, Cheney was preoccupied with the possibility of a far more lethal attack, this time with nuclear, chemical, or biological weapons: "We will work to prevent regimes that sponsor terror from threatening America or our friends and allies with chemical, biological or nuclear weapons—or allowing them to provide those weapons to terrorists. To the extent we define our task broadly, including those who support terrorism, then we get at states."[14] Cheney believed that Saddam was in league with Osama bin Laden and, despite the absence of intelligence proving an operational link between Iraq and al-Qaeda, clung to his conviction that Saddam would provide WMD to al-Qaeda.

Cheney's seniority, experience, and bureaucratic abilities gave him vast influence in the White House. During the first weeks of the administration, Cheney lobbied Bush to make him chair of the Principals Committee, which includes the heads of agencies involved in national security and is responsible for coordinating information and formulating foreign-policy recommendations to the president. This pivotal job is usually reserved for the national security adviser. Though Bush ultimately decided to preserve Condoleezza Rice's role, Cheney was given unprecedented permission to participate in all meetings of the committee. The Office of the Vice President (OVP) functioned like an independent body wielding enormous influence. Cheney asserted a major role in national security policy and created his own National Security Council (NSC) staff, headed by Scooter Libby.

Cheney and Rumsfeld share a common view of America's role in world affairs, a collaboration that dates back to 1969. America's retreat from Saigon had a profound effect on them both, and they blamed President Lyndon Johnson for allowing the domestic peace movement to undermine America's resolve. The "Vietnam syndrome"—a reluctance to use military power—caused a perception of weakness rather than strength and resulted in challenges to the United States. To Bush and his team, Bill Clinton epitomized the problems of political leadership. Halfhearted efforts in Haiti and Somalia had resulted in ignominy and failure. Cheney and Rumsfeld were both deeply skeptical about the U.S. military's role in nation-building.

In addition, Pentagon and OVP personnel had a long history of collaboration. Libby was a former student of Wolfowitz's at Yale University and was his top aide in the administration of George H. W. Bush. Wolfowitz was called the "intellectual godfather" of the war in Iraq.[15] The son of a Cornell University statistics professor, Wolfowitz entered government when he took a position in the Arms Control and Disarmament Agency. During the Ford, Carter, and Reagan administrations, he rotated between positions at the Pentagon and the State Department, including a stint as U.S. ambassador to Indonesia, the world's largest Muslim country. In Jakarta, Wolfowitz took an interest in the reform movement of Islam. He envisioned Iraq, like Indonesia under President Suharto, as a secular pro-Western anchor for U.S. interests in the Muslim world.

Wolfowitz's work on Iraq dated back to the Carter administration, when he drafted a report on security threats in the Persian Gulf that highlighted the danger of Iraq's military to Kuwait and Saudi Arabia. As undersecretary of defense for policy, Wolfowitz was involved in planning the Gulf War. Having urged Bush to march on to Baghdad, he thought the decision to leave Saddam in power was a colossal blunder. Cheney agreed: "Very seldom in life do you get a chance to fix something that went wrong."[16]

The link between terrorists and failed states or rogue regimes that sponsor terrorism became the "principal strategic thought underlying our strategy in the war on terrorism."[17] Administration hawks immediately honed in on Iraq.

Wolfowitz dispatched James Woolsey, the former CIA director, to London. It was rumored that Ramzi Yousef, the jailed mastermind of the 1993 World Trade Center bombing, was really an Iraqi agent who had stolen the identity of an Arab student in Wales. To no avail, Woolsey tried to dig up the fingerprints of the "real" Ramzi Yousef from the West Cardiff police. Wolfowitz was convinced that Iraq had operational ties to al-Qaeda, but the CIA did not believe it. The Agency maintained that Saddam's secular government would never collaborate with a radical Sunni group rooted in Wahhabism.

Rumsfeld wrote to George Tenet, the current CIA director, and suggested putting together a team of experts to conduct a "lessons learned" exercise. Undersecretary of Defense Douglas Feith's Policy Counterterrorism Evaluation Group would review CIA databases and information from the Defense Intelligence Agency (DIA) in search of links between terror groups and Middle Eastern countries. Using raw intelligence, CIA and DIA reports, as well as information from Chalabi's INC, Feith worked with David Wurmser, the special adviser to the undersecretary of state for arms control and international security, and F. Michael Malouf, a former Pentagon official, to produce a "link analysis" that asserted Iraq and al-Qaeda were working together. The CIA had drawn a different conclusion; Wurmser and Malouf alleged serious problems with the Agency's intelligence capabilities.

At the same time, the Office of Special Plans was established in the Office of the Secretary of Defense to bypass normal channels. It used Iraqi exiles of questionable reliability to produce reports on Iraq's illicit weapons programs. In a BBC interview, Feith admitted that the Office of Special Plans was given an ambiguous title: "We did not think it was wise to create a brand-new office and label it an office of Iraq policy."[18] Senator Jay Rockefeller, a Democrat from West Virginia, later accused Feith of running a rogue intelligence operation.[19]

The Office of Special Plans and John Hannah, a special assistant for national security in the OVP, were major recipients of an Information Collection Program run by the INC. Funded by the State Department until the end of 2002 and by the DIA thereafter, the program collaborated with William Luti, a former staffer of speaker Newt Gingrich and chief of Middle East policy at the Pentagon. Feith and Wurmser, both close associates of Richard Perle's, were extensively involved. Wurmser had a long history of working on Iraq. In 1990, he was employed at the Rendon Group, an American public relations firm in London that was contracted to make the case for going to war and creating an external opposition movement to Saddam. Using U.S. taxpayer funds for domestic propaganda, Wurmser oversaw a multimillion dollar campaign demonizing Saddam.

When Richard Perle was assistant secretary of defense, he was dubbed the "Prince of Darkness" for his fierce opposition to arms control agreements with the Soviet Union. Perle did not have an official position in the administration of George W. Bush, but he wielded great influence as chairman of the Defense Policy Board (DPB). Though Perle was offered a senior post in the Pentagon, he declined, citing family reasons. Congressional confirmation would, of course, require close scrutiny of his financial dealings. In 2003, Perle resigned the DPB chairmanship when he was charged with conflict of interest for representing a company seeking Pentagon approval for the sale of its foreign subsidiaries.

Perle's interest in Iraq dates back to his employment as an aide to Senator Scoop Jackson. In 1975, he had the senator's office intervene and arrange a visa for Mula Mustafa Barzani, the Kurdish freedom fighter, to visit the Mayo Clinic for cancer treatment. Perle also arranged CIA sponsorship for Barzani's activities.

Over the years, Perle stayed in close contact with Iraqi exile groups and, after the Gulf War, developed a close friendship with Ahmad Chalabi. "There must be a phase two," Perle insisted after the Taliban was toppled. "At the top of the list for phase two is Iraq."[20] Perle envisioned an open-ended war on terror that would dismantle shadowy terrorist networks and the regimes that harbor them. He argued that attacking Iraq not only would be good for the Iraqis but would also send a message to other rogue regimes—"You're next."[21] As the administration's internal feud escalated over what to do with Iraq, Perle blasted the CIA analysis of Iraq's WMD program, saying that it "isn't worth the paper it's written on."[22]

DIFFERENCES between the White House and the State Department came to a head as Powell was preparing his presentation to the UN Security Council on Iraq's WMD. When Libby gave him a script for presentation to the Security Council; Powell retorted, "I'm not reading this. This is bullshit."[23]

Insisting that all claims be verified by multiple sources, Powell rejected more than half of the original forty-five-page assessment on Iraq's WMD. Libby's text described a chronology of contacts between Iraq and al-Qaeda over many years, including a meeting between Mohammed Atta and an Iraqi intelligence officer in Prague just five months before 9/11. It accused Iraq of developing drone aircraft capable of spraying lethal chemicals and seeking Australian software to map America's east coast.[24] Minutes before Powell's presentation to the United Nations on February 5, 2002, Libby called Powell and urged him once again to emphasize the link between Saddam and al-Qaeda. Against his better judgment, Powell cited human sources who had described mobile germ weapons production labs and mobile warfare research facilities, even though the DIA found that the defectors who provided the information were lying.

Powell supported the president, but he was not gung-ho about the Iraq war. He feared that the coalition for Afghanistan would break up if the United States unilaterally extended the war on terrorism beyond al-Qaeda to other countries. Moreover, he worried that attacking Iraq would lead to more terrorism. As his regime crumbled, Saddam could transfer his WMD to Syria or give them to terrorists. Powell also worried about what would happen to Iraq after Saddam was overthrown. Without international cooperation to stabilize the country, violence could spiral out of control, resulting in bloody civil war and widespread regional instability. Powell's concerns mirrored those of U.S. allies in Europe. Prime Minister Jose Maria Aznar of Spain commented, "We need a lot of Powell, and not much of Rumsfeld."[25]

The neo-cons resented Powell for what they saw as his lack of vision and excessive cautiousness. The "Powell Doctrine" called for the overwhelming use of force, but only as a last resort. Averse to compromise, Powell's opponents criticized him for his dedication to diplomacy. To Perle, Powell was a "soft-liner."[26]

Perle and other neo-cons also questioned Powell's commitment to democracy in the Middle East. During the Gulf War, Powell worked closely with Saudi Arabia and other Arab regimes in the coalition. He forged close ties with governments in the Persian Gulf. When Powell became secretary of state in 2001, he was surrounded by Arabists whom the neo-cons blamed for giving authoritarian Arab governments a pass when it came to human rights. The State Department had long subscribed to the belief that stability was more advantageous than rapid and unpredictable reform. They reasoned that democratization could backfire in bringing anti-American elements to power.

I had many conversations with Marc Grossman, Ryan Crocker, and David Pearce about strategies for promoting democracy in the Arab and Muslim world. They never wavered in their commitment to human rights and democracy. However, they appreciated the importance of a patient approach that emphasized developing democratic institutions and strengthening civil society to buttress reforms.

Faisal al-Istrabadi, who went to Iraq to help draft the Transitional Administrative Law, insisted that State Department officials never doubted whether liberal democracy was possible in Iraq. "From Colin Powell on down, I've spent hundreds of hours with State Department people," he said. "I've never heard one of them say that democracy was not viable in Iraq. Not one."[27]

Nevertheless, Cheney and Rumsfeld distrusted those who were close to Powell. The neo-cons wanted to marginalize anyone who questioned their plans to reinvent Iraq and push radical reform across the Middle East. Because the Future of Iraq Project was led by State Department, Faisal maintained, at the Defense Department he was "seen as one of 'them.'"[28]

Cheney and Rumsfeld thought they understood the Muslim world. Wolfowitz may have dabbled in Islamic studies when he was in Jakarta, but it takes time to develop in-depth understanding. Tutored by scholars such as Bernard Lewis and Fouad Ajami, they listened only to what they wanted to hear.

State Department experts had a far better, though still incomplete, understanding of Iraq. They appreciated the difficulties of developing liberal democracy in the heart of the Arab world. State Department officials were concerned that precipitous elections could bring anti-U.S. elements into power. Building democracy would take time because democracy is a process, not an event. The difference between the State Department and the CIA on one side, and the Pentagon and OVP on the other, was the difference between pragmatists and ideologues. No matter what their policy disagreements, U.S. officials should never have allowed their personal feelings to poison the interagency process. But, of course, they did. Personal animosities combined with different postwar approaches would ultimately destroy the Future of Iraq Project.

Responsibility for the interagency breakdown rests with Condoleezza Rice. The job of the national security adviser is to maintain a level playing field and forge consensus between the president's national security team. When it came to policy, Rice was a manager, not a deep thinker. She had few opinions of her own; indeed, her primary concern was to preserve her relationship with the president. Inconsistency created the impression of an administration in disarray. The lack of clarity confused lawmakers on Capitol Hill and upset U.S. allies and potential partners.

As experienced bureaucratic in-fighters, Cheney and Rumsfeld were able to manipulate the debate so that their views would prevail. Though Rice is "like a daughter" to Powell,[29] she did little to prevent Cheney and Rumsfeld from marginalizing the secretary of state. David Kay maintained that Rice willfully suppressed Powell's more prudent approach to Iraq, leaving him "hanging out to dry." Kay accused Rice of botching the intelligence management of Iraq's WMD and turning a blind eye as hawks on the principals committee cherry-picked intelligence to justify policy decisions that had already been made. According to Kay, Rice's National Security Council was the "dog that did not bark."

The *New York Times* editorial board wrote: "At best, Ms. Rice was ignoring the facts that were right in front of her. In any case, she failed in her duty to keep the president from seizing upon the same unreliable intelligence to defend his policy of preventive war with Iraq before the American public and the world."[30]

The NSC cleared an address by Bush on October 7, 2002 that asserted, "Iraq has trained al-Qaeda members in bomb-making and poisons and deadly gases." He also stated, "We know that Iraq and the al-Qaeda terrorist network share a common enemy: The United States of America."[31]

CHAPTER 7

— ◆ —

AHMAD CHALABI

THE BUSH ADMINISTRATION NEVER HAD A PLAN OR program for running postwar Iraq; instead, it focused on a person—Ahmad Chalabi, who, it believed, could transform Iraq into a liberal democracy and support U.S. goals in the Middle East. U.S. officials did not trust unknown elements of the Iraqi polity, which they feared would be unfriendly to U.S. interests.

I first met Chalabi in 1993 when he gave me a tour of the Iraqi National Congress (INC) headquarters in northern Iraq. Chalabi is an impressive figure—elegantly dressed, strikingly intelligent, and compellingly articulate. In the mid–1990s, Chalabi became a regular in Washington's power circles. His lobbying efforts paid off when President Clinton signed the Iraqi Liberation Act of 1998, legislation that made regime change in Iraq the official policy of the U.S. government.

In 2002, a major battle broke out within the Bush administration over who would lead the Iraq if the U.S. went to war to remove Saddam Hussein. Chalabi's supporters poured resources into the INC. In turn, the INC provided "informants" and fed intelligence directly to officials at the White House and Pentagon. As a result, Chalabi's INC became a one-stop shop for information on Iraq.

The Kurds warned me not to trust Chalabi; they insisted that he would be an unreliable partner over the long term. But at the time, Iraqi opposition leaders were content to let Chalabi act as the front man. Only later did Iraqi leaders express concerns that Chalabi had supplied misleading information on Iraq's weapons of mass destruction (WMD), conjured a connection between Saddam and al-Qaeda, and exaggerated the feasibility of establishing a Western-style democracy in Iraq.

I never doubted Chalabi's commitment to create a "new Iraq," nor was I surprised when Chalabi emerged as a powerbroker on U.S. policy. It is understandable that Chalabi would tell people what they wanted to hear. His goal was to gain U.S. support for regime change and, if necessary, for military action. Chalabi's intelligence was embraced by U.S. government officials who found it convenient in justifying their aims. Among Washington insiders, no foreign national has ever evoked such strong feelings—both pro and con.

Administration officials did not publicly announce what leadership role they envisioned for Ahmad Chalabi after Saddam was deposed, nor did they tell me. But Chalabi's backers in the Pentagon and the Office of the Vice President (OVP) invested almost messianic qualities in the man. In October 2002, I addressed a group of European diplomats meeting U.S. officials to discuss postwar plans. Though I emphasized the importance of a broad-based and inclusive approach, a senior staffer in the office of the Secretary of Defense focused on Chalabi's leadership role: "Ahmad Chalabi is like Prophet Mohammed. At first people doubted him, but they came to realize the wisdom of his ways."

Chalabi became the poster boy for the "new Iraq"—modern, secular, democratic, and pro-Western. He convinced some U.S. officials that he could deliver America's vision for Iraq and the broader Middle East. Under Chalabi, Iraq's liberal democracy would pressure the leaders of Syria, Iran, and Libya to reform. Iraq's transformation would inspire moderate Palestinian forces; Iraq and Israel would establish diplomatic relations and other Arab countries would follow suit.

Smart U.S. officials allowed Chalabi to spin them because they badly wanted to believe what he said. Suspending their disbelief, some envisioned Chalabi as a Mesopotamian Spartacus mobilizing vast legions to take over and reshape Iraq. Chalabi systematically provided the rationale for going to war and promised that coalition forces would be greeted as liberators.

The information Chalabi provided also affected Pentagon plans for postwar Iraq. Rumsfeld's decision to send too few troops was influenced by Chalabi's claim that he controlled a vast underground security network whose members would stand up as soon as they saw the Americans. Either Chalabi's network did not exist or it did not materialize. As Saddam's regime began to crumble, the Pentagon did not have enough boots on the ground to meet security requirements. The U.S. failure to secure Iraq led to widespread instability, looting, and destruction. It also undermined a core recommendation of the Future of Iraq Project: Immediate and tangible benefits after liberation were vital for winning the hearts and minds of Iraqis.

Senator Joseph R. Biden, Jr., a Democrat from Delaware, was always skeptical about Chalabi: "I could never quite understand the incredible preoccupation of the administration with Mr. Chalabi and I think that reliance has done us a great deal of damage in terms of establishing legitimacy."[1] Biden was right.

AHMAD Chalabi grew up as a secular Shi'a in Baghdad. He was born to power in one of Iraq's wealthiest families. Chalabi's father, who enjoyed vast real estate holdings, was an important political figure who served as president of the Iraqi senate and adviser to the king. His grandfather also had an extensive history of public service in nine different cabinet positions. Accustomed to success and achievement, Chalabi presumed a right to join the ranks of Iraq's elite. He earned undergraduate and master's degrees in mathematics from the Massachusetts Institute of Technology and a Ph.D. in mathematics from the University of Chicago. Well-spoken and handsomely attired in expensive designer suits, he circulated comfortably in positions of power.

The Chalabi family fled Iraq after the 1958 revolution, when Ahmad was twelve years old. By 1977, Chalabi had moved to Amman and befriended the Jordanian royal family. He founded Jordan's third largest bank, the Petra Bank. After the bank's mysterious financial collapse, Jordanian authorities launched an investigation into the crash. On April 9, 1992, a military court convicted Chalabi in absentia of thirty-one charges, including embezzlement, theft, forgery, currency speculation, perjury, and self-dealing. He was sentenced to twenty-two years of hard labor and ordered to repay $230 million.

In response, Chalabi accused Iraq of a political frame-up and Saddam Hussein of orchestrating the Petra Bank's failure. In a civil suit filed against the Kingdom of Jordan, Chalabi charged the former Jordanian prime minister and director of Jordan's central bank with stealing the money. He also claimed that Jordan had convicted him out of fear that he would disclose illegal Jordanian arms sales to Iraq.

Allegations of fiscal improprieties have always dogged Chalabi. I do not believe, however, that Chalabi is driven by personal enrichment. For sure, Chalabi has lavish personal tastes. But he used his personal wealth primarily to advance his political objectives by cultivating a vast patronage system. He paid loyalists to build a network of activists committed to overthrowing Saddam. Like a tribal sheik, Chalabi understood that loyalty is dependent upon financial rewards; wealth was just a means to political power. Chalabi envisioned himself as Iraq's great leader—like Salladin, who unified the "land between two rivers" and then sent his armies into battle across the region.

When the INC was founded by exiles at a meeting in Vienna in May 1992, it was truly representative of Iraq's diverse ethnic and tribal groups. At the time, Arab Shi'a and Kurds were still reeling from Saddam's ruthless crackdown after the Gulf War. Iraqi opposition leaders told me they supported the INC because it vowed to get rid of Saddam Hussein's Ba'ath Party and establish a representative government based on the principles of democracy, federalism, parliamentarianism, and human rights.

In 1995, Chalabi hatched a plot to overthrow Saddam. Several high-ranking Ba'ath Party officials and generals of the elite Republican Guard were co-conspirators. The plan envisioned INC and tribal militias attacking three cities simultaneously. The coup plotters anticipated that the revolt would trigger a nationwide uprising, culminating in the overthrow of Saddam's regime.

The plan collapsed. Saddam infiltrated the cabal and arrested two hundred Iraqi military officers before the rebellion unfolded. When news of the debacle surfaced, I was horrified to learn that at least eighty officers had been executed. I was also deeply disappointed in the Kurds. Saddam's forces had taken advantage of a dispute between the Kurdistan Democratic Party (KDP) and the Patriotic Union of Kurdistan (PUK) to make a deal with the KDP that allowed the Iraqi armed forces to enter Iraqi Kurdistan. The INC headquarters in Erbil was overrun. Many dissidents—Kurds, Turkmen, Assyrians, and Arabs—were rounded up. Marc Grossman supervised the evacuation of 7,000 people from northern Iraq. U.S. employees, Iraqis with ties to the CIA, and Iraqis working for American non-governmental organizations were rushed across the border to Silopi in Turkey. There they were loaded onto buses that took them to an airfield where they boarded C–130 Hercules transport planes and flew to Guam, the first stop towards resettlement in the United States. Many of those left behind were executed; the others disappeared.

Whenever Chalabi failed, he always laid blame elsewhere. In this instance, Chalabi accused the CIA of incompetence and charged the

Agency with bungling the rebellion. The botched operation became known at the CIA as the "Bay of Goats."²

THE incident taught Chalabi an important lesson: Iraqis could not rid themselves of Saddam without international assistance. More than political support and covert operations, Chalabi needed a real army to invade Iraq. To this end, he intensified his efforts to cultivate political leaders and opinion makers in the United States.

Chalabi devoted himself to the study of U.S. domestic politics and the U.S. history of foreign interventions: "I followed very closely how Roosevelt, who abhorred the Nazis, at a time when isolationist sentiment was paramount in the United States, managed adroitly to persuade the American people to go to war," he said. "I studied it with a great deal of respect; we learned a lot from it."³ Chalabi also pored over documents describing postwar reconstruction in Germany and Japan. After getting the U.S. into Iraq, he hoped to keep it there to stabilize the country and consolidate his authority as Iraq's new ruler.

Private dinner parties in Washington's neo-conservative circles helped form the nucleus of a support group, including members of the Project for the New American Century (PNAC). However, Chalabi still needed a broad-based domestic constituency in favor of regime change. After assessing various lobbying strategies, Chalabi decided to use the model of the American Israel Public Affairs Committee (AIPAC). AIPAC, one of the strongest and most effective advocacy groups in the United States, lobbies the executive branch, Capitol Hill, the media, and various think tanks. It favors a multitrack approach through strategic coalitions and outreach across party lines.

More than inspiration, Chalabi also sought support in prominent Jewish circles. In June 1997, he delivered a rousing speech to the Jewish Institute for National Security Affairs, during which he promised to topple Saddam and establish an Iraqi government friendly to Israel. He pledged to rid the region of terror groups and to use Iraq as a base for undermining rogue states. He also proposed expanding economic ties between Iraq and Israel by restoring the Kirkuk-Haifa pipeline, which was shut down in 1948.

His vision for Iraq and the Middle East was warmly welcomed. Chalabi represented a heretofore unknown leader in the Arab world: He would not only defend U.S. interests in the region but also sign a peace treaty with Israel and pressure other Arab countries to abandon their hostility towards the Jewish state.

Chalabi's promises of support for Israel won him many friends on Capitol Hill. Effective outreach put him in touch with conservative think tanks such as the American Enterprise Institute. As a good news source, Chalabi also earned favor with key journalists, among them Jim Hoagland of the *Washington Post*, Judith Miller of the *New York Times* and Claudia Rossett of the *Wall Street Journal*.

He made Washington insiders feel that he was their most important contact with the Iraqis, and he convinced Iraqis that only he could give them what they wanted from the United States. Chalabi asserted that Iraqis were practically begging to be invaded; furthermore, after liberation, the country could be run on the cheap. There was nothing wrong with Chalabi's pro-Western positions; Arab reform and peace between Israel and her neighbors are noble goals. However, his backers failed to appreciate fully that Chalabi's self-interest was served by persuading the United States to invade Iraq. Chalabi's singular focus was to secure assistance in advancing Iraq's liberation.

Financial resources started pouring into the INC. The Chalabi patronage machine was well fueled. The gravy train started right after the Gulf War, when George H. W. Bush signed a covert "lethal finding" authorizing the CIA to "create the conditions for the removal of Saddam Hussein from power" and develop an external opposition to the regime. The presidential finding allocated $100 million to the goal of regime change in Iraq. Most of the money went to the Rendon Group in London. According to the INC's Francis Brooke, who worked on "perception management" at Rendon, "We tried to burn through $40 million per year. It was a nice job."[4]

The U.S. government funneled more than $100 million to the Iraqi National Congress between 1992 and 2004. After the Iraq Liberation Act of 1998, the State Department drew from a variety of accounts, providing $33 million to the INC. When the State Department suspended its support, Chalabi's network attacked the State Department. The Pentagon came to Chalabi's rescue: For two years, beginning in May 2002, the Defense Intelligence Agency (DIA) provided the INC with $4 million in monthly payments of $335,000.[5]

Corruption was inevitable with so much money kicking around. The INC spent all its funds in cash and kept shoddy records. When the CIA looked into INC finances, Chalabi "refused to cooperate with an audit because [he] argued it would breach the secrecy of operations."[6] According to the Agency's case officers, "There was a lot of hanky-panky with accounting: triple billing, things that were not mentioned, things inflated . . . it was a nightmare."[7] When INC accounting practices surfaced in the press, Richard Perle defended Chalabi and asked whether the United States required Charles de Gaulle to provide expense reports during his efforts to liberate France from Nazi Germany.

B EGINNING in 1998, the INC was gathering intelligence on Iraq's humanitarian requirements and also using intelligence to make the case for war. By the time George W. Bush was elected, the INC had developed an intelligence program with global reach. It paid special attention to raw intelligence and providing defectors with first-hand accounts of Iraq's WMD. After 9/11, Chalabi also used the INC's intelligence operation to assert an operational link between Iraq and the terror attacks.

Though the INC's information came with an overt agenda, administration hawks did not question its reliability, nor did they listen to concerns raised by the CIA and the State Department's Bureau of Intelligence and Research. In response to allegations that the INC was providing exaggerated and fabricated intelligence, Wolfowitz drew on his experience setting up parallel operations in the Reagan administration to create the Office of Special Plans (OSP), directed by Douglas Feith. The OSP was ostensibly established to provide objective intelligence, but it gathered intelligence with an objective: to justify military action against Iraq.

Chalabi's cohorts also set up parallel structures to circumvent U.S. laws prohibiting the use of taxpayer money for lobbying the government. Chalabi helped create the Iraq Liberation Action Committee (ILAC) and the Iraqi National Congress Support Foundation. According to its articles of incorporation, ILAC was formed "to work in support of the United States and international efforts to remove the regime headed by Saddam Hussein from power in Iraq" and to help "drafting resolutions, legislation, and regulations [and] engaging the United States in the promotion of democracy in Iraq."[8]

In 2001, the State Department's inspector general questioned whether the INC had violated lobbying laws and cited its relationship with ILAC. The inspector general determined that the INC had a relationship with ILAC "contrary to the proposal and assurances made" to State Department officials.[9] The audit also raised questions about $2.2 million in INC spending.

The following year, Chalabi got into more trouble by violating the INC's grant agreement with the State Department. On June 26, 2002, Entifadh Qanbar, the INC spokesman in Washington, D.C., sent a memo to the Senate Appropriations Committee titled "Summary of ICP Product Cited in Major English Language News Outlets Worldwide." It provided extensive details on the INC's use of U.S. government grants to develop information products.[10] The memo also highlighted the INC's effectiveness in placing news stories, claiming responsibility for 108 English-language reports between October 2001 and May 2002. Naming Bill Luti and John Hannah, the memo indicated that products were being passed directly to senior officials in the Pentagon and the OVP.

In addition to raw intelligence, the INC provided defectors offering firsthand accounts. Regarding WMD, the defectors claimed that Iraq had mobile biological warfare facilities disguised as yogurt and milk trucks. Code-named "Curveball," one informant maintained that WMD production and storage facilities were hidden beneath Saddam's presidential palaces and in the basement of a hospital in Baghdad. Abu Zeinab al-Qurairy claimed to have been employed at Salman Park where al-Qaeda was training Iraqi personnel. Khidir Hamza purported to be involved in Iraq's nuclear program and asserted that Saddam was on the verge of developing a nuclear bomb to use as blackmail. Sabah Khalifa posited that Iraq's security services were receiving WMD and anthrax training. Other false charges surfaced: Iraq had toxin-tipped scud missiles targeting Israel; Saddam's security services held eighty Kuwaitis captured in 1990; U.S. Navy Lieutenant Commander Michael Scott Speicher, missing in action after his war plane was downed during the Gulf War, was seen alive in Baghdad in 1998.[11]

None of the informants proved to be reliable assets. The CIA called Curveball a "fabricator";[12] Abu Zeinab was dismissed as a "bullshitter."[13] A senior U.S. intelligence official characterized information provided by the INC and its informants as "useless at best and misleading at worst."[14] The opinion was corroborated by the DIA, which indicated that the information was of "little or no value."[15]

Chalabi understood that putting information into print created the impression of multiple sources. In at least one instance, the INC made defectors available to the media immediately after they were debriefed by U.S. intelligence. Judith Miller traveled to Bangkok, where the INC arranged for her to meet Adnan Ihsan al-Haideri. But three days before

Miller wrote about him as a credible informant, al-Haideri had flunked a polygraph test. Miller published a series of spectacular reports based on information from informants provided by the INC. After it became known that Chalabi was her primary source, the *New York Times* published a formal apology for its coverage.[16]

Widening the rift between his supporters and detractors in the U.S. government, Chalabi provided information directly to the OVP and Feith's Office of Special Plans. The INC's information found its way into statements by U.S. officials. Coincidental with Bush's address to the UN General Assembly on September 12, 2002, the United States issued a dossier titled "A Decade of Deception and Defiance"; this work drew on a number of sources, including statements from informants handed over by Chalabi. The October 2002 National Intelligence Estimate incorporated the INC's raw information and other sources to make the case that Iraq possessed WMD and was actively pursuing the capability to develop a nuclear bomb.

A month after 9/11, two-thirds of Americans believed that "Saddam Hussein helped the terrorists in the September 11 attacks."[17] Cheney's ongoing allegations that Iraq was behind al-Qaeda's attacks did even more to generate public support for the Iraq war than concerns about WMD. False claims even found their way into Powell's carefully vetted presentation to the UN Security Council on February 5, 2003. In addition to satellite photography, Powell talked about "firsthand descriptions of biological weapons factories on wheels and rails."[18]

Chalabi's dissembling finally caught up with him. On March 3, 2004, U.S. senators wrote to the Government Accounting Office asking for an investigation into whether taxpayer funds were used by the INC to arrange meetings between Iraqi defectors and journalists, to propagandize the American public, and to influence Congress on matters concerning Iraq.[19] Chalabi was quick to defend himself: "We were not focused on WMD. The U.S. asked us. We didn't bring these people up. They asked us. They requested this help from us."[20] After the United States invaded Iraq, Chalabi showed no remorse about the credibility of his intelligence operation. "As far as we're concerned," he asserted, "we have been entirely successful. The tyrant Saddam is gone and the Americans are in Baghdad. What was said before is not important."[21]

Chalabi got what he wanted. The INC's advocacy helped administration hawks make the case for preemptive military action. With war looming, Chalabi turned his attention to plans for postwar Iraq: He wanted to make sure that the U.S. government put him in a position to dominate the transition and take power in Baghdad.

Although Ahmad Chalabi did not directly participate in any activities of the Future of Iraq Project, he carefully placed his proxies in positions that would allow them to steer the process. The Democratic Principles Working Group's coordinating committee was dominated by the INC. Salem Chalabi, Ahmad's nephew, and Kanan Makiya had spent a lifetime working to overthrow Saddam. Now was their chance to play a prominent role in shaping the new Iraq.

CHAPTER 8

——— • ———

WILTON PARK

THOUGH THE WORKING GROUP'S PREVIOUS MEETING in Surrey, England, had ended on a positive note, and the task forces struggled to maintain momentum and finish their reports. It was hard to keep everybody involved. The Iraqi participants were, after all, scattered over three continents and a dozen time zones. For the planning process to gain acceptance, participants had to feel that they were consulted and that their views were reflected in the final report.

A Foreign Service Officer named Yael Lempert coordinated input from the Iraqis. Lempert was the State Department's troubleshooter. A highly energetic and skilled member of David Pearce's staff, she was adept and well suited for the task; Lempert had an open, honest, and even-handed approach that enabled ready rapport with the Iraqi participants. A tireless worker, she had gained the trust of Pearce and her State Department colleagues, and she was on good terms with her counterparts in other agencies.

In between its first and second meeting, the State Department's Office of Northern Gulf Affairs tried to organize a weekly conference call with members of the Democratic Principles Working Group. Telephonic coordination did not go well and soon proved ineffective. In some instances, the call did not go through; in others, the connection was bad. Sometimes Iraqis dropped off the line in the middle of the discussion. Moreover, the Iraqis used the conference call to complain about process rather than to focus on work products. I was growing increasingly concerned about the ability of the Iraqis to come together and finish the task at hand.

So that Iraqis drafting the task-force reports could receive the necessary written feedback to complete their work, I prepared a survey for all members of the Working Group. The survey was designed to involve the participants and to consolidate their views. It was also intended to forestall criticism by giving every person a chance to contribute.

Only a few surveys were returned by the deadline. Some arrived too late to be incorporated. Other opinions were so fragmented that they were of little value. As a result, the coordinating committee took upon itself the responsibility of preparing the report.

In addition to Kanan Makiya, other committee members—Faisal al-Istrabadi, Rend al-Rahim, and Salem Chalabi—worked hard on the document. On October 4, 2002, the coordinating committee met to review progress. Of its ten members, eight attended; the notable exception was Ghassan al-Atiyyah, who deliberately absented himself because, he claimed, the draft had not been provided in time for him to respond adequately.

JUST after the Working Group's first meeting, Bush addressed the UN General Assembly on September 12. He warned the world body that, unless it enforced existing resolutions calling for the disarmament of Iraq, it would become an irrelevant entity. The White House released its National Security Strategy on September 20, 2002. Its Doctrine of Preemption affirmed America's right to attack potential foes before they could harm the United States.

The National Intelligence Estimate of October 1 included key judgments that influenced the Iraq war resolution pending in Congress. It concluded, "If left unchecked [Iraq] will have a nuclear weapon during this decade."[1] On October 7, Bush issued an ultimatum: "After eleven years during which we have tried containment, sanctions, inspections, even selected military action, the end result is that Saddam Hussein still has chemical and biological weapons and is increasing his capabilities to make more. And he is moving ever closer to developing a nuclear weapon." He continued, "The time for denying, deceiving, and delaying has come to an end. Saddam Hussein must disarm himself—or, for the sake of peace, we will lead a coalition to disarm him."[2]

Working Group members had been reluctant to be a part of a theoretical exercise. But by the time we met at Wilton Park, Surrey, Bush had dispelled their doubts: It looked as though the United States was really going to war. The moment was sobering because the Iraqi opposition had so far focused on advocacy. In the event of military action, postwar planning took on a greater urgency and required different skills.

If war was indeed imminent, Iraqis had a lot of work to do preparing for the transition.

I anticipated a showdown at Wilton Park. Despite the surprising degree of goodwill coming out of the first meeting, uneven participation during the drafting process had exacerbated differences. The worst possible outcome would be for participants to walk out and cause the effort to collapse. Although we had originally hoped the meeting would formally adopt the coordinating committee's report, my expectations were now low because of the difficulties in preparing for the meeting.

Salem Chalabi showed up in Wilton Park with several boxes containing copies of a bound glossy document titled "Transition to Democracy in Iraq." The imposing volume was a couple of inches thick. It did not, however, reflect the views of participants. Over breakfast, Kanan expressed frustration that those with dissenting opinions had not been more active making their case within the agreed-upon framework. He was also critical of the State Department for slowing the process; drafts were in English rather than Arabic.

I sympathized with Kanan's frustrations, but urged him to refrain from publicly criticizing Members of the Working Group. He would garner greater support if his colleagues assumed ownership of the document. Even if they had not participated, I assured Kanan, the Working Group would still embrace the report if they were given the opportunity to discuss it and make changes.

Kanan addressed the Working Group: "[The report] is a work in progress that represents the collective effort of all those individuals on the coordinating committee who committed time and effort to contacting their fellow task force members and producing it. It embodies input from the working group, Iraqis outside the working group, and non-Iraqi experts."[3] Describing the difficulties of communicating with so many over such great distances, he acknowledged that the report was not representative. Working Group members were surprised when the report was distributed, and many were seeing it for the first time.

To frame recommendations, the report used the resolution adopted at the Salahuddin conference in October 1992: It called for a democratic and federally structured Iraq with separation of powers and individual and group rights. Kanan explained that the report also took into account the meeting between Iraqi opposition groups and U.S. officials in Washington, D.C., on August 8, 2002, at which the opposition agreed to hold

a conference of free Iraqis before any action was taken in Iraq. The purpose of the conference would be to adopt a detailed program for Iraq's
transition from dictatorship to democracy.

Kanan further stated, "To prevent disarray and a repeat of 1991, a
temporary Iraqi authority must be on the ground and capable of operating as soon as the regime starts to disintegrate. Preparations for this
eventuality must be made in advance, before the fall of the regime."[4] In
a stirring appeal, he maintained that "Iraqis abroad, who are in a position
to act, are morally obligated to do so and to do so fast."[5] To this end, he
suggested that the Iraqi Opposition Conference adopt the report of the
Democratic Principles Working Group and move quickly to establish a
transitional authority made up of technocrats from the Iraqi diaspora
who were qualified to govern during a transition period that could last
up to thirty-six months.

The report was thorough and comprehensive. It addressed the issues
of democracy, human rights, security, and the political transition. Asserting a leading role for Iraqi exiles, the report posited that a transitional
authority should be established at the Iraqi Opposition Conference. The
conference would elect an assembly of about one hundred persons who,
in turn, would select an executive. Under U.S. protection, the Transitional Authority would assume power as soon as the outgoing regime
was dismantled. The executive would, upon entering Baghdad, become
head of the Provisional Government, and the national assembly would
be upgraded to a constituent assembly. The assembly's membership
would double by adding representatives, to include notables and local
leaders, from inside the country. Local elections for mayors, district officials, and regional administrators would take place within twelve months
of the transition.

In addition, the constituent assembly would appoint legal experts and
professionals to consider topics such as truth and reconciliation, amnesty,
a bill of rights, the rights of nationalities, and how federalism would work.
The constituent assembly's priority would be to develop, discuss, and approve a permanent constitution for Iraq. It would also establish committees to draft an electoral law, prepare a national census, and address other
transitional matters. Until Iraq's permanent constitution could be
adopted through a referendum, the transitional authority would use an
amended version of the 1925 Iraqi constitution as Iraq's governing law.
After the executive had established the Provisional Government, it

would be responsible for basic services and administration; it would also be responsible for reforming security-sector institutions and adopting a de-Ba'athification program: "Foreign troops, assisted by émigré Iraqis, will play the lead role in maintaining security in the initial phases."[6]

I leaned over and quietly complimented Kanan. "I've been working on the document my whole life," he replied. "It's been in my briefcase waiting for this moment."[7]

Some Iraqis objectioned. In particular, they were upset about the prominent role the report envisioned for Iraqi exiles. They viewed it as an attempt to hijack the Democratic Principles Working Group and secure its endorsement for the transition plan of the Iraq National Congress (INC).

Ghassan criticized the way the report was prepared as well as its conclusions. He complained about the rushed timetable and noted that dissenting views had largely been ignored. He also noted that the report's structure did not even correspond to the thematic categories of the Working Group's task forces.

Laith Kubba criticized Kanan's transition plan as unworkable. Laith believed that Iraqi exiles were too divided among themselves and did not command loyalty inside Iraq. As an alternative, he proposed an interim administration with three temporary councils, each with defined powers and responsibilities. A lower house of two hundred members would include representatives from within Iraq as well as the exile community. An upper house, or senate, would have one hundred seats for tribal and ethnic leaders as well as religious dignitaries. These two bodies would nominate members of a constitutional assembly and approve the draft constitution before submitting it to a public referendum.

Laith also proposed a third council that would focus on national security, its members to include select officers from the current Iraqi security establishment, as well as Kurdish peshmerga and militia from the Supreme Council for Islamic Revolution in Iraq. The security council would coordinate efforts to guard Iraq's borders and so prevent foreign fighters from entering the country. It would assert control over weapons depots and control armed groups to prevent crime and violence. Finally, Laith recommended that civilian bureaucrats retain their jobs to ensure the unbroken provision of essential services. A presidential troika, including a Sunni, a Shi'a, and a Kurd, would appoint cabinet ministers and provide executive leadership.

The Kurds objected to both proposals. They did not accept Kanan's vision of a transitional authority dominated by exiles. Having suffered from Saddam's heavy hand, the Kurds were not willing to entrust their future to an exile politician who might abrogate their hard-fought progress towards self-rule. Laith's plan, they said, relied too much on central authority and failed to articulate power sharing between Baghdad and the regions. The Kurds believed that their interests would be swamped in councils dominated by Arabs and exiles. They also thought Laith's proposal too cumbersome; the joint presidency would end in gridlock. It would be impossible to quickly establish complicated governance structures while keeping Iraq stable and meeting humanitarian needs.

The Working Group could have gone on venting differences and debating transitional plans. Its purpose, however, was not to negotiate the mandate of a transitional authority but to agree on guiding principles in laying the groundwork for Iraq's peaceful and democratic future.

Pearce had let the conversation go too long. During a coffee break, I urged him to steer the meeting back on track by reminding the Iraqis of the Working Group's original purpose and asking the task forces to report on their work. After that, we could discuss strategies for linking the Working Group with the Iraqi opposition's political conference. Pearce agreed, and, after the break, each task force presented its findings.

CIVIL SOCIETY, CIVIL AND POLITICAL RIGHTS

The task force embraced the rule of law and recognized that civil and political rights are fundamental to good government. Iraq's future constitution would adopt human-rights precedents from the 1925 constitution and include a bill of rights reflecting international standards embodied in the UN Declaration on Universal Human Rights.

Though individual rights enable group rights, special protections for the rights of nationalities would be needed. These protections should accord with provisions in the Copenhagen Convention of the Commission on Security and Cooperation in Europe. Self-determination does not imply a right to sovereignty or statehood: An individual could have a strong sense of group identity and still be loyal to the state.

Special protections would be needed for vulnerable groups. Women have always played a leading role in Iraqi society and their rights should be promoted in accordance with the Convention on the Advancement of Women. To redress ethnic cleansing by the regime, displaced persons should have the right to return to their homes, reclaim property, or receive compensation. Religious freedom would be protected, and the right to receive a religious education guaranteed.

The task force highlighted the prevention of torture and safeguards against inhumane treatment during detention. It emphasized the role of civil society in holding government accountable. Because Iraq's civil society had virtually collapsed under decades of authoritarian rule, measures would be needed to revitalize independent media, political parties, watchdog groups, professional associations, and other nongovernmental organizations. Civil society should also participate in discussions about the permanent constitution.

Participants could not agree, however, on whether the new constitution should make Islam the official state religion. They also wrestled with the balance between individual and group rights: The extraordinary protections of group rights could cause disunity and accelerate fragmentation.

HUMAN RIGHTS AND THE RULE OF LAW

The task force recognized that human rights and the rule of law are the cornerstones of peace, progress, and development. To these ends, it affirmed that democracy is the most effective system of governance. Iraq would need checks and balances, as well as provisions separating powers between the executive, judicial, and legislative branches.

Given Iraq's history of dictatorship, military authorities would have to be subordinate to civilian leaders if democracy was to flourish. Measures would also be needed to professionalize the armed forces and, in establishing an all-volunteer army, former members of the armed forces should be given technical training to help ease their integration into civilian life. Iraq's new security services would be accountable to a military council defining their mission, force levels, and budget.

Without a system of transitional justice, widespread revenge-taking, vendettas, and vigilantism could disrupt public order and social cohesion. To promote national healing, the truth-and-reconciliation process would include a body to investigate war crimes and identify the worst criminals. A list of the "Most Wanted" should be prepared and offenders held accountable. Security agencies involved in atrocities, such as the Mukhabarat and military intelligence, should be disbanded and so-called lustration laws adopted to remove those who had committed atrocities.

To strengthen the administration of justice, responsibilities between the Ministries of Justice and Interior must be delineated. Military courts would be replaced with civilian courts, and judges would be selected on their merits and their commitment to fairness and impartiality. The army and police would also be trained in human rights and international humanitarian law. Legislative oversight would establish transparency and impose limits on expenditures. A National Human Rights Commission would monitor compliance with constitutional requirements, and an ombudsman would adjudicate complaints.

Participants disagreed about de-Ba'athification. They discussed two options: either bar all high-ranking Ba'ath Party officials from office, or make allowances for individuals who joined the party because they had no choice. Some were concerned that eliminating the armed forces and intelligence agencies could jeopardize national security. The task force could not agree on whether to reform or disband all organs of the security sector, nor did it define a balance between the need for justice and reconciliation. Some argued that all persons who had committed or were knowledgeable about atrocities should be prosecuted; others preferred some kind of amnesty.

FEDERALISM

The task force supported federalism consistent with the Salahuddin Declaration of 1992. It agreed that federalism would not compromise national unity, nor would it promote fragmentation if an essential role was preserved for the central government (e.g., national defense, monetary policy, and the energy sector).

Federal structures should reflect group affinities and regional interests but must not be ethnically homogeneous. Consistent with the goal of promoting human rights through decentralization, federal units would enable nationalities to assume responsibility for administration at the local level. Resource-sharing with the regions should be based on their size, population, and contribution to the national treasury. A bicameral legislature with an upper and lower house would assure proportional and regional representation.

Despite agreement on the principle of federalism, the task force thought that defining details of a federal arrangement should be delayed until a competent body was established to manage the return of displaced persons, conduct a population census, and develop demarcation procedures. However, it agreed that deferring decisions should not be misunderstood as a lack of support for federalism.

Participants did not reach consensus on how many federal units should be established. Some Iraqis wanted three provinces, others wanted five, and some insisted on eighteen. Pointing out that Iraq is Kurdish and Arab, the Kurds argued that there should be one Kurdish entity and Iraqi Arabs could sort out for themselves the number of federal units in the rest of the country. In response, Turkmen and Assyrians insisted that they should control a federal entity where they constitute a majority. Some task-force participants believed that Iraq's eighteen governorates should be preserved.

TRANSITIONAL ISSUES

The task force agreed that legitimacy would be enhanced by making sure the transitional authority included a broad representative group of Iraqis. Decisions affecting the transition must be carefully considered because they send a message to all Iraqis. Trends established at the outset would shape subsequent events.

In addition, the manner in which Saddam was deposed would affect transitional strategies. If the United States invaded, the transitional authority would be dominated by the United States. Regardless, the transitional authority must be temporary and include checks and balances. A legal instrument would be needed to define the duration and scope of operation and lend it legitimacy.

While structures should reflect the country's requirements, public order, reconstruction, and humanitarian assistance would be priorities. One of the transitional authority's first tasks would be to conduct a census in preparation of elections. Regarding a legal framework establishing more permanent governance, regulations on the formation of political parties would be required, as well as an electoral law. Iraq's permanent constitution should be approved in a popular referendum.

The task force disagreed sharply on the division of transition responsibilities between Iraqis inside the country and those outside, although it was felt that both groups have vital skills. The proposal to convene a conference of Iraqi exiles that would select an interim assembly and executive was hotly debated. Some were afraid that an unelected provisional government would deprive Iraqis inside the country of full democratic participation.

In exploring the establishment of an advisory council, discussion also bogged down over the selection process. The Iraqis agreed, however, that the council's legitimacy would be compromised if members were appointed by a foreign power. There was consensus on the need for an international security force, but the Iraqis disagreed about whether it should be led by the United States. They also debated an appropriate role for the national army and regional militias.

Disagreement also arose over a role for the United Nations. Some Iraqis thought the United Nations should lead the Transitional Authority; others questioned the world body's legitimacy, criticized its management of the Oil for Food Program, and disparaged the integrity of UN staff in Iraq. They worried that an open-ended international presence would foster resentment and violence. Some participants argued that the duration of the transitional authority should be determined by deadlines, but others suggested performance milestones.

T HE Democratic Principles Working Group was not authorized to finalize a transition plan, nor was it mandated to set the agenda of the Iraqi opposition's broader political conference. When INC members on the coordinating committee sought an endorsement of their plan to establish a provisional government dominated by exiles, other Iraqis pushed back.

In between meetings and at Wilton Park, Ryan Crocker and Pearce were far too timid about confronting Kanan and his cohorts. The Future of Iraq Project was the State Department's responsibility. However, Crocker and Pearce bent over backwards to avoid provoking Kanan lest he complain to the Office of the Vice President (OVP) and the Pentagon. Pearce should have vigorously insisted that the drafters keep it brief and focus on principles rather than detailed transition plans.

When Iraqis disagreed on substance, Pearce reverted to the process of team building. When it became clear the report could not be finalized at the Wilton Park meeting, I urged Pearce to focus on procedures and a timetable for obtaining additional ideas before completing the document. It was agreed that written comments should be submitted to the coordinating committee by October 21. The coordinating committee would have two weeks to integrate comments so that the report reflected the full range of opinions. After the revised text was distributed on November 9, there would be one week to submit dissenting opinions for inclusion in the annex of the final report.

At one point during the discussion, Kanan and I stepped out for a walk in the garden. He was fuming after a particularly testy confrontation with his colleagues: "How dare they object to the plan when they have none of their own?" he complained, reminding me of assurances by the OVP.

I told Kanan to tread softly. Sure, he could go to his friends in the Bush administration and seek their endorsement of a provisional government. But the plan would lack legitimacy without backing from the Working Group. Moreover, a breakdown would raise questions about whether the Iraqis were ready to govern themselves. At least publicly, the Bush administration was still insisting that it had not yet decided to go to war. Not only would a breakdown send the wrong signal to European countries and to Iraq's neighbors, it could also undermine congressional support for military action.

I suggested to Kanan that he focus on the big picture. He had written eloquently of "a historic opportunity that is as great as anything that has happened in the Middle East since the fall of the Ottoman Empire and the entry of British troops into Iraq in 1917. Once the regime of Saddam Hussein is removed from power, Iraq can be remade out of the ashes of thirty years of brutality, domestic and foreign wars, nightmare weapons, and near total economic collapse."[8] I assured him that the Working Group might still adopt the coordinating committee's original report and, if it did, the report would set the agenda for the political conference.

DESPITE my hopeful words, I feared the worst. The Wilton Park meeting revealed deep divisions in the Iraqi opposition. It also exposed the INC's weaknesses. Chalabi's cadres could not convince their colleagues to support a transition plan dominated by exiles. The Bush administration started to worry that the process was out of control.

I, too, worried that the Iraqis were not ready for prime time. Problems that surfaced in the Democratic Principles Working Group were a microcosm of problems in the Future of Iraq Project as a whole, as well as issues that would undermine Iraq's future democratic development. Iraqi political factions and ethnic and religious groups were deeply divided. The gap between exiles and other Iraqis was more of a chasm than a subtle difference of opinion. The sharp differences would be made public a month later at the London Opposition Conference.

CHAPTER 9

THE OPPOSITION
CONFERENCE

U.S. POLICY CHANGED COURSE AFTER WILTON PARK. Feuding by members of the Democratic Principles Working Group underscored the difficulty of relations among factions of the Iraqi opposition. High expectations that a unified Iraqi front would embrace liberal democracy had confronted the reality of internecine Iraqi politics.

The Pentagon had no doubt that the United States would prevail militarily against Iraq. However, postwar planning had revealed fissures that made Iraq's political transition look increasingly uncertain. Worried supporters of Ahmad Chalabi in the U.S. government, began to doubt the ability of the Iraq National Congress (INC) to gather support for a provisional government dominated by exiles. The Bush administration was still committed to regime change, but it needed a broadly representative political conference to demonstrate that Saddam Hussein's opponents were capable of speaking with one voice. The Democratic Principles Working Group had shown that it was impossible to predict what might happen when Iraqis get together. A big conference was even more risky. Guidelines would be needed to keep the meeting from taking an unforeseen turn and discrediting the administration's approach to Iraq.

In mid-November 2002, David Pearce and Bill Luti led a U.S. delegation to London for meetings with Iraqi opposition leaders. They delivered a strong message: President Bush had decided that it would be premature to establish a provisional government until Saddam was removed from power. To prevent the Iraqis from trying to play one agency off against the other, they delivered a letter articulating the administration's unified position. The letter was signed by Deputy Defense Secretary Paul D. Wolfowitz, Deputy Secretary of State Richard L. Armitage, and I. Lewis Libby, Dick Cheney's chief of staff. It affirmed Washington's opposition to forming a provisional government or creating an interim national assembly until after Saddam was deposed.

In addition, the letter prescribed an agenda for the upcoming Iraqi Opposition Conference. To minimize disagreements, the administration wanted the Iraqis to focus only on broad principles guiding their efforts going forward. Pearce also presented a memorandum called "Vision Themes," which summarized some of the major points discussed by the Working Group. U.S. officials wanted a unified opposition message of commitment to a democratic, multiethnic Iraq that would preserve its territorial integrity, live at peace with its neighbors, disavow weapons of mass destruction (WMD), and comply with UN Security Council resolutions. They also hoped that the conference would establish an advisory group to work with Dr. Zalmay Khalilzhad, Bush's new "special envoy and ambassador-at-large for free Iraqis."

Reaction to the letter was mixed. Some Iraqis agreed that it was premature to create a provisional government while Saddam was still in power. Others resented U.S. efforts to dictate ground rules and provide written instructions. Iraqis agreed on one critical point: None would tolerate a U.S. military occupation or the appointment of a U.S. viceroy to govern Iraq. Jalal Talabani expressed the sentiments of all Iraqi opposition figures: "If we don't accept an Iraqi general, how are we going to accept a U.S. general?"[1]

Ahmad Chalabi was furious with the United States for its decision to scale back the role of the Iraqi exiles. Despite backing from Dick Cheney and the Pentagon, Chalabi had failed to win support for his transition plan. Unwilling to accept the latest decision, Chalabi shifted tactics; he abandoned his effort to secure the administration's endorsement for a government-in-exile and focused instead on persuading the conference to endorse a transitional authority to be formed just before the U.S.-led invasion. Chalabi concluded that his best chance to establish himself in power would come before Iraqis in Iraq could organize themselves. He envisioned himself at the head of a nucleus transitional authority that would follow on the heels of U.S. forces entering Baghdad.

THE State Department welcomed Khalilzad's appointment as special envoy. The Bureau for Near Eastern Affairs (NEA) was glad that someone finally had a clear mandate to "serve as the focal point for contacts and coordination among free Iraqis for the United States government and for preparations for a post–Saddam Hussein Iraq."[2] Even though the real center of political gravity on Iraq policy was in the Pentagon and the Office of the Vice President, the NEA had become the regular port of call for Iraqis seeking contact with the administration. With Khalilzad's appointment, Ryan Crocker and his colleagues could simply refer appointment requests to the National Security Council.

Zalmay Khalilzad—known to friends as "Zal"—was well-suited for his new responsibilities. He has a long history of friendly relations with the neo-cons, having served with Richard Perle and Paul Wolfowitz in the Reagan administration as assistant undersecretary of defense for policy planning from 1991 to 1992. Khalilzad was a founding member of the Project for the New American Century. In the mid-1990s, Khalilzad also developed ties to Dick Cheney, who was then chairman of Halliburton. At the time, Khalilzad was consulting with Unocal, which had signed letters of agreement with the Taliban to build an 890-mile-long, $2 billion natural-gas pipeline from Turkmenistan across Afghanistan to Pakistan; Halliburton is in the pipeline business and wanted a piece of the contract.

Born in the northern Afghan city of Mazar-e-Sharif, Khalilzad grew up in Kabul and, after emigrating to the United States, received a Ph.D. from the University of Chicago. Khalilzad is a traditional man with thick dark hair, aquiline features, and penetrating eyes. In 2001, George W. Bush asked him to serve as the U.S. envoy to Afghanistan. Khalilzad played an important role at the Bonn Conference, a "loya jirga" that helped reconcile the different ethnic factions to establish an interim Afghan government. Not only did he have experience with post-conflict transitions, but Khalilzad's Farsi language skills and Afghan sensibilities endeared him to Iraqis. He appreciated the importance of local customs. Khalilzad was prepared to spend all day drinking tea with Iraqis to garner their support for Bush's plan.

Convening the London Opposition Conference became an end in itself for the Bush administration. Just staging the event was a major accomplishment. The conference had been postponed several times and the venue was moved from Brussels to London. The Belgian government had originally offered to host the meeting, but withdrew its offer at the last minute. Belgian officials had second thoughts about hosting a conference the goal of which was the overthrow of Saddam Hussein when the government's official policy was to support the disarming of Saddam through UN weapons inspections.

The day before the conference, Pearce asked me to drop by the Churchill Hotel and brief Khalilzad on the Democratic Principles Working Group. Several Iraqis were lounging in the lobby, drinking espresso. Ghassan al-Atiyyah stepped out of the elevator just as I arrived and told me that Khalilzad was holding court in the suite upstairs. The Bush administration needed Iraqis to legitimize the goal of regime change, and, according to Ghassan, Khalilzad was interviewing candidates for an Iraqi coordinating committee to advise the U.S. government.

I briefed Khalilzad on the Working Group, describing the method, nuance, and outcome of its activities. Khalilzad said that the United States intended to continue its collaboration with task forces set up by the Iraqi opposition and "integrate them in our plans as we prepare for liberation."[3]

Khalilzad was focused on personalities more than on process. He had instructions from the White House to select Iraqis for the coordinating committee. In addition, he wanted the Iraqis to adopt guidelines for regime change, as well as principles for governing postwar Iraq. He told the Iraqis, "I'm here to make sure you don't fail."[4]

I feared that Khalilzad was too focused on the end-game and would bully the Iraqis. I also worried that Khalilzad's antagonism towards Iran would prejudice his working relations with Iraq's Arab Shi'a. Annoyed that Iraqi opposition leaders had met in Tehran a week before the London Opposition Conference, Khalilzad was critical of Iran's conservative clerics, who, he believed, were trying to manipulate Arab Shi'a as a bulwark against America's influence in Iraq. Hamid al-Bayati, the U.K. representative of the Supreme Council for Islamic Revolution in Iraq (SCIRI), encapsulated the dissatisfaction of many Iraqis: "We want the Americans to help us overthrow Saddam. They seem to want to do it themselves."[5]

AFTER leaving Khalilzad's suite, I went to find Hoshyar Zebari at the Hilton Hotel. Zebari is adept in the art of politics. He worked closely with U.S. officials to make them feel they were choosing the participants and setting the conference agenda. At the same time, Zebari inspired confidence among Iraqis on the conference preparatory committee. Without his steady hand, the U.S. government might have canceled the meeting or Iraqi factions might have balked. Zebari did yeoman's work by balancing competing constituencies and addressing seemingly irreconcilable demands.

As I entered the Hilton lobby, I spied Zebari smoking a cigarette near the conference registration desk. Hundreds of Iraqis were queuing up for their blue all-access registration passes. The scene was colorful and chaotic: Sheikhs, mullahs, and tribal leaders had virtually taken over the hotel.

Pearce had gone through an exhausting process in selecting participants. He carefully considered not only the total number but also the proportional representation of different groups and political factions. Once the proportions were figured out, individuals had to be identified and arrangements made for their travel and attendance. It was originally thought that 150 Iraqis would attend; by the time of the conference, 330 had been invited. After weeks of wrangling about names and numbers, hundreds of Iraqis simply showed up, demanding to participate.

A few days before the conference, Iraq had provided a 12,000-page report in response to the UN's demand for a full and final disclosure of its WMD program. U.S. officials called the report a whitewash, insisting that Saddam had missed his last chance to avoid military action. Iraqis understood the historic nature of the moment and showed up in droves. Everyone wanted to be a part of the last opposition meeting before liberation.

Zebari had hired a security firm to manage the registration and ensure the delegates' safety. However, security staff became so exasperated with the crush of registrants that they abandoned the pre-cleared list and started issuing blue badges to invited guests as well as their friends. The agenda was also fluid. One day before the conference, speakers and schedules still had not been determined.

NBC hired me as a Middle East expert in mid-2002; I had special permission from the State Department to give electronic interviews without clearance from the U.S. government. NBC scheduled me to report from the conference on camera twice a day. Neither NBC's producers nor its reporters knew what was going on with the conference. Hundreds of media representatives from all over the world had shown up, but there was no press guidance. Well past midnight, Zebari had still not announced a start time, nor had he distributed an agenda. When it came to arrangements, I had some useful information thanks to my meetings with Khalilzad, Pearce, Samantha Ravich, and others; Zebari was also keeping me informed about developments. I made a point of being as forthcoming as possible with journalists whom I respected, such as Trudy Rubin of the *Philadelphia Inquirer.*

Well after midnight, the lobby bar was overflowing with delegates, guests, and journalists. Many Iraqis were dressed in business suits. Sheikhs wore traditional garb. Clerics were clad in their religious turbans.

I was approached by a tourist from South Carolina who asked what was going on. I explained that Iraqis were meeting to plot the overthrow of Saddam Hussein. Noting his anxious reaction, I assured him that the group did not include terrorists. His family vacation should go forward without a hitch.

T HE following morning, the media packed a conference room to attend a press conference that was called for 11:00 A.M. The announcement was distributed by Burston Marsteller, a public-relations firm under contract to the INC. The briefing was conducted by Ahmad Chalabi and his INC cohorts, Kanan Makiya and Rend al-Rahim.

When I entered the press hall, Kanan was giving a talk on the "Transition to Democracy in Iraq." Kanan was summarizing the INC's plan for a nucleus transitional authority to be installed in Baghdad. Though the Democratic Principles Working Group had not authorized the report, Burston Marsteller was handing out fact sheets presenting its conclusions.

I was shocked that Chalabi would hold a press conference to present the Working Group's report as the agenda for the whole conference. I quickly found Zebari and told him what was going on. Zebari rushed into the room just as the panel was finishing. Though he rarely gets upset, he was infuriated by the INC's attempt to hijack the conference. He stepped up to the microphone and announced that Chalabi's press briefing was not authorized by the conference secretariat and that the conference agenda had nothing to do with the report.

By then, other Working Group members had filtered into the room. Laith Kubba was particularly irate: "I was a member of that working group," he told the journalists huddled around him. "The draft has not been endorsed." The press conference was part of a plan "to empower one small group," Laith charged. "They are blackmailing and manipulating the process to shove their plan down everybody's throat and embarrass the Americans."[6]

Members of the media were confused; Zebari tried to explain that most Iraqis preferred to form a transitional authority—but only after Saddam had been removed. For their part, Iraqi Kurds already governed their affairs and did not want to surrender control to ambitious exiles. Shi'a leaders and reformed Ba'athists also wanted to wait. Zebari was concerned about U.S. plans for a coordinating committee. Announcing a provisional government would send the wrong signal to Iraqis in Iraq. He said, "This is no Bonn Conference. We are just going to issue a statement of principles."[7]

Zebari and other members of the conference preparatory committee were also wary of being perceived as puppets of the Americans. He fumed, "It was unfortunate that some people claimed to represent the conference when they do not."[8]

I pulled Kanan aside and asked what was going on. He was ashen and perspiring profusely. "This is a complete disaster for Iraq," he complained. "I personally am going to blast the organizers of the conference when I give my talk. They essentially implant the seeds of division in the hearts of Iraqis before we even start."[9] I told Kanan that his unauthorized press conference could also have disastrous consequences. The INC's attempt to set the agenda had further divided Iraqis; it had also conveyed disarray to the media and foreign observers, who were already skeptical about the ability of Iraqis to overcome their differences.

THE London Opposition Conference convened later that day under a large banner in Arabic and English that read: "For the salvation of Iraq and for democracy." A recitation from the Holy Qura'n was greeted with replies of "God is great." Then a series of speakers addressed the plenary.

Regarding the conference, Bakr al-Hakim, SCIRI's leader, pointed out that "people said it could not be done. We proved them wrong."[10] Another prominent Shi'a leader, Muhammed Bahr al-Ulum, affirmed, "Differences of opinion are healthy. We reject those who say we cannot stand together. Blood has covered the land of the Euphrates." He added, "Shame on you, Saddam, for causing the people to suffer."[11] Al-Ulum continued, "We must return to the body of Iraq its spirit, its soul. We must tear a black page from our history."[12] Sharif Ali, the first cousin of King Faisal II, described the conference as a "sure step towards our beloved Baghdad. We will turn prisons into hospitals, schools, and universities. These are not dreams. They can be achieved if we trust each other."[13] Underscoring the independence of Iraqis, Jalal Talabani stated, "This is not an American show." He also recognized the limitations of Iraqi exiles: "The conference does not represent all the opposition. Iraqis within Iraq can not participate because of repression, but they will play an important role in Iraq's future democracy."[14] Ayad Allawi, head of the Iraqi National Accord, a London-based group set up by MI5, Britain's security agency, to infiltrate Iraq's security services, seconded Talabani's message: "It's normal that to participate in government you must have a presence in the country." He affirmed, "We have assets on the ground."[15] Speaking of Iraq's future governance, Ahmad Chalabi said that "federalism will bring unity to Iraq. It is a way to strengthen sovereignty and guarantee the rights of all."[16] Chalabi added, "Regretfully, the United States has let down the Iraqi people many times."[17] Chalabi made a point of thanking Iran for hosting Iraqis, expressed gratitude for Tehran's help over many years, and acknowledged assistance from Syria, calling on President Bashar al-Assad to continue his father's support.

When the most prominent Iraqis had spoken, Khalilzad addressed the plenary: "Some critics say that you are not ready for democracy, but free Iraqis inspire hope. Iraq and the United States share the goals of democracy, security, and a free and just society. We reject any form of dictatorship. Human dignity is non-negotiable." Khalilzad also underscored the U.S. commitment to "restore Iraq to its proper place in the community of nations—free from sanctions and fulfilling its international obligations." As a warning, he added, "Resolution 1441 is the final chance for Saddam to take the path to peace. The world is resolved to act militarily if he does not."[18]

Except for the morning session, U.S. officials were conspicuously absent from the plenary. Khalilzad told me he wanted to keep a low profile so that it would not appear as though he was controlling events. Khalilzad retreated to his suite at the Churchill while a cavalcade of Iraqis made their way to the podium during the next two days.

KHALILZAD was working behind the scenes to shape the coordinating committee. Up to that point, U.S. officials had stayed in contact with only a few Iraqi opposition groups. They wanted to broaden their cooperation with the Iraqi opposition. They also hoped that the coordinating committee would put the United States in good stead with other Iraqis after the war. If the coordinating committee proved amenable to U.S. plans, it might be upgraded into the nucleus of a governing authority that would act as America's partner in governing Iraq.

Despite the flowery affirmations of the Iraqis addressing the plenary, not all were sanguine about the conference. Laith Kubba, for example, was concerned about a power struggle for the composition of the coordinating committee: "The unstated assumption is that the committee will be important in the making of a new government. Some people think of it as the nucleus of a new authority. . . . This is why there are fights."[19]

Some Iraqi groups boycotted the conference because they saw it as window dressing for a U.S. takeover of Iraq. Al-Da'wa, the Iraq Communist Party, Arab nationalist parties, and Islamic groups all refused to participate. Other Iraqis attended reluctantly. Some Shi'a stormed out, claiming that the conference had been "cooked" by the Bush administration.[20] Tensions were further exacerbated when a bomb threat emptied the hall and the bodyguard of a tribal chieftain was arrested for carrying a concealed weapon.

Despite the precarious show of unity, Iraqis disagreed sharply on the size and allocation of seats on the coordinating committee. This is when the bickering over the draft statement of principles spilled into public view. In protest of efforts by influential tribal leaders and conservative mullahs to enshrine Shari'a law, more than a hundred liberal Iraqi intellectuals organized a parallel forum to discuss their own statement of principles. They also met with Khalilzad to demand that secularism be enshrined in the conference's conclusions.

There were other disputes. Independent Kurds tried to adopt a federal plan that specifically included Kirkuk in Iraqi Kurdistan. Khalilzad turned to Barzani and Talabani to suppress the renegade Kurdish initiative. Arguments also flared over what should be done about the Ba'ath Party and the role of reformed Ba'athists. A schism arose between Iraqi exiles and everyone else. The vast majority of Iraqis rejected plans for a nucleus transitional authority led by the INC.

The deepest divisions at the London Opposition Conference occurred over the size and composition of the coordinating committee. Disputes over representation in governing bodies would recur at every critical juncture in Iraq's transition to self-rule. Such disagreements would occur over and over during Iraq's torturous political transition.

As the majority in Iraq, Shi'a groups demanded most of the seats on the coordinating committee. As the leading Shi'a political party, SCIRI insisted upon the largest block of seats allocated to the Shi'a. The INC was jockeying for representation. Ayad Allawi and former Ba'athists associated with the Iraqi National Accord also demanded a leading role. As Iraq's third-largest ethnic group, Turkmen wanted proportional representation. Kurds resisted, claiming that the Turkmen were exaggerating their numbers. Except for the Kurds, who had achieved de facto independence, few Iraqi parties could claim significant support from within Iraq.

KHALILZAD and the Americans kept a close watch on the proceedings and worked behind the scenes to ensure an acceptable outcome to the Bush administration. Concerned about Khalilzad's heavy-handed tactics, many Iraqis came to me with complaints about intimidation. I went to Khalilzad's suite to let him know what I was hearing.

I found Khalilzad in a lather over Iran. He was convinced that Iran was working behind the scenes to upset the conference by hardening the demands of Iraq's Arab Shi'a. He believed that Iran wanted to establish a theocracy in Iraq modeled on Iran's. In so doing, Iran would dominate Iraqi politics and establish a Shi'a zone of influence stretching from Tehran to Basra and Baghdad, all the way to Beirut.

Khalilzad called an impromptu press conference in his suite to discuss developments. While we waited for the journalists to arrive, I warned him not to be too confrontational. Public criticism could backfire and harden Arab Shi'a recalcitrance.

Before Khalilzad publicly accused Tehran of meddling in the conference, I offered to try to fix the problem by working my channel with Javad Zarif, Iran's former deputy foreign minister and permanent representative to the United Nations. To preempt criticism by administration hardliners, I always notified Marc Grossman and Bill Burns, the assistant secretary of state for Near Eastern affairs, of my private contact with Iranian officials.

SCIRI was the primary stumbling block; Bakr al-Hakim refused to provide the names of SCIRI's representatives to serve on the coordinating committee. Khalilzad was convinced that SCIRI would not move without permission from Tehran. Someone floated the idea of finalizing proportions and group assignments but deferring the selection of committee members. I strongly opposed the proposal, arguing that the committee would never come into existence unless its membership was agreed upon at the London Opposition Conference. To avoid a breakdown, the conference was extended for twenty-four hours.

Despite Khalilzad's mediation, the Iraqis could not agree on the size or composition of the coordinating committee. Khalilzad called the six major opposition groups to his hotel suite at 4:00 A.M. on December 17. He warned them that they risked irrelevance unless they could agree on the committee's composition. He and Luti berated the Iraqis for allow-ing a deadlock over unimportant details.[21]

Though Khalilzad's intimidating tactics were resented, they seemed to work. Within a few hours, the Iraqi groups agreed to expand the coordi-nating committee to sixty-five seats. About half were reserved for Shi'a; SCIRI received the most. To broker the deal, the Kurds gave up some of their quota.

Lempert and I commented on how remarkable it was to see Kurds mediating between Arab groups and exhibiting their leadership. I also mentioned that negotiations over the committee were just a snapshot of the difficulties to be faced in forming a representative government inside Iraq.

The conference adopted two statements articulating a shared political vision for the future and describing a general framework for governing Iraq. The political statement, strongly supportive of the Shi'a, called for a unified, democratic, federal, and parliamentary government to replace Saddam. The conference "condemns the desecration of religious author-ity, the violation of sanctuaries and scholarly institutions, and interven-tion in their affairs. It condemns the killing of prominent clergy and the torture and arrest of many thousands. It condemns violations of the shrines in noble Najaf and other holy cities [and] the portrayal of Iraqi Shi'a as non-Arabs and the maligning of their Iraqiness."

The statement identified Islam as the state religion and emphasized its importance as one of the basic sources of legislation: "The Islamic faith is one of the fundamental characteristics of the Iraqi state and the rulings of the Islamic Shari'a are a principal source of legislation." The statement also upheld the "noble values of Islam and its example of tolerance, its charitable principles and its teachings with due respect to all other heav-enly religions and other creeds."[22]

Chalabi backed Shi'a efforts to enshrine the role of religion in Iraqi gov-ernance. In doing so, he sought to leverage U.S. support by demonstrating affinities for Iran. Knowing how much radical Islam concerned the Bush administration, Chalabi repeatedly played one side off against the other.

The conference endorsed a governance structure for Iraq, including a provisional national assembly, an executive, and a government of tech-nocrats. The assembly would be "representative of the national, religious, political, social, and geographic components of the Iraqi people." Its members would include "experienced and qualified people to undertake legislative roles during the transition period and to monitor the work of

the executive body."[23] The executive council would include three leaders "with honorable pasts and who are known for their integrity." It
would act as the head of state during the transition. In addition, the transitional government would include "qualified and experienced specialists
representing the components of Iraqi society."[24]

A committee of specialists was envisioned to prepare a constitution
for the transition period. Once duly constituted, the national assembly
would appoint "academics and law scholars, as well as politicians and religious scholars representing the ethnic, political, and religious diversity
of Iraq for the purpose of drafting a permanent constitution which will
be presented in a referendum to be endorsed by the people."[25] The conference defined the transitional period as the time between the establishment of a coalition authority and the holding of parliamentary
elections, which should occur within two years.

The Iraqi opposition was united in demanding immediate control of
the country when the regime crumbled. They rejected all U.S. efforts to
establish either a military transitional government or a transitional body
under the supervision of a U.S. general. Over U.S. objections, the coordinating committee agreed to meet again on January 15 at a location under
Kurdish control in northern Iraq.

VIRTUALLY sidelined during the intense late-night negotiations to
establish the coordinating committee, Ahmad Chalabi stalked the
halls of the conference. Instead of trying to help overcome factional
differences, he counted on a breakdown to restore his leadership.

The London Opposition Conference was a huge setback for Chalabi.
Unable to control events, he disparaged the outcome. He was joined by
Kanan, who criticized the conference for failing to appoint a nucleus
transitional authority. Kanan condemned "the appointment by the U.S.
of an unknown number of quislings palatable to Arab countries of the
Gulf and Saudi Arabia" and accused the State Department of appeasing
the existing bankrupt Arab order: "Bureaucrats responsible for this plan
are drawn from parts of the administration that have always been hostile
to the idea of a U.S.-assisted democratic transformation."[26]

When plans for a government-in-exile fell apart, Chalabi demanded
his own militia so that he could garner credibility with Iraqis. In the
middle of the opposition conference, a U.S. Army general arrived to finalize arrangements for training a 5,000-man INC militia called the
"Free Iraqi Forces."

Despite disarray and delays, Zebari put a brave face on the proceedings: "We have proven our critics wrong by organizing and financing this conference."[27] Ayad Allawi maintained that "the conference was useful in showing unity of purpose."[28] U.S. officials also counted the conference a success. However, Chalabi's backers in the Bush administration were disturbed by his inability to gain support from other Iraqis. They were most troubled by the dominance of Arab Shi'a. SCIRI had proved itself a powerful force; its allegiances to Tehran were far deeper than its ties to Washington.

The London Opposition Conference had revealed the difficulties of achieving consensus among Iraqis. Forging a common vision would take time, but administration hawks knew that time was not on their side. Waiting could undermine the push towards war and eventually weaken the case for invading Iraq.

Although the conference exposed the complicated power-sharing issues that would be faced in Iraq, Bush was apparently unaware of the animosity between Iraqi factions. Less than a month after the conference, Kanan was invited to watch the Super Bowl at the White House; he told me later that he had to explain to the president of the United States the differences between Arab Shi'a, Arab Sunnis, and Kurds.

CHAPTER 10

— •—

THE ENEMY OF
MY ENEMY

IN THE MIDDLE EAST, WHERE "THE ENEMY OF MY ENEMY is my friend," the United States and Iran found common cause in confronting al-Qaeda, overthrowing the Taliban, and getting rid of Saddam Hussein. In May 2003, the Bush administration suspended dialogue with Iran, thereby forsaking that country's assistance in positively influencing Arab Shi'a in Iraq. U.S.-Iran cooperation would have been especially valuable in mitigating the uprising of Iraqi Shi'a that erupted in April 2004.

In his State of the Union speech on January 29, 2002, Bush said that

states like [Iran, Iraq, and North Korea] and their terrorist allies constitute an axis of evil. By seeking weapons of mass destruction, these regimes pose a grave and growing danger. They could provide these arms to terrorists, giving them the means to match their hatred. They could attack our allies or attempt to blackmail the United States. In any of these cases, the price of indifference would be catastrophic. Time is not on our side. I will not wait on events while dangers gather. I will not stand by as perils draw closer and closer. The United States of America will not permit the most dangerous regimes to threaten us with the world's most destructive weapons.[1]

Javad Zarif, Iran's deputy foreign minister, was "totally shocked" by Bush's remarks. He complained "Iran offered a helping hand and it was chopped off."[2]

Al-Qaeda is a radical Sunni organization engaged in a holy war with the West as well as with Shi'a Muslims. Al-Qaeda committed many

103

atrocities against the Iranian people, including a bomb attack on the Imam Reza Shrine, the holiest sanctuary in Iran. Hassan Rowhani, the secretary general of the Supreme National Security Council, insisted that Iran was involved in a "serious struggle against al-Qaeda."[3]

Iran and Afghanistan, which harbored al-Qaeda, were bitter rivals. Like al-Qaeda, Afghanistan's Taliban rulers subscribed to a Sunni fundamentalist sect called Wahhabism. The Taliban deplored Iran's support of northern warlords who resisted Taliban control. In August 1998, tensions between Iran and Afghanistan spiked when Taliban guards killed ten Iranian diplomats and one journalist at the Iranian consulate in Mazar-e-Sharif.

DESPITE distrust and the absence of formal diplomatic relations, U.S. and Iranian officials interacted on Afghanistan through the United Nations "six plus two" framework that brought together the United States, the United Kingdom, and Afghanistan's immediate neighbors. The "Geneva process," which began several months before 9/11, was led by Francesc Vandrell, a skilled UN diplomat in the Department of Political Affairs. Ryan Crocker represented the United States. The Iranian delegation was headed by a director general from the foreign ministry and included a team of experts on Afghanistan.

The Geneva process catalyzed a debate in Tehran about relations with the United States. According to Zarif, "We did not want to be America's enemy." Though Iran's leaders "did not think the U.S. was trustworthy or serious about relations," they decided that Iran's national interests could be advanced through contact. During the months between 9/11 and the Bonn Conference on Afghanistan's political transition, in November 2001, Iranian officials debated different approaches. All Iranian factions opposed direct negotiations. One faction emphasized building trust, another argued for guarantees before even considering U.S. needs.[4]

During and after the Afghanistan War, Crocker met regularly with his Iranian counterpart. Iran agreed to look the other way if U.S. warplanes or missiles entered Iranian air space; Iran also promised not to interfere with search and rescue operations of downed U.S. pilots on Iranian soil. Through various UN agencies, the United States and Iran also developed a protocol for assisting refugees fleeing the conflict.

Both countries were preoccupied with al-Qaeda. After the Taliban fell, Iran arrested five hundred al-Qaeda operatives as they made their way from Afghanistan into Iran. Though there was no public acknowledgement, the United States welcomed Iran's decision to send some back to their countries of origin. No matter their helpfulness, Iranian officials feared that, after Syria, Iran was next on America's list of countries targeted for regime change.

O F A L L Iran's enemies, though, Saddam Hussein was the most despised. In 1980, Iraq invaded the Sha'at al-Arab and so launched a bloody eight-year war in which more than 500,000 Iranians died. During my trip to Iran in 2003, I was struck by the deep scars left by the Iran-Iraq War. Every Iranian city displays billboards showing the images of hometown heroes martyred during the conflict. Almost every Iranian family lost a loved one in combat. Among the survivors, many were maimed by land mines or damaged by chemical weapons, which Iraq deployed to offset Iran's numerical advantage.

Iranian leaders vilified the United States as the "Great Satan," not only for supporting Israel but also for aiding Saddam in the Iran-Iraq War. As President Reagan's special envoy, Donald Rumsfeld visited Baghdad in 1983 to finalize arrangements for financing, food shipments, and military assistance. The United States also supplied Iraq with some of the chemical weapons that were used against Iran and the Iraqi Kurds.

There was no love lost between Saddam and Iranian leaders. Iran was unwilling to assist U.S. war operations in Iraq, but took steps to secure its interests in the event of U.S. military action. Iranian officials wanted to ensure a friendly regime on its border by creating conditions so that Iraq's Shi'a majority would hold power in the new Iraq.

Deep ties bind Shi'a in Iran and Iraq. After Saddam seized power in 1968, many Shi'a scholars feared persecution by the Ba'ath and moved their seminaries from Najaf, in Iraq, to the Iranian holy city of Qum. Iran's population of 65 million makes it the center of Shi'a Islam. Iraq has the second largest Shi'a population, about 15 million. Although there is no formal head of the Shi'a clergy, its hierarchy is determined by the intellectual initiative of clerics (*Ijtihad*). The wisest and most charismatic have the largest following and receive the largest monetary donations.

Even though Iranians are Persian and Iraqi Shi'a are Arab, Shi'a unity has been forged from more than 1,500 years of persecution as a minority in the Muslim world. Martyrdom is a powerful force among Shi'a, who share a common identity and unity that transcends national borders.

Born in Iran, Ali al-Sistani moved to Najaf as a young man and later emerged as Iraq's most influential cleric. After achieving the rank of grand ayatollah in the 1990s, he began making substantial financial contributions to clerics in Iran, establishing ties with the Supreme Leader and the Guardian Council. Assistance went both ways; Zarif maintained, "We have been helping the Iraqi opposition—Kurdish parties, most Shi'a groups and some Sunnis—for decades."[5]

Iranian-backed Iraqi groups include the Supreme Council for Islamic Revolution in Iraq (SCIRI), which, with elements of the Da'wa Islamic Party, was exiled to Iran during Saddam's rule. Though SCIRI's leaders are closely connected with the Iranian establishment, they claim that "SCIRI is not related to the Iranian government and has different opinions and positions."[6] SCIRI admitted to accepting funds from Iran, but insisted that the money came from individual donors, not official sources. SCIRI also pointed out that it received funds from individuals in several Gulf States, not just Iran. The money was used to support SCIRI's Badr Brigade, a highly disciplined fighting force of thousands. Though SCIRI agreed to disband the Badr Brigade after coalition forces entered Iraq, the militia reappeared immediately after Bakr al-Hakim, SCIRI's leader, was assassinated in August 2003.

Hamid al-Bayati, SCIRI's London representative who later became Iraq's deputy foreign minister, is an adept diplomat who navigated between SCIRI's Iranian sponsors and advocated cautious cooperation with the American authorities. U.S. officials did not protest publicly when Bayati and other members of the Iraqi opposition met in Tehran just a week before the London Opposition Conference in December 2002. Privately, though, the Bush administration was incensed when the Iraqi opposition and Iran came together to reject a U.S. military government in Iraq. Ahmad Chalabi insisted, "Our alliance with Iran is not temporary."[7]

Because Iran's greatest fear was a post-Saddam power vacuum, Iran emphasized influencing events in Iraq by working with Iraq's Shi'a political parties. Iran espoused majority rule for Iraq because democratization would empower Iraq's Shi'a majority to take control of the central government. According to Tehran, the optimal outcome would be a Shi'a-led Iraq at peace with its neighbors and foreswearing weapons of mass destruction. A friendly regime in Baghdad would also allow Shi'a pilgrims access to the holy shrines in Najaf and Karbala. In addition, it would protect Iran's commercial interests and promote trade across the nine-hundred-mile Iran-Iraq border. Iran hoped to reopen the Basra pipeline, which transported Iraqi oil to Iranian ports; resume electricity sales; and restore rail, road, and communications links.

When it came to security, Iran was wary of an open-ended U.S. military presence in Iraq. It felt threatened by the presence of U.S. forces in countries on each of its borders. Iran tried to achieve a difficult balance. It did not want to destabilize Iraq to such an extent that the country descended into civil war, but it wanted to cause enough instability to create difficulties for the U.S. occupation.

AT THE second "six plus two" meeting in March 2002, Zarif found Zalmay Khalilzad "extremely tough" and "totally pre-occupied with al-Qaeda." Khalilzad acted as though "Iran only responds to threats of force." Zarif "sensed an obsession with Iran that could lead to policies that are destructive to both the U.S. and Iran."[8]

Instead of grasping that "Iran is the closest natural ally of the U.S. in Iraq," Zarif concluded that Khalilzad saw Iran as a threat.[9] The United States was worried that Iran would export its Islamic revolution. Left unchecked, Iran would emerge as the powerbroker in Iraq's elections and succeed in establishing Shari'a law as the basis for Iraq's constitution. Donald Rumsfeld issued a warning: "A vocal minority clamoring to transform Iraq in Iran's image will not be permitted to do so. We will not allow the Iraqi people's democratic transition to be hijacked . . . by those who might wish to install another form of dictatorship."[10]

US officials accurately assessed that Iran wielded enormous influence in Iraq. It had spent decades harboring and financing the Iraqi opposition. SCIRI's Badr Brigade was trained and equipped by Iran's revolutionary guards; Farsi-speaking fighters had joined its ranks. Iran was infiltrating Iraq with intelligence agents for months before the Iraq war.

After the Taliban was defeated in November 2001, al-Qaeda members fled across the rugged Afghanistan border to Iran. Though Iran's official policy required Taliban to be arrested, some members of the Iranian military (*Pasdaran*) and intelligence services (*Ittila'at*) accepted bribes to allow their transit through Iran into Iraqi Kurdistan. Ansar al-Islam, which was called Jund al-Islam at the time, welcomed their Wahhabi brothers into their Islamist militia. Ansar fighters went back and forth between Iraq and Iran to buy supplies and receive medical attention in Iranian hospitals.

The Bush administration was increasingly preoccupied with limiting Iran's influence in Iraq. Rumsfeld declared, "Interference in Iraq by its neighbors or their proxies will not be permitted. Indeed, Iran should be on notice that efforts to try to remake Iraq in their image will be aggressively put down."[11]

Instead of attempting to cooperate with Iran when cooperation could advance U.S. interests, the administration was busy plotting strategies to overthrow the mullahs in Tehran. Rumsfeld described interagency deliberations that discussed "whether it might be better to deal with the president, the so-called moderate reformer; or deal with the clerics, or not deal with either."[12] Though the State Department advocated a dialogue with the reformers, it was decided that the United States should emphasize direct contact with the Iranian people "over the heads of their leaders."[13]

The Pentagon objected to the Geneva process and tried to kill it. According to Zarif, in May 2002 the neo-cons sent him a message: They wanted to call the shots; Iran should break off contact with State Department officials and open a back-channel through the Pentagon. [14] The neo-cons estimated that it would take Iran three years to develop a nuclear weapon. Given the slim prospects for domestic political change in Iran, they argued that the United States should be thinking about preemptive action against selected nuclear sites.

Nothing poisoned U.S.-Iran relations more than the Bush administration's flirtation with Tehran's sworn enemy, the Mujahadeen e-Khalq (MEK), also known as the People's Mujahadeen. Founded in the 1960s, the MEK blended Marxism with revolutionary Islam. Its leader, Massoud Rajavi, supported Khomeini's revolution in 1979 but, after a falling out, Rajavi plotted against the Islamic regime. Driven out of Iran, the MEK survived for two decades under the patronage of the Ba'ath Party. Saddam gave them money, weapons, and a military base. The MEK became part and parcel of the Iraqi military, reporting directly to Saddam, not the Iraqi defense minister.

In 1997, the State Department placed the MEK on its list of foreign terrorist organizations. The neo-cons, however, advocated taking the group off the terror list and using it as a fighting force to overthrow the regime in Tehran. But their plan was impractical. The MEK was despised by both Iraqis and Iranians.

U.S. policy also undermined Iran's moderates. According to Behzad Nabavi, the deputy speaker of the Iranian parliament, "Reformist politicians endured a huge setback after President Bush named Iran part of the axis of evil. Every time the United States has threatened Iran, hard liners intensify their crackdown."[15] Nabavi saw "no problem in official negotiations with the United States" despite opposition from the regime. "What we can do as members of parliament is to speak to American citizens, diplomats, intellectuals, and congressmen," he said. "This would be very helpful in cracking the wall of mistrust that President Khatami mentioned exists between our two countries."[16] President Mohammad Khatami, elected in May 1997, pursued a more conciliatory foreign policy. However, Iran is firmly under the control of the Supreme Leader, Ayatollah Ali Khamenei, who distrusts U.S. intentions.

They do not admit it publicly, but many Iranians welcomed U.S. military action in Iraq. They hoped that Saddam's overthrow would allow freedoms to flourish in the region. Reforms in Iraq could have a liberalizing effect on Iran, thereby creating a space for debate and freer discussion about Islam.

Sayyid Hussein Khomeini, the grandson of Grand Ayatollah Khomeini, called Iran's clerical rulers "the world's worst dictatorship" and accused them of exploiting his grandfather's name "to continue their tyrannical rule." He maintained: "Secularism is not blasphemy. We want a secular constitution and to separate religion from the state. That would be the end of despotism."[17] Regarding regime change in Iraq, he asserted that "if it was necessary to come from abroad, especially from the United States, people will accept it."[18] When I met students from Isfahan University, they were excited by the idea of the United States coming to liberate them.

After the Taliban was overthrown, Iranian authorities detained many al-Qaeda members in Sistan Baluchistan. Zarif stated. "Iran probably captured more al-Qaeda people in the past fourteen months than any other country. We have a number of people who are in custody right now, and we are continuing our efforts to first of all establish their identities and second, to try and see whether we can, in interrogation, get information from them which may be helpful to friendly governments."[19] It was believed the detainees included Saif al-Adel, al-Qaeda's security chief, and Saad bin Laden, Osama's son.

U.S. officials criticized Iran for failing to hand over prominent al-Qaeda personalities. Rumsfeld was asserting that al-Qaeda was "busy" in Iran.[21] Iranian officials reprised by refusing to deport al-Qaeda detainees until the United States repatriated members of the People's Mujahadeen from Iraq to Iran.

The Bush administration also maintained that Iran was still a state sponsor of terrorism. On January 3, 2002, the Israeli Coast Guard boarded the *Karine A*, an Iranian merchant vessel, and discovered a huge arms cache being smuggled to the Palestinian Authority.[20] Israeli and U.S. officials were incensed. Washington was also increasingly concerned about Iran's uranium enrichment activities, which it believed were part of a clandestine program to develop a nuclear bomb.

KHALILZAD was a lame duck when he and Zarif met again on May 3, 2003. Pentagon political appointees and their allies in the White House decided that it was too much for Khalilzad to be responsible for both Afghanistan and Iraq. They wanted one of their own in Khalilzad's position. Even Khalilzad, a proven neo-con, was not ideologically pure enough for the job. Besides, he had raised doubts about Ahmad Chalabi's fitness to rule Iraq.

According to Zarif, Khalilzad's "portfolio was taken away from him" on the day before their May 3 meeting. Nonetheless, Zarif conveyed Tehran's willingness "to provide advice and information" on developments in Iraq. He offered to "bring people outside the foreign ministry to join the next meeting."[22] Presumably, he was offering to provide the United States with intelligence from "facilities infiltrated during Saddam's years."[23]

The proposed meeting never occurred. Rumsfeld announced that the U.S. had intercepted phone conversations implicating al-Qaeda members in Iran with the Riyadh bombings on May 12, 2003. The Bush administration broke off bilateral contact just as the full-blown insurgency was getting under way in Iraq.

U.S. policymakers were obsessed by Iran's influence in Iraq. The image of Shi'a masses storming the U.S. Embassy in Tehran in 1979 and leading blindfolded Americans from the building had stuck in their craw. Indeed, many key decisions were influenced by fears of Iran and a Shi'a takeover in Iraq. But in attempting to allay its worst fears, the Bush administration would help realize many of them.

CHAPTER 11

— • —

A WAR WITHIN A WAR

U.S. OFFICIALS COUNTED ON TURKEY FOR SUPPORT AND as a launch point for U.S. forces into northern Iraq. Ankara was not favorably disposed. Turkish officials were concerned that attacking Iraq would spark a civil war. If Iraq fell apart, an independent Iraqi Kurdistan would emerge, inspiring unrest among Turkey's 15–20 million Kurds.

Turkey was also concerned that Iraqi Turkmen—ethnically and linguistically related to their Turkic brethren—would end up an oppressed minority in Iraqi Kurdistan. The fates of Iraqi Kurds and Turkmen are inseparably linked. Kurds and Turkmen not only share the same land, religion, and way of life but also a commitment to fostering democracy in Iraq and building a tolerant and multiethnic society. Both had suffered atrocities committed by the Iraqi regime. Despite their common destiny, Kurds and Turkmen remained fundamentally wary of one another.

The Iraqi Turkmen Front (ITF) is a political party financed and coordinated by the government of Turkey. The ITF claims to be the sole representative of the Iraqi Turkmen, but Iraqi Kurds and some Turkmen dispute its legitimacy. According to Massoud Barzani, the ITF was a stalking horse for Turkey's interests in Iraqi Kurdistan. Fomenting conflict between Kurds and Turkmen would be used by Turkey as a pretext to reassert control over the rich Kirkuk oil fields. By occupying parts of Iraqi Kurdistan, Turkey would also be in a position to eradicate its nemesis, the Kurdistan Worker's Party (PKK), a terror group that waged a separatist struggle from its mountain bases in southeastern Turkey and along the Turkey-Iraq border between 1984 and 1999.

Behind the Arabs and the Kurds, Turkmen are the third-largest ethnic group in Iraq. The ITF claim Turkmen represent 12 percent of Iraq's population. In response, the Kurds point to the 1997 census, which showed that there were only 600,000 Turkmen.

After the London Opposition Conference, U.S. officials intensified efforts to secure Turkey's support. To avoid a breakdown between Kurds and Turkmen that might upset negotiations between Turkey and the United States, I proposed to David Pearce that the State Department establish a task force as part of the Democratic Principles Working Group to focus on Kurdish-Turkmen issues. A structured dialogue could help bridge the gap between Barzani's Kurdistan Democratic Party (KDP) and the ITF; Pearce agreed.

Hoshyar Zebari immediately confirmed the KDP's participation. I also spoke with Barham Salih. Though almost all Iraqi Turkmen lived in KDP-controlled territory, he agreed that the Patriotic Union of Kurdistan (PUK) would attend the meeting. Orhan Ketene, the ITF's Washington representative, was interested, but deferred a decision until he had spoken with Sanan Ahmet Aga, secretary general of the ITF. When Pearce made it clear that the initiative enjoyed full backing from the U.S. government, the ITF agreed to participate.

I N January 2003, Kurds and Turkmen met at the Royal Horseguards Hotel in London. Mustafa Ziya, the ITF's Ankara representative, traveled to London with Ketene and two other ITF officials. Zebari led the KDP group; Favad Ma'soum, the PUK's London representative, Mikael McKowan, the State Department's Iraq desk officer, and an official from the Turkish embassy in London also attended. The meeting was called "Mapping the Issues." It was an informal gathering; no members of the media were invited.

After describing ground rules, I asked Ziya and Zebari to describe their visions for future governance in Iraq. Zebari described Iraq as a federal democratic parliamentary republic with extensive arrangements for self-rule and power sharing with federal entities; Iraqi Kurdistan would be constituted with Kirkuk as its capital.

Ziya is a controlled and calculating politician who carefully calibrates his words. In response, Ziya warned: "Federalism is dangerous now." He insisted that "if Kurds have a federal state, then the Turkmen should have one as well." The ITF envisioned Iraq "united and democratic with equal political and cultural rights guaranteed in the constitution [and] proportional representation in both the central government and national parliament."[1]

Conflicting property claims make Kirkuk a lightning rod for conflict. Fearing they would lose legitimacy if they gave up Kirkuk, Kurdish political leaders insist upon Kirkuk as the capital of Iraqi Kurdistan. Kurdish peshmerga vowed to retake the city upon liberation. Turkmen groups also stake a claim.

Though Zebari and Ziya did not agree about how to handle Kirkuk, they concurred on the need to reduce communal tensions. Ziya proposed enhanced autonomy for Turkmen. Zebari acknowledged that "Kurdistan" does not mean that the region is Kurdish. Rather than focus on intractable issues, such as Kirkuk, they identified Erbil as a potential model for joint administration.

They also agreed on the need for an orderly process to return hundreds of thousands of Kurds and Turkmen driven from Kirkuk over generations. An internationally supervised population census would be conducted once displaced persons had returned to their homes. Until a demarcation process could be undertaken by a legitimate Iraqi body, they supported Colin Powell's proposal that the United States hold Iraq's oil reserves "in trust" for the Iraqi people.[2]

Zebari and Ziya agreed on other confidence-building measures, such as general education conducted in native languages. Zebari asked for names of Turkmen charged with crimes and promised to investigate allegations of KDP bias. He also requested a list of illegally confiscated properties and the names of civilians evicted from their homes so that the KDP could launch an investigation and provide for their safe return. They agreed to establish a hotline for future discussion.

The meeting proved that the participants "can interact in a civilized way as one team united in a greater purpose," according to Zebari. "Our mutual interest is greater than past prejudices."[3] Ziya also thought that the workshop had been successful and proposed a second meeting in Erbil. I urged him to brief Turkish officials as well as the ITF leadership. It was important that Turkey help bring agreement between Kurds and Turkmen.

TURKEY was always one of the strongest and most reliable allies of the United States. During the Gulf War, President Turgut Ozal acted decisively to support the international coalition. Recep Tayyip Erdogan's Justice and Development Party (AKP) won a sweeping electoral victory in February 2003. It came into power promising reform, but its first months were defined by missteps over Cyprus and Turkey's accession to the European Union. Most of all, the AKP was ill-prepared to deal with the imminent war in Iraq.

The Pentagon's battle plan envisioned stretching Iraq's defenses through a two-pronged offensive, with troops entering Iraq from Turkey in the north and from Kuwait in the south.

In the past, the Turkish General Staff (TGS) was irrefutably in charge and Turkish generals always cooperated with the U.S. Department of Defense. However, the AKP introduced a new variable into decisionmaking. The Iraq war was profoundly unpopular with Turkish citizens who believed that aggression against Iraq was unjustified and illegal. Many Turks thought that the United States took their support for granted.

Ankara was caught between its domestic political priorities and its strategic relationship with the United States. In the event of war, Ankara feared that Iraqi Kurds would take advantage of the power vacuum to establish an independent Kurdish state. They believed that the peshmerga would seize Kirkuk and other oil-rich regions to attain the means for economic independence and, in the process, commit ethnic cleansing against Iraqi Turkmen. Ugur Ziyal, Turkey's undersecretary of foreign affairs, argued that federalism in Iraq would incite separatism among Turkey's Kurds and be a catalyst for terrorism by the Kurdistan Worker's Party (PKK). According to Turkish officials, "We see northern Iraq as an issue directly related to Turkey's national interests and security. We hope that groups in northern Iraq do not resort to provocative statements. It is more appropriate for all to see Turkey as a party to regional cooperation, rather than a hostile party."[4]

To mollify concerns about the emergence of an independent Iraqi Kurdistan, Zalmay Khalilzad was charged with mediating a security agreement between the Iraqi Kurds and Turkey. Khalilzad met Turkish officials, Kurdish representatives, and the ITF in Ankara on February 6, 2003. Kurdish leaders insisted they had no intention of declaring an independent Kurdish state, but they vehemently objected to Turkish forces on their territory.

Khalilzad tried to dissuade Nechervan Barzani, Massoud's nephew, and Jalal Talabani from taking steps that might antagonize Turkey. Whether the Kurds liked it or not, he warned, "Turkish troops are going to cross the border."[5]

Zebari reacted sharply: "We will oppose any Turkish military intervention. No one should see us as bluffing on this issue. Any intervention
under whatever pretext will lead to clashes."[6] Sami Abdul-Rahman complained that "Turkish troops will be a boot on our chest meant to strangle
our people."[7] Reflecting Kurdish public opinion, the Women's Union of
Kurdistan declared that "Turkey is worse than Saddam."[8] Turkey was harboring "grandiose dreams of re-annexing the old Ottoman villayet of
Mosul," accused Najmaldin Karim's Kurdish National Congress of North
America. "The United States wants the Kurds to jump from the frying
pan into the fire willingly; or else, they might be shoved into it."[9]

Barham Salih tried to be more accommodating: "There has to be a
compromise on all sides," he said. "Our claim to Kirkuk is based on history, geography and population, and we want to incorporate it into our
region. But we'll adopt a democratic way for people to decide what they
want, rather than simply say the area is ours."[10]

Ankara was inflexible. As Egeman Bagis, Erdogan's adviser on foreign affairs, explained, "If the United States feels they need to come 10,000 miles
away to Iraq to protect their citizens from another September 11, isn't it
right that Turkey, which is right on Iraq's border and is a long-standing ally
hosting U.S. forces, should be concerned? If Saddam is armed with
weapons of mass destruction, Turkey has a right to be in Iraq."[11]

The TGS also maintained that the situation in northern Iraq directly im-
pacted on Turkey's security. It demanded that U.S. troops stay south of the
36th parallel and act as a buffer to prevent the Kurds from occupying Mosul
and Kirkuk. A Joint Operation Headquarters would be set up in Diyarbakir
and a Turkish general assigned to the U.S. Central Command in Qatar.
Kurdish peshmerga would be subject to inspection by Turkish troops, who
would also carry out search-and-destroy missions against the PKK.

When General Fevzi Turkeri insisted that Turkish troops would not
submit to foreign control, Khalilzad responded, "All combat forces in the
area have to be under coalition command."[12]

I sent a memo to Ryan Crocker on February 11 reporting on my conversations with Kurdish leaders; they said, "If we have to choose between
Turkish domination and what we have now, then we'd rather live with
Saddam. Peshmerga will not stand for this. We will fight them."[13] I
pointed out that the Kurds were worried about the number, distribution,
duration, and command of Turkish forces. They were also dismayed by
the Pentagon's decision not to use Kurdish peshmerga the way Northern

Alliance fighters were used in Afghanistan. Tens of thousands of Kurds took to the streets across Iraqi Kurdistan to protest Turkey's demands.

To address both Turkish and Kurdish concerns, I recommended that the combined U.S.-Turkish force be predominantly American; that Turkish troops be restricted to a narrow security belt on the Iraq-Turkey border; and, in accordance with NATO procedures, that Turkish troops be placed under an overall U.S. command. I also urged the U.S. government to issue a public statement reaffirming Iraq's territorial integrity and emphasizing that a Turkish deployment would be of limited scope and duration. I suggested that a Joint Security Committee be formed, to include U.S., Turkish, and peshmerga commanders, which would meet regularly, assess security conditions, and serve as a platform for resolving potential conflicts. I also proposed the creation of a "Kirkuk Humanitarian Coordinating Committee" that would bring local actors together with international humanitarian agencies and donor countries for preparedness and contingency planning.

T HE Turks thought they could dissuade The U.S. from going to war by blocking the northern attack option. But if Bush did go to war, Erdogan wanted to make sure that Turkey had a seat at the table: "If we stay out of the equation from the start of the operation," he reasoned, "we won't have any control over its later developments."[14]

Initial military plans had 92,000 troops and support personnel in the U.S. Army's Fourth Infantry Division transiting through Turkey. To approve the deployment, the Turkish Grand National Assembly (TGNA) was scheduled to vote on February 18. However, the vote was postponed until March 1, 2003. In the interim, Foreign Minister Yasar Yakis went to Washington to discuss the terms of Turkey's participation.

When Yakis met Colin Powell on February 24, 2003, they discussed the size and nature of an economic assistance package, the military aspects of Turkey's deployment, and the political issues concerning Iraq's future. Yakis sought $92 billion—$1 billion for every 1,000 troops to set foot on Turkish soil. He also insisted that an equal number of Turkish troops be permitted to enter northern Iraq to control the border, manage the flow of refugees, and assist in the event of a humanitarian emergency.

The United States finally agreed to provide a grant of $6 billion, which could be used to leverage credits and bring the total value of the package to $24 billion. Additional compensation included $2 billion for military assistance. Qualified Industrial Zones for Turkish textiles and military equipment would generate an additional $1 billion; Turkish companies were also promised reconstruction contracts.

Ankara was not satisfied; U.S. aid was tied to conditions of the International Monetary Fund's economic-reform program for Turkey. The package required congressional approval, which could be held up by the Greek American or Armenian American lobbies. Furthermore, the AKP leadership was dissatisfied with Washington's vague assurances about security and governance in postwar Iraq.

ON February 24, 2003, Khalilzad and David Pearce stopped in Ankara on their way to the Iraqi opposition meeting in Salahuddin. Turkey refused to allow Khalilzad's security detail to accompany him, insisting that only Turkish Special Forces could serve as bodyguards. Khalilzad was incensed.

After the London Opposition Conference, I tried unsuccessfully to discourage Zebari from going ahead with a follow-up meeting. "What for?" I asked. Another meeting would muddy the waters, and I was concerned that Ahmad Chalabi would use it for one last power grab before military action.

Sure enough, Chalabi convened opposition leaders in Tehran and from there they traveled to Salahuddin. Though Kanan Makiya suggested that they might flaunt U.S. instructions and establish a provisional government, Talabani demurred: "There is no intention to declare a provisional government at this time," he said. "We believe that following liberation we can discuss that."[15]

To the dismay of the U.S. military planners, the meeting endorsed "an organized popular uprising. This will be achieved through close cooperation with the masses in cities and armed forces loyal to the people who are all committed to the dignity of Iraq and its glorious heritage." In response, Khalilzad insisted that Iraqis should "move" only when ordered to do so by General Tommy Franks; Donald Rumsfeld was even more dismissive: He told the Iraqis just to "stay home."[16]

In Salahuddin, the Iraqi opposition was more concerned about Turkey's saber-rattling than about Saddam. While pledging to support Iraq's unity and territorial integrity, Talabani also gave a warning: "The most dangerous aspect of the coming conflict lies with foreign powers who will try to enter Iraqi lands."[17] Zebari stated: "The Iraqi opposition is united in opposing any intervention. As opposed to Kurds versus

Turks, this is the unanimous view of the whole opposition. This could have serious consequences for the campaign in Iraq. It would be a destabilizing factor. There would be problems and there would be clashes."[18]

Arab Shi'a also opposed Turkey's intervention. Abdul Aziz al-Hakim of the Supreme Council for Islamic Revolution in Iraq asserted, "One of the biggest dangers of the war is foreign domination."[19] Hamid al-Bayati hinted that the Iraqi opposition might seek help from Iran if Turkey sent in troops: "[The Kurds] have an option to allow the Badr brigade to enter."[20] Moreover, he warned that Turkey's military intervention could prompt Iran to cross the border, seizing sections of eastern Iraq in order to target the People's Mujahadeen. Zebari asked, "If no one else respects Iraq's territorial integrity, why should we?"[21] He added, "Any unilateral military intervention would lead to Iranian intervention."[22]

Khalilzad tried to placate Iraqi concerns, declaring, "The United States is opposed to a Turkish unilateral role." [23] He insisted, "We are confident that any coalition operations undertaken will be fully coordinated, that there is no intention by Turkey to act outside of this framework in northern Iraq, and that there will be full withdrawal of all coalition forces when the job is done."[24] Just hours before the TGNA voted whether or not to approve the transit of American troops, his statement was widely reported in the Turkish media. Editorials also criticized the exclusion of a Turkmen representative from the leadership committee: "People feel [Khalilzad] is saying one thing here and another thing there. There is a serious lack of communication," wrote Ilnur Cevik, editor of the *Turkish Daily News*.[25]

The United States turned a deaf ear to Turkey's concerns about going to war in Iraq, even though 94 percent of Turks did not want U.S. troops in Turkey[26] and 50 percent viewed U.S. policies as the greatest threat to Turkey's security.[27] Erdogan tried desperately to balance domestic political pressures with the importance of maintaining good relations with the United States. Always pragmatic, Erdogan pledged to support "the temporary deployment in Turkey . . . of a maximum of 62,000 military personnel and air elements of no more than 225 planes and 65 helicopters for a period of six months."[28]

On March 1, the TGNA failed to approve the measure by just three votes. Erdogan blamed the United States for rushing the vote in parliament before he could gather enough support. By taking Turkey for granted, the Bush administration had cast doubt on the strategic partnership between the United States and Turkey. It had alienated the Turkish public by insinuating that Turkey's reluctance was a bargaining ploy for more economic aid. One U.S. official characterized Turkey's demands as "extortion in the name of alliance."[29] Racist depictions in the U.S. press of Turks as carpet salesmen and bazaar hagglers were deeply offensive. Turkey's deputy permanent representative to the United Nations appeared on television and announced, "We are not prostitutes."

The outcome was a staggering setback to U.S. war plans. It also rocked Turkey. Within forty-eight hours, the Turkish stock market had plunged 12.5 percent and the Turkish lira fell 5 percent on fears that the United States would withdraw its aid package of $26 billion—the equivalent of $97,000 per person.

U.S. officials immediately started angling for a new vote in the TGNA. Meanwhile, the Pentagon kept twenty-four cargo ships carrying vehicles, supplies, and equipment of the U.S. Army's Fourth Infantry Division off the Turkish coast. The Pentagon was anxious to start the military campaign and avoid summer heat and sandstorms. Unless Turkey reversed its decision, the battle plan would have to be amended. Cargo ships could be re-routed through the Suez Canal to Kuwait. Given the backlog, the Fourth Infantry Division might arrive late, or not at all, if Turkey refused to open a land bridge.

Erdogan also visited Washington, D.C., and argued against removing Saddam during his meeting in the Oval Office on March 10, 2003. Bush and his national security advisers made the case for Turkey's participation. Erdogan was noncommittal and warned that a Shi'a regime with strong ties to Iran would emerge. He said that no decision could be made without authorization by the Turkish parliament and left the meeting convinced that the United States would not attack Iraq without Turkey. He was sure he had convinced Bush that doing so would be riskier, take longer, and result in more casualties.

Despite the Pentagon's urgency, Erdogan was in no rush. On March 18, Khalilzad returned to Ankara with a package intended to address Turkey's security concerns: Up to 20,000 Turkish troops would follow on the heels of U.S. forces and establish a twenty-kilometer buffer zone on the border. The peshmerga would be placed under U.S. command and kept out of Mosul and Kirkuk. U.S. and Turkish forces would jointly supervise the arming and disarming of the peshmerga. The United States also agreed to look the other way while Turkish troops hunted down remnants of the PKK. In addition, Khalilzad reaffirmed the U.S. commitment to Iraq's territorial integrity and, to keep order when the fighting ended, he proposed a commission managing the return of refugees and sorting out competing property claims between the Kurds, Turk-men, and other northerners.

General Franks tried to pressure Ankara by insisting that the United States could prosecute the war without Turkey. The 173rd Airborne Brigade and some special forces were already on the ground in Kurdistan. The United States could use air transport to deploy the 101st Airborne into northern Iraq. The Fourth Infantry Division had been re-directed to Kuwait. In addition, war ships from the USS *Harry S. Truman* and USS *Theodore Roosevelt* carrier battle groups were on their way from the Mediterranean to the Red Sea, where they could launch long-range tomahawk missiles traversing Saudi air space. When the Turkish parliament voted on March 19, Turkey was the last NATO country to approve overflight by U.S. war planes.

The next day, the TGS upped the ante and demanded a written guarantee that Turkish troops would be allowed to occupy northern Iraq. U.S. officials were outraged; Colin Powell held an impromptu press conference to condemn the Turkish position. "It feels like the Turks have taken a hot poker and stuck it in my eye," a senior administration official told me. "Don't they watch CNN? Don't they know that the war has already started?"[30]

Meanwhile, Turkish forces were massing on the Iraq-Turkey border. Colin Powell feared a war within a war. Two NATO allies could end up fighting each other instead of Iraqi forces: "We have made it clear that the situation in northern Iraq is volatile and it would be better if there were no Turkish forces as part of any military operation that might take place," he warned.[31] In less diplomatic language, U.S. officials threatened to intercede if Turkey invaded northern Iraq.

With the onset of war, the United States found itself more isolated than ever. Though the Turks ultimately allowed overflights, the damage was done. Failure to open the northern front had huge implications for the conduct of military operations, as well as for postwar planning. It forced the United States to focus entirely on the south, stretching supply lines and making U.S. forces more vulnerable to attack. The Fourth Infantry Division never made it into the theater of combat while major military operations were under way; had it been in play, the coalition might have been able to control the situation and establish better security. The breakdown in U.S.-Turkish relations also poisoned the prospect of Turkish help with stability operations after the war.

CHAPTER 12

OFFICE OF
RECONSTRUCTION AND
HUMANITARIAN
ASSISTANCE

WHILE ZALMAY KHALILZAD WAS IN ANKARA TRYING TO hammer out the details of security cooperation between Turkey and the Kurds, members of Congress were sharpening their knives for a hearing on postwar Iraq. Douglas Feith and Marc Grossman testified about postwar plans before the Senate Foreign Relations Committee on February 11, 2003. The briefing was remarkably short on details. Although some facts were unknowable until the United States was actually on the ground, the Pentagon gave no details about postwar security arrangements and declined to estimate the costs of securing and rebuilding Iraq. Senators were visibly irritated.

Grossman was the first witness. Grossman has impeccable credentials on Capitol Hill, where he has appeared dozens of times during his career as a Foreign Service Officer. Grossman also enjoys credibility with the Washington bureaucracy. He earned his reputation by never pulling punches or obfuscating the truth.

The United States would "stay as long as necessary in Iraq, but not one day more," Grossman asserted.[1] Reflecting our conversations on the subject, he described principles, strategies, and potential milestones central to Iraq's democratic development. In phase one, the United States would focus on stabilizing Iraq. Providing security, stability, and order would lay the groundwork for phase two, during which authority would progressively be given to Iraqi institutions. In phase three, Iraqis would draft a new democratic constitution. Once the constitution was debated and approved, Iraq would hold free and fair elections: "I think you would agree [this] is the way for any future Iraqi government to be truly legitimate," Grossman said.[2]

It was important to win hearts and minds. "What we learned in Afghanistan," he added, "was that if we could quickly do things to show people that there's tangible benefit to change, then we're able to bring people along."[3] The sequence of events mirrored deliberations of the Democratic Principles Working Group.

Douglas Feith elaborated on planned stability operations for when coalition military forces had defeated Iraq's armed forces: "A lot depends on what the nature of the war is, how much destruction there is, how much cooperation one gets, how many Iraqi units defect. The most you can do in planning is develop concepts on how you would proceed, not rigid plans based on some inflexible assumptions about how future events are going to unfold."[4]

Senators wanted more information. Feith's sound bites sounded more like slogans for the evening news than a serious consultation with the U.S. Congress. Senator Joe Biden put it bluntly: "One of the things [we] are worried about is that you don't have a plan."[5] Biden pressed for details, but Feith focused on broad goals and he would not elaborate on how to accomplish those goals. For example, he did not discuss how the United States would protect oil fields and secure borders. He did not describe plans for managing ethnic conflict and population flows. He provided no details about securing weapons of mass destruction and controlling weapons-storage facilities.

In contrast, U.S. Army General (Ret.) Anthony Zinni laid out a coherent checklist of security challenges, including the need to "maintain law and order, provide for a force protection, do peacekeeping, protect threatened groups, and deal with civil unrest and acts of retribution, counter external threats, and develop local security capabilities."[6] Zinni was speaking from first-hand experience gained during the Gulf War. Feith had never been closer to Iraq than Ankara, which he had visited in his private capacity as a registered foreign agent for the Turkish government.

Other committee members expressed concerns. Senator Richard Lugar, a Republican from Indiana and chairman of the Senate Foreign

Relations Committee, stated that "success in Iraq requires that the administration, the Congress, and the American people now think beyond current military preparations and move toward the enunciation of a clear post-conflict plan for Iraq and the region. We must articulate a plan that commences with a sober analysis of the costs and squarely addresses how Iraq would be secured and governed."[7]

In the Gulf War, friends and allies had covered 88 percent of the costs. Senator Chuck Hagel, a Republican from Nebraska, asked, "Aren't we wiser to bring our coalition partners along rather than laying down a timeline?" Because the Bush administration had failed to secure broad international support, Hagel was concerned that the United States would be forced to assume the entire panoply of postwar responsibilities. He was also concerned by the administration's defiant posture: "Either you do it our way or we'll do it."[8]

Regarding costs, Feith affirmed that it would require a supplemental appropriation for fiscal year 2003. However, he demurred from estimating potential costs and said that the budget would depend on the length and intensity of the war. Feith quoted Donald Rumsfeld, who had said, "I have no idea whether it's going to last four days, four weeks, or four months."[9]

Senator Christopher J. Dodd, a Democrat from Connecticut, was annoyed by the administration's reluctance to provide details: "It's very important to level with the American public. It's going to be very costly and take a long time."[10]

In response to questions about foreign debt, war reparations, and paychecks for the Iraqi civil service, Feith insisted that Iraq's vast oil wealth would generate enough revenue to cover reconstruction and sustain government operations. He repeated the administration's mantra: Iraq's oil assets are national assets; they belong to the people of Iraq; the United States will protect Iraq's oil fields from acts of sabotage so that oil production can be resumed as quickly as possible to help provide for the Iraqi people. Senator Barbara Boxer, a Democrat from California, asked about the condition of Iraq's oil industry. She wanted to know what it would cost to rehabilitate Iraq's energy sector, debilitated as it was from years of sanctions and war. Feith suggested that it would cost between $8 billion and $10 billion to repair Iraq's oil infrastructure. But he had no answer when asked who was going to pay for it.

Senator Hagel wanted more information on the U.S. exit strategy and timetable for drawing down forces. He warned, "Every day you get past three months, you've got to expect peacekeepers to have a bull's eye on their back."[11] Feith acknowledged Hagel's concern, but would not speculate on how long the occupation might last. Hagel then asked, "Which nations have committed specific resources to postwar Iraq?"[12] "There's a great sensitivity that many countries are not interested in having their role publicized," Feith replied. "They're not interested in making public commitments until other things have happened."[13]

Grossman explained that the Bush administration had approached fifty-one countries and asked for their support in three categories, one of which was post-conflict support. He also pointed out that without the UN's endorsement at the outset, it would be difficult to involve the world body in the immediate postwar period. Anticipating that the United Nations would suspend its activities in the event of war, the Pentagon was establishing a civil-military operations center to coordinate the provision of U.S. relief supplies until the UN and nongovernmental organizations (NGOs) could resume their programs. With about 60 percent of Iraqis getting their food from the UN's Oil for Food Program, the United States was counting on UN specialized agencies to restart food distribution as soon as possible.

When Senator George L. Voinovich, a Republican from Ohio, wanted to know about the administration's contact with Iraqi exiles, Feith replied, "We are not going to impose particular people or even a particular governmental system on the Iraqis. I think we recognize it would not be the right thing to do and it would not probably be something that we could pull off if we attempted it."[14] He added, "Our goal is to transfer as much authority as possible, as quickly as possible, to the Iraqis themselves. But the United States will not try to foist onto those who are not in a position to carry them burdens that can't be managed."[15] Senator Sam Brownback, a Republican from Kansas, cautioned, "You've got to have some leadership arise, Iraqi leadership arise to run Iraq."[16] To which Grossman reiterated, "The United States will not support a government-in-exile to be foisted upon the Iraqis."[17]

Grossman further explained that the transition strategy would be advised by a consultative council made up of Iraqis representing all groups and parties. The United States would also establish a judicial council to suggest necessary revisions to Iraq's laws and institutions, as well as a constitutional commission, which would draft a new constitution for submission to the Iraqi people for ratification. Because it depended on stability conditions, the transition could take place at different rates in different parts of the country, but town and district elections would be held soon after liberation. Feith insisted, "We're not going to show up there and then try to figure out what to do."[18] He also maintained that Iraq's governmental structures would be salvageable. After eliminating Ba'athists implicated in atrocities, the major institutions and ministries would remain in place and continue to perform essential functions just as before.

Biden was skeptical: "Even if you find this bevy of incredibly neutral technocrats and bureaucrats who will be accepted by the Kurds, the Shi'a, and the Sunni who are not part of the security apparatus, to keep the water running, the lights on the traffic flowing. They have to answer to somebody. Who's that going to be? I can't fathom when we're three weeks away from war or five weeks away from war possibly, you don't know the answer yet."[19] Biden wanted to know whether the Bush administration envisioned a U.S. general in charge. Would it adopt a MacArthur model for Iraq, similar to that used in Japan after World War II? Would NATO help provide security or train Iraq's new armed forces? What reconstruction role was envisioned for the European Union? Would the United Nations facilitate a political dialogue establishing Iraq's new government?

Grossman drew distinctions between Afghanistan and Iraq. As he pointed out: "In Afghanistan you had no bureaucracy to speak of, no money, but there was a loya jurga process. In Iraq there is a talented bureaucracy . . . and there's money from oil [but] no equivalent of the loya jurga."[20]

Senator Lincoln Chaffee, a Republican from Rhode Island, observed, "A worse case would be that this isn't viewed or interpreted as liberation; it's interpreted by many people not only in Iraq but around the region as a war on Islam."[21] In contrast, the neo-cons believed that success in Iraq would have a positive effect across the region. According to Paul Wolfowitz, "It is a war to liberate perhaps the most talented population in the Arab world, people who are ready to build a society and a government that could become a model for the future for others."[22] Interagency disputes occur in every administration. However, differences were on clear display when Grossman and Feith appeared before the Senate Foreign Relations Committee on February 11.

To leverage U.S. diplomacy, the U.S. Congress gave Bush the authority to disarm Saddam Hussein. In October 2002, it appropriated $65 billion for Iraq, $62.6 billion of that sum intended for military operations. The balance would be channeled through the Pentagon for relief and reconstruction. By early 2003, many members of Congress felt misled by Bush's assertion that war was a last resort. They were determined not to be left out of the loop.

National Security Presidential Directive 24 gave the Pentagon overall responsibility to help meet the humanitarian, reconstruction, and administrative challenges facing Iraq in the aftermath of combat operations. To manage Iraq's transition, President Bush established the Office of Reconstruction and Humanitarian Assistance (ORHA) on January 21, 2003. ORHA was placed under the supervision of Douglas Feith. It was headed by Jay M. Garner, a retired three-star army general with thirty-five years of service. It was envisioned that ORHA would be staffed by officials from departments and agencies throughout the government. Whether civilian or military, all officials reported through General Tommy Franks, the head of the U.S. Central Command (CENTCOM). ORHA would plug right into CENTCOM's operations for a seamless liaison with the Office of the Secretary of Defense (OSD). According to Feith, "ORHA will serve as the U.S. government nerve center for this effort going forward."[23] The establishment of ORHA represented a bureaucratic victory for the Defense Department; Garner was Rumsfeld's guy. The neo-cons were running the show.

ORHA was formed to do the job started by the Future of Iraq Project. However, it did not avail itself of previous planning, nor did it make use of those in the State Department knowledgeable about Iraq.

ORHA essentially had to invent itself from scratch. Given that it was established just eight weeks before the invasion of Iraq, it faced daunting challenges. James Dobbins, who supervised postwar relief and reconstruction in Haiti, Somalia, Bosnia, and Kosovo, observed, "Rather than use the structures that had done our nation-building for the past decade, we created a completely new structure. We transferred responsibilities from State and the Agency for International Development to the Department of Defense for things the Department of Defense had never been responsible for."[24] One of the cardinal rules in post-conflict peace building is to apply lessons learned from comparable operations. Instead, the Pentagon decided to erase the U.S. government's institutional memory and go it alone.

ORHA's organizational chart divided Iraq into three sectors. Responsibility for the northern sector was assigned to Bruce Moore, a retired general; Roger "Buck" Walters, another retired general, oversaw the south; and Barbara K. Bodine, a former U.S. ambassador to Yemen who had served in Baghdad in the 1980s, supervised the central region. ORHA's activities were also organized functionally. George F. Ward, a former U.S. Marine and ambassador to Namibia, supervised humanitarian activities; Lewis W. Lucke, a U.S. Agency for International Development (AID) veteran, was in charge of reconstruction; and Michael Mobbs, a former law partner and special adviser to Feith, managed civil administration. Regional offices would be staffed with representatives from each of the functional pillars. Fully loaded, ORHA would have a staff of about 450, including more than one hundred Iraqi expatriate technocrats identified by the OSD's Iraqi Reconstruction Development Council. ORHA was also charged with establishing links to UN specialized agencies, counterpart offices in the governments of coalition countries, and NGOs. Despite the enormous scope of activities, ORHA was envisioned as a lean operation relying on private contractors to do much of its work. I spoke with contacts at the UN, Scandinavian aid agencies, and leading humanitarian NGOs. ORHA never contacted them.

The Future of Iraq Project had been in operation for more than a year, but Garner did not even learn about it until a rehearsal of the postwar mission was held at the National Defense University on February 21–22, 2003. About two hundred people from different government agencies participated. Peeling back the onion on the myriad layers of postwar issues, Garner learned that there were far more questions than answers.

With ORHA getting a late start, Garner desperately needed qualified staff to ramp up operations. Though Garner wanted to incorporate part of the Future for Iraq Project into his planning, Tom Warrick was a problem. Warrick begrudgingly shared information with his counterparts in other agencies. Also, he had publicly criticized the Defense Department in an Iraqi-American forum in Michigan, when he stated that "if you work with Paul Wolfowitz, the State Department will not give you anything."[25] The OSD sidelined Warrick. In addition, Rumsfeld turned down Garner's request to hire thirty-two State Department experts on Iraq, including Meghan O'Sullivan—who would later appear mysteriously in Iraq and then emerge as staff of the National Security Council and Condoleezza Rice's principal adviser on Iraq.[26] George Ward observed that ORHA had "few experts on Iraq on the staff."[27] Tim Carney, Wolfowitz's personal addition to ORHA, groused, "There were scarcely any Arabists in the beginning." Though Garner was in desperate need of expertise, he was "instructed by Secretary of Defense Rumsfeld to ignore the Future of Iraq Project."[28]

Why were State Department experts frozen out of ORHA? According to Carney, Pentagon political appointees said that "Arabists were not welcome because they did not think Iraq could be democratic."[29] U.S. Middle East policy had always emphasized stability and, to this end, previous administrations typically found themselves allied with autocratic regimes. Several former ambassadors who doubted that Iraq could be transformed into a model democracy did not meet the ideological litmus test. Some State Department officials were blacklisted for not supporting Ahmad Chalabi. They were victims of the ideological rivalry that caused a virtual collapse of interagency process. By February 2003, State and Defense Department officials were barely on speaking terms.

Garner stepped into the interagency morass with the best of intentions. Upon his appointment, he remarked: "What better day in your life can you have than to be able to help somebody else, to help other people, and that is what we intend to do."[30] Garner brought a reputation as a good listener and a history of involvement in the region. He was beloved by Iraqi Kurds for carrying out General John Shalikashvili's 1991 humanitarian relief operation in northern Iraq. Reflecting on Operation Provide Comfort, which resettled hundreds of thousands of Kurds after the Gulf War, Najmaldin Karim said of Garner, "He is very capable and competent. I think he's a good man."[31]

Not everyone welcomed Garner's appointment. Particularly in the Arab world, concerns were voiced about his ties with U.S. defense industries and his staunch support of Israel. To run ORHA, Garner took a leave of absence from the presidency of SY Coleman. Owned by the U.S. defense giant L–3 Communications, SY Coleman specializes in missile systems, including the Patriot and the Arrow defense system that was sold to Israel for $2 billion. The *Jewish Forward* greeted Garner's appointment with the headline: "Pro-Israel General Will Oversee Reconstruction of Postwar Iraq."[32] In addition, Garner and prominent neo-cons served on the board of the Jewish Institute for National Security Affairs. In 2002, he was one of forty-two retired U.S. military officers who issued a statement praising the Israeli military for "remarkable restraint" in response to the Palestinian Intifada.[33] Many Muslims perceived him as Israel's agent in Iraq; Iran's Supreme Leader Ayatollah Ali Khamenei said, "The Iraqi administration should be elected by the

Iraqi people and not run by an American military officer with ties to the Zionist regime."[34]

Though ORHA was supposed to operate for only three months, the international community was worried about an open-ended U.S. military presence in Iraq. Garner spurred concerns by announcing that ORHA would stay for "as long as it takes."[35] His deputy, Buck Walters, also fueled suspicion: "I took a one-year leave of absence, but this organization is going to be here for a while."[36]

GARNER placed priority on earning the trust of Iraqis by keeping up a steady flow of aid. Portable generators would be needed if the utility system went down. Potable water and emergency food rations should be stockpiled to meet the basic needs of Iraqis. To this end, ORHA pledged to work within the letter and spirit of international humanitarian law. In collaboration with the United Nations, ORHA developed a structure to coordinate humanitarian assistance at the national and local levels. Coordinating mechanisms sought to inform policy decisions and match humanitarian requirements to assets. ORHA also planned to coordinate donors and to create a registration process for non-government organizations (NGOs).

Many obstacles impeded humanitarian NGOs in Iraq. The International Rescue Committee (IRC) carefully considered its involvement. In December 2002, when the Bush administration released $11 million for humanitarian activities, the IRC discussed whether to accept earmarked funds from the U.S. government. Staff members were concerned that signing a grant agreement with the State Department's Office of Northern Gulf Affairs implied support for U.S. policies. The IRC's Sandra Mitchell complained about a lack of "openness": "In meeting with State Department officials, we were repeatedly told that they themselves didn't know what some of the plans were, because the humanitarian response was so interwoven into the military plan."[37] From the available information, and in keeping with its relief mission, the IRC ultimately decided to accept the State Department's financing for stockpiling humanitarian supplies and developing emergency plans for water and sanitation. However, the IRC and several other NGOs insisted that their agreements include a provision stating that they would report only to civilian agencies.

At the February 11 hearing, Grossman described weekly meetings with thirty NGOs; each complained that their efforts at relief and development were hampered by restrictions imposed by the Treasury Department's Office of Foreign Assets Control. With sanctions on Iraq, NGOs faced a long and cumbersome process when seeking approval for operations in Iraq. Though Grossman pledged to enhance the role of NGOs, the NGO community was wary of being seen as pawns of the U.S. government and, in particular, the Department of Defense.

The Pentagon's plan to unify reconstruction and the humanitarian response with security represented a break from the tradition of multilateral post-conflict activities. Civilian agencies typically managed humanitarian efforts. In Iraq, however, the Bush administration had decided that the military would take the lead. Though humanitarian NGOs had learned to coordinate emergency relief operations with U.S. and international peacekeepers in Bosnia, Kosovo, and East Timor, NGOs had never been in a situation where the military maintained complete control. They worried about becoming targets of Iraqi insurgents resisting occupation. Impartiality is essential for humanitarian workers, and relief organizations bend over backwards to maintain neutrality. The decision to establish one command for all aspects of the post-conflict response put private humanitarian agencies at risk. It also minimized contributions from donor countries, which were wary of collaborating with the U.S. military. For example, the European Union made only a modest pledge of 100 million euros because it was concerned about the "independence and integrity of delivering humanitarian aid."[38]

Congress tried to bar the Pentagon from controlling the $2.5 billion emergency supplemental earmarked for humanitarian purposes in Iraq. Representative Jim Kolbe, a Republican from Arizona and member of the House Appropriations Committee, stated that "the secretary of state is the appropriate manager of foreign assistance and is so designated by law."[39] Grossman maintained that the U.S. Agency for International Development had "laid out a very detailed plan for their operations in the first month, months one to three, and three to six, in areas of water sanitation, public health, humanitarian, seaports, airports, establishing food distribution, emergency electricity."[40] That was before Feith commandeered the reconstruction account.

Working with Iraq's existing governmental structures was fundamental to ORHA's success strategy. "We wanted to take over the ministries, remove the senior Ba'athists," said Colonel Paul Hughes. "We intended to keep everybody else in place as much as we could, and have them continue functioning under the guidance of what we called senior ministry advisers."[41] As well as hand-picking key ORHA officials, the Pentagon wanted certain exile Iraqis, whose names Feith provided Garner, to act as de facto ministers for each of Iraq's ministries. The Pentagon affirmed that the "DoD is not hiring or contracting with the Iraqi National Congress (INC) members as such, but some of the Iraqi expatriates working with DoD may be INC members."[42]

Chalabi's backers in the Bush administration never wavered from their commitment to installing him in power. After Bush decided against establishing a government-in-exile, Chalabi pushed his backers to endorse the formation of a nucleus provisional government. When this failed, the Pentagon reverted to Plan C.

As part of a "rolling transition," ORHA would hand over power to an interim Iraqi administration that would run day-to-day affairs and reconstitute Iraq's military. Nine months later, a constitutional assembly would meet to draft Iraq's new constitution. Once the constitution was written, a sovereign administration would be established and elections organized within two years. Chalabi's backers reasoned that giving Chalabi and the Iraqi National Congress control of Iraq's reconstruction would eventually put him in a position to assume political leadership in Iraq.

ORHA's planning for the "day after" was based on a set of assumptions that all proved to be wrong. The United States anticipated oil-field fires, a massive humanitarian crisis, widespread revenge attacks against former leaders of Saddam's government, and threats from Iraq's neighbors. None of these events came to pass. From ORHA's inception, it scrambled to get ready. As Garner admitted, "This is an ad hoc operation glued together over about four or five weeks' time. [We] didn't really have enough time to plan."[43]

CHAPTER 13

— —

BASIC NIHILISTIC
IMPULSE

O N MARCH 19, 2003, PRESIDENT GEORGE W. BUSH
ordered a decapitation strike targeting Saddam Hussein. Accelerating war plans, two F–117 stealth fighters dropped precision ordnance, and U.S. war ships in the Persian Gulf and the Red Sea launched Tomahawk cruise missiles targeting Dora Farms, where U.S. intelligence believed Saddam was conducting a leadership meeting. Special Forces dropped behind enemy lines to secure the Rumaila oil fields as well as other oil fields in the country. On March 20, the ground war of "Operation Iraqi Freedom" began. Despite sand storms and occasional fierce fighting, U.S. troops took control of the Baghdad airport on April 5. Four days later, they entered Firdos Square and pulled down the statue of Saddam.

Jay Garner and his staff were languishing at a five-star hotel in Kuwait and trying to keep a low profile. Garner was itching to receive country clearance and start operations in Iraq. However, General Richard Myers, chairman of the U.S. Joint Chiefs of Staff, insisted that Garner did not need to be in Iraq to work. "It does not really matter where General Garner and his group are because they are, in fact, acting now."[1]

Meanwhile, Garner watched with dismay as the basic nihilistic impulse of Iraqis led to chaos and looting across the country.[2] He denied that America was at fault for the situation: "Much of the looting occurred on the streets before the military had taken those streets," he insisted. "In places where the military was there at the time the looting occurred, they were still fighting the combat operation."[3] The Third Infantry Division's "After Action Report" contradicted Garner's claim: "Higher headquarters did not provide the Third Infantry Division (mechanized) with a plan for

Phase IV (stability operations). As a result, Third Infantry Division transitioned into Phase IV in the absence of guidance."4

Tom Warrick had provided the Office for Reconstruction and Humanitarian Assistance (ORHA) a list of sites to be secured—infrastructure, administrative facilities, financial institutions, religious sites, and cultural monuments, including the Iraqi National Museum. The military went out of its way not to bomb these sites, but Warrick's list was either ignored or never conveyed to field commanders. Lacking instructions and with no one in charge, U.S. troops simply stepped aside when the looting began. Among all of Iraq's government facilities, field commanders protected the oil ministry only, an action which, of course, reinforced perceptions that the United States was after Iraq's oil.

The first days of liberation were an unmitigated disaster. Looting effectively gutted every government institution in Baghdad and in cities across Iraq. "They stole everything," Garner reported. "They stripped the wiring out of the walls, took the plumbing, and they torched the buildings."5 Looters dismantled the electricity grid, creating power shortages that shut down refrigeration, lighting, and water systems. Frenzied mobs ransacked hospitals, stealing medicines and even patients' beds. The crowd surged into the universities at Baghdad and Mosul and robbed them of computers and office furniture. The mob took anything that was not bolted to the floor. Cultural institutions were stripped. The National Library was ransacked; every book ever published in Iraq as well as rare manuscripts and newspapers from the last century were destroyed. Historical records dating from the Ottoman period disappeared. Looters also entered the National Museum, stealing and destroying 10,000 historical objects, including some of the finest artifacts from the Mesopotamian collection. Seals put in place by the International Atomic Energy Agency were broken at the al-Qaqaa weapons-storage facility and looters took tons of high-quality explosives used to detonate nuclear devices. Even the Tuwaitha nuclear complex was left unguarded; looters were able to steal yellowcake and other radiological materials. Though the looting was worse in Baghdad, it was rampant across the country. Lamented ORHA's Colonel Paul Hughes: "As Baghdad goes, so goes Iraq."6

I T is unclear whether the chaos was random or if Saddam loyalists had orchestrated the events to undermine U.S. efforts. What is clear, however, is that the looting had a devastating effect on the postwar administration of Iraq: Seventeen of Baghdad's twenty-three ministry buildings were destroyed. The professionals upon whom the United States was relying to rebuild the country were demoralized. The unrest undermined confidence and respect for the U.S. authorities. In a country where conspiracy theories abound, many Iraqis suspected the United States of orchestrating the mayhem. They could not comprehend how the powerful U.S. military could vanquish Saddam's Republican Guard yet fail to prevent civil unrest.

The Pentagon did not deploy its own military police, nor did it ask the United Kingdom to send military police units to Iraq. Field-tested on the streets of Northern Ireland, British military police are known for their effectiveness in post-conflict situations.

Garner tried to accentuate the positive. In his testimony to the House Budget Committee, he observed that "the crisis so many predicted never materialized."[7] Many of America's worst fears—more than 1 million persons displaced by the war, oil fires, and frontline states invading Iraq—had not been realized.

Garner also compared prewar conditions to current circumstances. Before the war, only 60 percent of Iraqis had access to safe drinking water, ten of Basra's twenty-one potable water treatment facilities did not work, and 70 percent of sewerage treatment plants were in urgent need of repair. Raw or partially treated sewerage was dumped into the Tigris and Euphrates Rivers; from there, it polluted Iraq's main water supplies. Before the war, 80 percent of Iraq's electrical system was operating at half its capacity of 5,500 megawatts. Power and fuel shortages were widespread, including scarce supplies of liquefied petroleum gas. In addition, 70 percent of children younger than five years suffered from malnutrition. Of the country's 25,000 schools, 80 percent were in poor condition. Some had as many as 180 students in each classroom and there was an average of one textbook for every 6 students.

Very little humanitarian aid was delivered during the early days of the war because military operations and logistical problems made it difficult to open supply routes. Garner pointed out that ORHA was working with the World Food Programme to distribute emergency rations. It was taking steps to rehabilitate Iraqi ministries and pay civil servants using frozen Iraqi assets and money gathered in Iraq. Garner described his efforts to work with technocrats who were untainted by their association with the Ba'ath. He also described reaching out to members of the Iraqi armed forces to seek their participation in reconstruction: "We are encountering some barriers in getting assistance to the Iraqi people," Garner acknowledged. "The primary barrier is security. It is not the threat of leftover forces continuing the fight, but from looters and other personnel using lawlessness to their advantage."[8] He also noted: "Every day we delay we're probably losing some momentum."[9]

Garner's realistic assessment was trumped by Donald Rumsfeld. In response to a question about looting at the Pentagon's daily press briefing, Rumsfeld replied, "Freedom's untidy. Free people are free to make mistakes and commit crimes and do bad things."[10]

Rumsfeld was determined to transform the U.S. military into a leaner and faster force and to make Iraq a showcase of the Pentagon's accomplishments. Military professionals anticipated that Rumsfeld's highly mechanized war plan would leave the United States with too few ground troops to impose order after the war. At a congressional hearing, Army Chief of Staff General Eric Shinseki was asked how many troops would be needed to stabilize Iraq. He replied, "I would say what's been mobilized to this point, something on the order of several hundred thousand soldiers."[11] Paul Wolfowitz dismissed the career military officer, claiming that Shinseki was "wildly off the mark."[12] He added, "There is no plan that could have achieved all the extraordinary speed of the plan and, at the same time, have been able to flood the country with 100,000 policemen. Choices had to be made."[13] Expressing a belief that was widespread among both the military's top brass and enlisted soldiers, ORHA's Tim Carney claimed that the Pentagon's "flawed policy and incompetent administration [had] marred the follow-up to a brilliant military campaign."[14]

O N April 6, the Pentagon flew Ahmad Chalabi and seven hundred of his Free Iraqi Forces to Iraq. The Office of the Secretary of Defense wanted Chalabi and his militia airlifted directly into Baghdad, but the move was vetoed by General Franks, who instead dropped him in Nasariyah. Nobody at the White House or the State Department was notified in advance; Condoleezza Rice was visibly startled by press reports. Colin Powell learned about it by reading the newspapers. Upon arriving on Iraqi soil, Chalabi announced that he and his men had come to join the fight with coalition forces.

U.S. policymakers envisioned a series of meetings in liberated parts of the country, culminating in a big Baghdad conference at which the Iraqi interim authority would be declared. The UN secretariat had not been informed about the plan when I went to see Louise Frechette, the deputy secretary general, on April 16. Mme. Frechette chaired the UN working group on Iraq. Rather than Iraq's political transition, she was focused on restarting UN weapons inspections. A UN spokesman, Ahmad Fawzi, explained that the United Nations would "do what the Security Council asks it to do. [However, t]he UN will not be subjugated to the occupying power on anything it does in Iraq."[15]

More than three weeks had passed since the onset of military operations. When Garner finally entered Iraq on April 9, 2003. He traveled to the port of Umm Qasr on the Euphrates River and then to Nasariyah. Though Garner was the official host of a conference involving about eighty Iraqis in Nasariyah on April 15, Zalmay Khalilzad ran the meeting. British officials worried that the meeting would founder if Iraqis thought the event was orchestrated by Washington. Sure enough, thousands of Shi'a gathered in peaceful protest of America's role; the Supreme Council for Islamic Revolution in Iraq refused to participate and issued a blunt statement: "We refuse to put ourselves under the thumb of the Americans."[16] Chalabi was not asked to attend but announced that he had refused Garner's invitation. Other Iraqi National Congress (INC) representatives were in the tent.

Amid questions about its purpose and place in U.S. postwar plans, Garner called the Nasariyah conference to order; Khalilzad explained that the meeting was the first in a sequence of regional conferences leading up to the establishment of an interim authority. To allay fears of a long-term U.S. military occupation, Khalilzad insisted that "the United States has absolutely no interest in ruling Iraq."[17] And in the *Wall Street Journal*, he wrote:

> Our meeting here in Nasariyah, with representatives of the Iraqi people, is the first in a series of consultations with Iraqis in different parts of the country. None of these meetings will choose a government for Iraq. Rather, they will be forums for Iraqis to discuss their ideas about the formation of the Iraqi Interim Authority, and to foster an Iraqi National dialogue. . . . The coalition supports the formation, as soon as possible, of the Iraqi Interim Authority a transitional administration, run by Iraqis, until a government is established by the people of Iraq through elections. The Interim Authority should be broad-based and

fully representative. It will also be temporary. Iraq in the past has had interim constitutions that lasted too long, and transitional leaders who overstayed their welcome.[18]

Iraqis were skeptical of U.S. intentions. Iraq's infrastructure was already run down by years of neglect, sanctions, and war. Baghdad's ransacking completely undermined the Bush administration's plan to demonstrate immediate material benefits from liberation. With coalition forces still involved in combat operations, Garner did not even enter Baghdad until April 20, more than one month after the start of combat operations.

ORHA had started too late to become fully operational. According to Colonel Hughes, "ORHA had a great deal of responsibility but very few resources and literally no field authority to make decisions."[19] Major Jeff Jurgensen admitted: "In many ways we are learning as we go."[20] Carney complained that the U.S. military simply did not understand or give enough priority to our political military mission. "For a group devoted to getting Iraq up and running, we had surprising difficulty getting ourselves up and running. There were no lights. We used Port-a-Johns. No one had thought about laundry for our civilian team, so a contractor drove clothes to Kuwait to be washed, a five-day round trip."[21]

To make matters worse, ORHA's staff had little on-the-ground knowledge of Iraq. Few spoke Arabic. ORHA staff was sequestered in one of Saddam's huge palaces and had sparse interaction with Iraqis. There was no way to communicate except by using Thuraya satellite phones, which did not work indoors. ORHA needed translators, escorts, and military transport. However, field commanders had scant appreciation for ORHA's efforts and rarely ever showed up at meetings. Carney observed,

> Few in the military understood the urgency of our mission, yet we relied on the military for support. We were not being treated seriously enough by the command given what we are supposed to do. The Defense Department was in charge. The Pentagon was using the same military staff structure it used during the war. Garner was subordinate to the combined forces land component commander, whose staff generally had little respect for ORHA and little grasp of our civilian mission.[22]

To illustrate obstacles, Carney described how twenty ORHA staff members showed up at the airport in Kuwait City to catch a flight to

Baghdad. A general's plane had broken down, so he commandeered theirs. When the ORHA group finally arrived in Baghdad, the military convoy scheduled to pick them up at the airport had returned to base. The group waited several hours at the airport before being able to arrange surface transport into the city.

I N April 2003, the United States had 150,000 troops in Iraq; in addition, 23,000 troops, most of whom were British, came from other countries. The international community was deeply divided over the U.S.-led military action. The Bush administration's effort to secure troops from other countries was hampered by its perceived failure to gain an explicit authorization for military action from the United Nations.

United Nations Security Council resolution 1441 was adopted unanimously on November 8, 2002. It warned of "serious consequences" if Iraq refused to fulfill its disarmament obligations.[23] To accommodate Tony Blair, who was under political pressure in Britain to seek a second resolution mandating the use of force, the United States, Britain, and Spain tabled such a resolution on February 24, 2003. Russia and France threatened a veto, but there was no need. The resolution fell far short of the nine votes necessary for approval. As Powell admitted, "It was a failure."[24] Lacking UN "cover," the failure made it even harder for governments to provide troops to the U.S.-led coalition.

The Bush administration further undermined its efforts to broaden the coalition by announcing that regulations permitted only U.S. companies to bid on reconstruction contracts using U.S. funds. Moreover, only coalition countries were allowed to bid on contracts paid for by the Development Fund for Iraq (DFI), which was capitalized with seized Iraqi assets and money left even in the UN Oil for Food escrow account. More questions about the U.S.-led reconstruction effort arose when the administration awarded Halliburton and Bechtel multibillion-dollar deals without going through a competitive bidding process. The need for immediate action and security clearances were among the reasons put forward by the administration, but the explanation did little to quell concerns.

Though the number of countries participating in Bush's "coalition of the willing" exceeded the number of states his father had assembled for the Gulf War, the group was a coalition of convenience rather than of commitment. Few countries rushed to join the coalition; therefore, the U.S. used a combination of perks and punishment to induce countries to participate. Small states, such as Azerbaijan, Macedonia, and Palau, joined the coalition but offered little tangible assistance.

In early April, the leaders of France, Germany, and Russia met in St. Petersburg to discuss Iraq's reconstruction. Arguing that prolonged U.S. military control would be opposed by Iraqis and antagonize the Arab world, they issued a joint statement calling on the United Nations to take the lead in determining Iraq's future. President Jacques Chirac of France said, "We are no longer in an era where one or two countries can control the fate of another country. Therefore, the political, economic, humanitarian, and administrative reconstruction of Iraq is a matter for the United Nations and for it alone."[25]

The following week, UN Secretary General Kofi Annan attended the Athens summit meeting of the European Union (EU). As part of its public diplomacy, the State Department arranged for me to give a series of lectures in Greece on postwar reconstruction plans; I encountered adamant opposition from Greek officials, intellectuals, and think-tank representatives. They complained that unilateral action was in violation of international law and that UN weapons inspectors should have been given more time to do their work. Their objections mirrored concerns that were raised across Europe. It was no surprise when the EU, with Greece occupying its rotating presidency, issued a strong statement calling on the United States to turn over control of Iraq to the United Nations.

Even commonsense initiatives, such as lifting UN sanctions so that Iraq could sell its oil to help pay for reconstruction, ran into problems. Bush declared, "Now that Iraq is liberated, the United Nations should lift economic sanctions on that country,"[26] but the international community responded skeptically; indeed, many countries saw it as a ploy by Iraq's occupying power to dominate the country's oil sales and use the proceeds to enrich U.S. corporations.

AFTER just a few months as ORHA administrator, Jay Garner was replaced. The Bush administration chose Ambassador L. Paul Bremer III for the job and claimed that the change had been planned all along. Garner was replaced because the administration was unhappy about developments and wanted to change course. Ideologues disapproved of Garner's efforts to rehabilitate Ba'ath Party technocrats and reform elements of the Iraqi armed forces. They also disapproved of delays in assigning key posts to Iraqi exiles associated with the INC. After the war, Garner complained bitterly about the Pentagon's failure to appreciate the importance of ORHA's mission and to provide adequate resources to do the job.

ORHA's staff welcomed Bremer's appointment. Despite their loyalties to Garner, they saw it as recognition by the Bush administration that the reconstruction effort needed a more competent and much greater civilian authority. With postwar plans in ruins, Bush appointed Bremer to salvage hopes for a "new Iraq."

— ■ —

CHAPTER 14

DE-BA'ATHIFICATION

PRESIDENT BUSH WAS FLANKED BY HIS NATIONAL security team in the Rose Garden of the White House. Journalists huddled at the foot of a lectern bearing the presidential seal. Sounding upbeat and positive, Bush squinted into the morning sun while reading a script announcing Ambassador Bremer's selection as civilian administrator of the Coalition Provisional Authority (CPA), which superseded the Office for Reconstruction and Humanitarian Assistance (ORHA). Bremer stood steadfast by Bush's side as the president described him as "a man of enormous experience" and "a can-do type person." Bush affirmed that Bremer "goes with the full blessings of this administration, and the full confidence of all of us . . . that he can get the job done."[1] Wearing his signature tan hiking boots and a blue suit complete with a stylish handkerchief in the pocket, "Jerry" Bremer—as he is known— arrived in Baghdad on May 11, 2003.

Bremer had received degrees from the Institut d'Études Politiques de Paris, Yale, and Harvard. He had enjoyed a distinguished career in the Foreign Service before retiring in 1989 to become the managing director of Kissinger Associates. Though Bremer spoke some Arabic and Farsi, he was not an Iraq specialist. His experience was in counterterrorism and internal security. Bremer served as ambassador-at-large for counterterrorism in the Reagan administration. In 1999, Bremer was appointed chairman of the National Commission on Terrorism. He also co-chaired the Heritage Foundation's Homeland Security Task Force, which created the blueprint for the White House's Department of Homeland Security. Bremer had a reputation as a hard-nosed manager.

Because he came out of the State Department, his appointment was intended to allay the perception that Iraq was run by a MacArthur-like military man.

Though Marc Grossman spoke highly of Bremer, the appointment was a surprise. Bremer was a less strident neo-con than Paul Wolfowitz and Richard Perle, but he was still ideologically in line with the White House and the Pentagon. Bremer's predictions about a terrorist attack on the homeland had been prescient. He was also on record as calling for regime change in Iraq. According to Bremer the United States should "finish the job we left unfinished in 1991, because Saddam Hussein still considers himself to be at war with us."[2]

Despite Bremer's credentials as a civilian, his appointment brought no change in the chain of command. The CPA was a proxy of the U.S. Department of Defense; Bremer reported to Donald Rumsfeld, who reported to the president.

Though Bremer had never run an enterprise as vast as the CPA, he had a work ethic and temperament ideally suited to the job. He also had a reputation for achievement and extraordinary competence. According to a former U.S. official who is one of his admirers, "Bremer is a control freak. Put him in a hierarchy, and he will bend it to your needs and purposes."[3]

Bremer's State Department experience suggested that he would bring political and diplomatic skills to his assignment as civilian administrator for Iraq. However, his iron will made him seem more like a viceroy than a partner to the Iraqi people. By the end of his tenure on June 28, 2004, Iraqis were complaining to me about his imperious and authoritarian ways. Arab Sunnis were angered by Bremer's decrees dismantling institutions they had dominated for decades. Arab Shi'a blamed Bremer for failing to build bridges to prominent clerics such as Grand Ayatollah Ali al-Sistani. The Kurds were upset by Bremer's efforts to strong-arm them into power-sharing concessions with other Iraqis. As the *Washington Post*'s Jim Hoagland commented, "He has come to personify America's good intentions, brash attitudes, and manifest shortcomings in Iraq."[4]

B REMER'S legacy will forever be defined by his first days in office; this is when he decided to dismantle the Ba'ath Party and ban the Iraqi armed forces. His unwillingness to hand over power to Iraqis further fueled resentment. The absence of a credible political process restoring sovereignty deeply embittered Iraqis towards the United States.

On May 16, 2003, Bremer issued a decree that "disestablished" the Ba'ath Party. Eliminating the party's structures and removing its leadership from positions of authority was intended to "ensure that a representative government in Iraq is not threatened by Ba'athist elements returning to power and that those in positions of power are acceptable to the Iraqi people." All senior party members holding the rank of regional command member *(Udw Qutriyya)*, branch member *(Udw Far)*, section member *(Udw Shu'bah)*, and group member *(Udw Firqah)* were removed from their positions and banned from future employment in the public sector. Reversing Jay Garner's more inclusive approach, Bremer thought a more thorough purge could be accomplished by dismissing all Iraqis in the top three levels of management at every government ministry and government-affiliated institution. Overnight, 120,000 Iraqis—including teachers and doctors—were dismissed from their jobs.[5]

Influenced by Ahmad Chalabi and his neo-con backers, Bremer made the decision to purge Iraq of the Ba'ath Party. The Bush administration condoned Bremer's "de-Nazification" approach even though it did not distinguish between individuals who had committed atrocities and those who were deemed guilty merely through association. As a result, tens of thousands of qualified Iraqis were kept from helping build the new Iraq. Bremer's ban appeared like an effort to marginalize Arab Sunnis, who dominated the Ba'ath Party. This perception was most widespread in the Sunni triangle north and west of Baghdad.

The Ba'ath Party was founded in Syria in 1941. Its message of Arab unity and independence struck a chord in the post-colonial period, and Ba'athism spread across the Arab world. The Ba'ath Party of Iraq represented a state ideology promoting social order. However, under Saddam Hussein, the party became a Stalinist instrument of control, repression, and subservience to the ruling elite. After seizing power in 1968, Iraq's Ba'ath Party took steps to consolidate its control. The Interior Ministry proved to be the most notorious actor in Iraq's culture of violence. The Republican Guards also committed atrocities in their genocidal campaigns against the Kurds and Shi'a, including the marsh Arabs. The secret police had a special reputation for cruelty and viciousness. Chaired by Saddam Hussein, the Revolutionary Command Council (RCC) became the epicenter of power.

Though the Ba'ath Party ruled by decree, it tried to create a veneer of legality to justify its abuses. Article 37 of Saddam's Provisional Constitution eliminated checks and balances by centralizing legislative, executive, and judicial functions within the RCC. Article 47 empowered the RCC to determine the parliament's schedule, thereby turning it into a rubber stamp of the party. To reduce challenges from Iraq's Shi'a majority, Saddam pushed through a controversial law to secularize the state and reduce the role of religion *(Qanum al Ahwad al Shakhsiyya)*. The party also controlled bodies that would normally serve civil society, such as professional unions and women's associations. It manipulated the media and used the arts and academia as propaganda tools. There were no political parties other than the Ba'ath. Dissent or criticism of the regime was considered a capital crime.

Not all of the Ba'ath Party's two million members, which included many technocrats, joined for ideological reasons. Some joined out of fear for their safety. Many joined because they had no choice, to earn a living, or out of professional ambition. Membership in the Ba'ath Party was a prerequisite for employment in the civil service. For example, university professors, doctors, and engineers were almost all party members. Thanks to its oil wealth, Iraq emerged as perhaps the most well-educated and technocratic country in the Arab world.

Bremer's blanket approach to de-Ba'athification excluded Iraqi civil servants who had valuable skills, historical knowledge, and experience. It failed to consider that not all party members were guilty of crimes against humanity. It did not address Iraqis who had attained senior positions in the party but did not have positions of power in the government. Nor did it consider that not all officials who committed atrocities were prominent in the party hierarchy. Take Saddam's sons, for example: Qusay was a member of the RCC, but Uday held no important rank in the party. Many business elites involved with the Hussein family did not join the party, but were accomplices in sustaining the regime's terror infrastructure.

The Bush administration believed that de-Ba'athification was not just about punishing the guilty; it was about distributing power to Iraqis who subscribed to its vision of the new Iraq. As Rumsfeld affirmed, "The coalition will work with forward-looking Iraqis and actively oppose the old regime's enforcers—the Ba'ath party leaders, Fedayeen Saddam, and other instruments of oppression—and make clear it will eliminate the remnants of Saddam's regime. Those who committed war crimes or crimes against humanity will be tracked down and brought to justice. De-Ba'athification may cause some inefficiencies, but it is critical to removing pervasive fear from Iraqi society."[6]

Getting rid of the Ba'ath army also eliminated opponents to the liberalization of Iraq's national economy. Modeling its approach on Poland's shock therapy, the neo-cons wanted to remove all remnants of state economic control. They believed that privatization would open Iraq to foreign investment, bring in foreign companies, and create an Iraqi bourgeoisie whose prosperity would inspire Syrians, Iranians, and others to seek the same.[7]

De-Ba'athification served another purpose central to the Bush administration's plans: Getting rid of the Ba'ath Party would eliminate Chalabi's competitors for political power. Chalabi believed that allowing the Ba'athists to remain in government was "like allowing Nazis into the German government after World War II."[8]

Chalabi's Free Iraqi Forces (FIF) acted more like Ba'athist thugs than liberators. After being air-lifted to Nasariyah, the FIF looted and pillaged as they made their way to Baghdad. Chalabi exacerbated the antipathy of Iraqis when, on May 20, he took over the posh Baghdad Hunting Club, an establishment for Ba'athist elites. Chalabi instructed his militia to seize twenty-five tons of documents from the Iraq Intelligence Ministry. When Bremer appointed Chalabi to run Iraq's de-Ba'athification program, Chalabi used the records of membership, services, and payments to advance his political agenda.

Tim Carney lamented, "There was so much reliance on Chalabi in those early days."[9] Chalabi infiltrated the CPA by establishing close ties with professional staff at all levels. Bremer developed a "list of Iraqis they wanted to work with for positions in the government of post-Saddam Iraq [that] included Chalabi and all of the members of his organization."[10]

He also convinced Bremer to install family members and INC cohorts to key posts such as oil minister, finance minister, and trade minister, as well as governor of the central bank. Appointed by Bremer to head the Iraqi Governing Council's Finance Committee, Chalabi used the position to influence its staffing and operations. He also steered several large reconstruction contracts to firms with which he had business or that employed members of his family. For example, the CPA agreed to pay $327 million to Nour USA for supplying equipment to the Iraqi armed forces; Nour also set up a subsidiary called Erinys, which won an $80 million contract to provide security to Iraq's oil sector. Burnishing Chalabi's reputation as Iraq's powerbroker, the INC became a one-stop shop for foreign companies wanting to do business in Iraq.

As the occupying power, Bremer's decree banning the Ba'ath Party was well within the bounds of the CPA's authority. Changing the attitudes of Iraqis would prove more challenging. Several generations of Iraqis had been inculcated with strident nationalism. Ba'athist values were taught in schools and emphasized in the workplace. Building on the anticolonial movement of the 1950s and 1960s, Ba'athism and Iraq's national identity became synonymous. Both were fundamentally about asserting independence from Great Britain and establishing equality with the West. Iraqi nationalism was strongest among the beneficiaries of Ba'athist rule.

IRAQIS involved in the Future of Iraq Project understood the difficulties of eradicating Ba'athism. The Democratic Principles Working Group recognized that accountability and justice were integral to healing and reconciliation. Without a system for prosecuting persons who committed atrocities, there would be acts of revenge, personal vigilantism, and collective punishment. Iraq's democratization would be impeded.

The Working Group recommended that the worst offenders be brought to justice through international courts, specially constituted Iraqi bodies, or a combination of the two. Taking into account the hierarchy of crimes, it also proposed that lesser offenders be dealt with through lustration laws or by way of truth and reconciliation. To complement punitive measures, amnesty arrangements were also discussed for those who had carried out the regime's policies but were not directly involved in atrocities.

During the period when Zalmay Khalilzad had served as special envoy to the free Iraqis, the U.S. government adopted many recommendations made by the Future of Iraq Project. After the Nasariyah meeting, Khalilzad laid out an approach to de-Ba'athification:

There will need to be accountability and reconciliation in Iraq. What should be done to the top leadership of the Ba'ath Party will be an important issue that Iraqis will need to decide collectively. The special position and privileges of the Ba'ath party have already stopped as a matter of practice. That will need to be translated into law. Iraqis, as a society, must decide how to treat differently those who led the crimes of the past regime, on the one hand, and those, on the other, who joined the Ba'ath party at the lowest levels and are not necessarily culpable in any crimes. There should be room for those Iraq civil servants—teachers, police, and irrigation engineers, for example—who in the past have done their best to serve their country, not Saddam's tyranny.[11]

After Khalilzad, Garner pursued a similar course. However U.S. policy changed when Bremer arrived in Baghdad.

B REMER'S decree banning the Ba'ath Party was followed on May 23 by an edict specifically targeting the Iraqi armed forces: "Recognizing that the prior Iraqi regime used certain government entities to oppress the Iraqi people and as instruments of torture, repression, and corruption," the CPA issued a list of disbanded entities that included the Revolutionary Command Council, the Ministry of Defense, the National Security Bureau, and the Special Security Organization, all branches of the armed forces, and all intelligence agencies and paramilitary groups such as the Saddam Fedayeen and Saddam's Lion Cubs *(Ashbal Saddam)*. It cancelled military subscription and offered a "termination payment." However, Iraqis with the rank of colonel or higher were considered to be senior party members and were denied payment. In a move that Iraqis saw as vindictive, benefits to widows of deceased senior party members were cut off. The decree also announced the establishment of the New Iraqi Civil Defense Corps as the first step in forming a national defense capability for the new Iraq.[12]

The decision to disband the armed forces sent shock waves through Iraqi society. During the war, the Pentagon dropped leaflets encouraging Iraqi soldiers to defect and go home. Their light resistance made military victory easier. After liberation, they expected a role in the new Iraq; but instead, Bremer sent a pink slip to 400,000 army personnel. Nine thousand military officers were members of the Ba'ath Party who deserved dismissal. However, Bremer did not distinguish between the officer corps and the rank and file, or between those who were drafted and those who were career soldiers. Military institutions were by and large led by Arab Sunnis, whereas mandatory subscription made foot soldiers of the Shi'a and Kurds.

At the beginning of the Iran-Iraq War, the armed forces numbered 242,000. By the beginning of the Gulf War in 1990, the number of men under arms was between 1 and 1.5 million. By 2002, the armed forces had been reduced to about 500,000. At the top of the structure was the National Security Council run by Saddam and Qusay. The intelligence directorate *(Mukhabarat)* dealt with external and internal opposition threats. The general security directorate *(Mudirriyat al-Amn al-Amm)* was responsible for internal security of the state. The special security directorate *(Mudirriyat al-Amn al-Khass)* provided presidential security and managed special weapons programs and counterintelligence against other directorates. The military intelligence directorate *(Mudirriyat al-Istikhbarat al-Askariyyah)* gathered information about external threats as well as about Iraqi military officers. In addition, Saddam maintained a private security force of trusted insiders and family members from Tikrit.

The decision to disband the armed forces contradicted the advice of Iraqis participating in the Future of Iraq Project. The Democratic Principles Working Group had recommended that Iraq's new government subordinate the military by conforming it to practices in democratic societies. The Working Group called for constitutional limits on the military budget and the elimination of military courts that had usurped functions of the judicial system. Participants agreed unanimously on the need to abolish the Republican Guard and to downsize and retrain the regular Iraqi army. Guidelines were proposed for governing the activities of the intelligence agencies so that they could still contribute to national security without abusing human rights. Participants also called for sustaining, reinvigorating, and retraining the police force so that it could keep order in the aftermath of regime change. However, disbanding the entire army was never considered.

The Future of Iraq Project's Defense Working Group also offered specific recommendations. It envisioned Iraq's approximately 100,000 career soldiers forming the leadership nucleus of a new, defensive military force removed from political activities. After screening, Republican Guard members would be transferred to the new Iraqi army. Special Forces would be reorganized to perform peacekeeping duties, participate in counterterrorism, interdict drug smuggling, provide security for Iraqi institutions, and protect infrastructure such as oil pipelines. Vetted military intelligence units would assist U.S. forces with security and reconnaissance against terrorist organizations.[13]

Rehabilitating the armed forces dovetailed with the vision themes presented to Iraqi opposition groups before the London Opposition Conference in December 2002. "When regime change comes," the paper read, "we are confident that the Iraqi military will join in the liberation of their country. We are also confident that they will refuse any order to target civilians or use weapons of mass destruction. A reformed Iraqi military should continue to have an important role in a post–Saddam Hussein Iraq."[14] The London Opposition Conference Political Statement "affirmed the need to restructure the army institutions and the Iraqi armed forces on a sound, professional and patriotic basis, away from militarization of the society, interference in internal disputes, and ethnic and sectarian discrimination." It also thought to "do away with the oppressive agencies that were founded by the regime to harass and terrorize citizens, and to restructure and reform the security apparatus in a way that is lawful and protects both civil and human rights of its citizens as well as the security of the country."[15]

Bremer's decree banning the armed forces flew in the face of advice from both Iraqis and U.S. experts. Other U.S. experts also agreed on the need to find a constructive role for the Iraqi armed forces. In his testimony to the Senate Foreign Relations Committee on February 11, 2002, Colonel Scott Feil (Ret.) indicated that "those internal security forces performing day-to-day enforcement of civil and bona-fide criminal law as opposed to political oppression must have their leadership changed, but the bulk of the rank and file will be essential to preserving order." In addition, Feil highlighted a role for the 70,000-man National Police Force and the Frontier Guard in maintaining civil order and making sure that terrorists did not cross into Iraq from neighboring states.[16] Garner echoed Feil's recommendations:

One of our goals is to take a good portion of the Iraqi regular army—I'm not talking about the Republican Guards, the special Republican Guards, but I'm talking about the regular army—and the regular army has the skill sets to match the work that needs to be done in construction. So our thought is to take them and they can help rebuild their own country. We'd continue to pay them. And these committees will nominate work for them to do, do things like engineering, road construction, work on bridges, remove rubble, de-mine, pick up unexploded ordnance, construction work. . . . Using the army allows us both to demobilize it immediately and put a lot of unemployed people on the street.[17]

The decision to ban the armed forces dismayed U.S. field commanders, who had reservations about excluding the military and skilled professionals from reconstruction, especially in the Sunni heartland. Major General John R. S. Batiste, commander of the First Infantry Division, said, "There are a number of Sunnis who are very good, courageous, and determined people, which, if given a chance, would be part of the solution in Iraq. These are proud officers with enormous energy and capability. If we harness their capability, it'd be a good thing." Brigadier General Carter F. Ham agreed, stating, "I'd like to see a policy that deals with individual cases rather than have a blanket policy."[18] Coalition partners also raised concerns. General Sir Mike Jackson, head of the British army, told the House of Commons Defence Committee that "the British approach to post-conflict situations was doctrinally different to that of the United States."[19]

Faisal al-Istrabadi, a member of the Democratic Principles Working Group, thought that "it was an atrocious decision" to disband the army: "I don't understand why you take 400,000 men who were highly armed and trained, and turn them into your enemies. Particularly when these are people who didn't fight."[20] Major Mohammed Faour, a former member of Iraq's Special Forces and a participant in the Future of Iraq Project's Defense Working Group, insisted that ex-officers were ready and willing to work for the Americans: "You can't put half a million people with families and weapons and a monthly salary on the dole. You can't do this in any country. They'll turn against you."

Just as Faour predicted, thousands of former Iraqi soldiers and officers gathered almost daily outside the gates of the CPA. One of their banners read, "Dissolving the Iraqi army is a humiliation to the dignity of the nation."[21] Not only did the decree turn 400,000 former soldiers against the U.S.-led coalition, but if you consider that an average Iraqi family includes six persons, the decision directly affected the lives of 2.4 million people, or roughly 10 percent of Iraq's population.

Not all Iraqis condemned the decree. Qubad Talabani, the Washington representative of the Patriotic Union of Kurdistan, stated:

> Ambassador Bremer's decision to disband the Iraqi army was a brave and just decision that no Iraqi leader could have done. The Iraqi army was not an Iraqi army, it was Saddam's army. However, Bremer made a grave error, deciding not to pay the salaries and pensions of those disbanded. When the army officers looked around and saw most of their civilian colleagues lining up for paychecks, they were infuriated, and with their arms by their sides, some former army officers took it upon themselves to join the insurgency.[22]

Bremer defended the decision, maintaining that the army had dissolved itself in the immediate aftermath of combat and there was no Iraqi military left to rebuild. His claim was disingenuous. The CPA had lists of former soldiers that they later used to provide severance pay. In addition, Bremer tried to deflect criticism by asserting that the decision was made at "very high policy levels" and was intended to convey a "highly symbolic" message about the demise of Saddam's regime. "We had concluded, talking to Iraqis, both in and out of the military, that people above the level of lieutenant colonel, because they had been in the army for so long, were essentially not going to be re-treadable into the new army," Bremer explained. "We had to create an entirely new institution."[23]

To soften the impact, that summer Bremer promised to pay the disbanded military additional stipends and invited members below the rank of lieutenant colonel to join the New Iraqi Corps. Almost one year later, the CPA came almost full circle by trying to reconstitute elements of Iraq's army and inviting former Ba'ath Party members back to their jobs if they could prove they were party members in name only.

Yet the decision came too late. The Bush administration had committed one of the greatest errors in the history of U.S. warfare: It unnecessarily increased the ranks of its enemies. Embittered Arab Sunnis, who had dominated the military establishment, would reemerge to lead the insurgency against U.S. troops in the Sunni triangle. Mistakes disbanding the armed forces and concerning de-Ba'athification would have lasting and far-reaching ramifications.

CHAPTER 15

— —

OCCUPATION

BREMER STATED, "OCCUPATION IS AN UGLY WORD. NOT one American feels comfortable with it, but it is a fact."[1] Until sovereignty was restored, Bremer envisioned that a U.S. military administration would run Iraq, guarantee security, oversee reconstruction, and organize elections. Bremer had a seven-step plan to hand over sovereignty to Iraqis. Starting with the establishment of an advisory council. However, Iraqis reacted angrily when Bremer announced that the transition to self-rule could take several years.

Bremer's decree banning the Iraqi armed forces was a tactical miscalculation with serious strategic consequences. Former members of the armed forces joined the legions of unemployed sitting at home and festering rage. At the same time, the Bush administration called on Iraqis to defend their country against insurgents, who were increasingly active blowing up water mains, oil pipelines, and electric towers, and attacking military convoys. Colonel Paul Hughes commented, "One of the cardinal sins in combat is to lose contact with the enemy. We had no knowledge about what they were doing. And these are trained soldiers. Some of them were not trained very well but they all had access to arms and people who would lead them."[2]

With 65 percent of Iraqis unemployed, ample recruits were ready to join the insurgency. Many of the dismissed Ba'athists and senior military officials were Arab Sunnis to whom Saddam had bestowed power and privilege. Suddenly, they were disgraced and destitute. Moreover, their future was uncertain in a country dominated by Arab Shi'a and Kurds.

The initial spasms of violence were concentrated in the Sunni triangle, where many former Ba'athists felt a sense of hopelessness that led them

155

to take up arms against the United States. "Instead of us using these personnel against terrorism, terrorists are using them against us," said Major Mohammed Faour. "This is a tragedy. We could use these people. They are military people. They are professionals. They are used to obeying orders. They need money. They need the lives they had before."[3]

Responding to Iraq's difficulties, Donald Rumsfeld invoked Thomas Jefferson: "We are not to expect to be translated from despotisms to liberty in a featherbed." Rumsfeld affirmed:

> The Coalition Provisional Authority has the responsibility to fill the vacuum of power in a country that has been under dictatorship for decades, by asserting temporary authority over the country. The coalition will do so. It will not tolerate self-appointed "leaders." The coalition will maintain as many security forces in Iraq as necessary, for as long as necessary, to accomplish these stated goals—and no longer. Coalition countries will seek to provide a secure environment, so that Iraqis will be able to take charge of their country as soon as possible.[4]

THE Bush administration had goals for Iraq, but no coherent strategy for accomplishing them. Its policy was based on a combination of naïveté, misjudgment, and wishful thinking. Vengeful insurgents found common cause with al-Qaeda elements, who were able to enter Iraq because the United States did not have enough troops to secure Iraq's borders with Syria and Iran. The chaos was exacerbated by up to 100,000 common criminals that Saddam had let out of jail just before the war. By creating chaos and inflicting casualties, they hoped to break U.S. will and drive the coalition out of the country. That summer, violence started to spiral out of control as the insurgency spread and suicide attacks started.

Even as violence was worsening, the Bush administration accentuated its accomplishments in Iraq. Rumsfeld pointed out:

> Thousands of lower level Ba'ath Party loyalists have been rounded up or otherwise dealt with. The Iraq Central Bank has been made independent. Iraq has reentered the world oil market. All of Iraq's universities have reopened. Power and water are, in most places, at pre-war levels, and we're making progress in Baghdad. The food distribution system has been re-

started. Nearly all of Iraq's 240 hospitals and 1,200 clinics are open. Over 100 newspapers have begun publishing.[5]

To influence Iraqi public opinion favorably, the Defense Department launched the Iraq Media Network, which reached 60 percent of the population, and twenty-four-hour radio. The Coalition Provisional Authority's (CPA) newspaper had a circulation of 60,000. According to the Pentagon, the Iraqis had a favorable prevailing view: "Notwithstanding all the difficulties we have, we're glad that you're here."[6]

In response to congressional criticism that the Bush administration did not have a plan to stabilize Iraq, Bremer explained: "My motto is strategic clarity and tactical flexibility. We need to be very clear where we are headed in our strategy on security, on economy, and on political developments. And we are very clear on that. And we need to have a plan, but we need to be tactically flexible as the situation evolves on the ground."[7]

Bremer described the CPA's agenda. First, the coalition would establish a safe and secure environment. Second, it would expand essential services. Third, it would stimulate the economy to create jobs and economic growth. And fourth, the CPA would steward Iraq's transition to democratic self-rule. Bremer recognized that security, reconstruction, and governance were interconnected. Sabotage worsened electricity problems, electricity shortages enhanced security risks, and reconstruction failures undermined the political transition. "Our task," said Rumsfeld, "is to try and create an environment that is hospitable for the Iraqi people to fashion a new way of governing themselves and be on our way."[8]

Initial looting appeared to be mostly random; but on closer inspection, at least some of the ransacking was orchestrated to undermine the occupation. Despite Bush's claim of "mission accomplished," Rumsfeld acknowledged that "while major combat activities have ended, the war continues."[9]

Though field commanders had little sense of the insurgency's leadership, organization, or financial sources, they believed that insurgents were organized at the regional level in a cellular structure in what amounted to a classical guerrilla campaign. After drive-by shootings or attacks using rocket propelled grenades, insurgents simply faded into the local population. Attacks were not just hit and run: Explosive devices used in combination with tactical activities implied some level of coordination. "There is an element of sophistication to what the enemy is doing," said Air Force Lieutenant General Norton A. Schwartz. "They have adapted over time, and, as a result, so are we."[10]

Pentagon civilians resisted use of the term "guerrilla war" to avoid the negative connotations of an open-ended and unwinnable conflict. Rumsfeld explained that he had looked up "guerrilla war," "insurgency," and "unconventional war" in the Pentagon dictionary. He preferred to call it an unconventional war because opposition forces were not an organized army. In addition, he pointed out that the insurgency did not qualify as a classical guerrilla operation because the majority of Iraqis did not support it. Assistant Defense Secretary Lawrence DiRita elaborated: "It's a low-intensity conflict in our doctrinal terms, but it is a war, however you describe it."[11]

Insurgents attacked pipelines, utility grids and other infrastructure. Convoys were targeted making the drive from the airport to Baghdad a dangerous gauntlet. Soft targets of the international community were also hit. Asked about the escalating violence, Bush replied "Bring 'em on."[12]

THE Iraqis themselves were increasingly targeted. Kidnappings and car-jackings became common occurrences. Women were too scared to leave their homes. Fearing that their daughters would be raped, fathers dropped them at school and then waited for them all day in 120-degree heat. Iraqis judged the United States by its ability to deliver security, services, and jobs. They were glad to be rid of Saddam, but they longed for the stability that had existed under the Ba'athist regime. As violence mounted, Iraqi resentment of the United States also increased.

In a country where conspiracy theories abound, many Iraqis believed the United States was holding Saddam as a trump card. Others feared that the United States would leave the job unfinished, as it had done in 1991, and that a Saddamist would return to power. Paul Wolfowitz tried to assuage their concerns: "If the Ba'athists have any staying power, let there be no doubt—we have more."[13]

With conditions worsening and Iraqis growing increasingly disaffected, the Pentagon commissioned an independent assessment of conditions in Iraq. The report concluded that "Iraqis uniformly expressed the view that the window of opportunity for the CPA to turn things around in Iraq is closing rapidly. The potential for chaos is becoming more real every day. The next three months are critical."[14]

Support for the Iraq war was also slipping in the United States. The administration cast the Iraq war as part of the broader war on terror. U.S. officials refused to acknowledge that the occupation had inspired the insurgency. Nor did it let on that the U.S. invasion had made Iraq the central front in the war on terror.

Rumsfeld insisted on staying the course:

> Coalition forces will continue to root out, capture, and kill the remnants of the former regime until they no longer pose a threat to the Iraqi people. . . . As we do, it is important not to lose sight of the fundamental fact that our country is still very much engaged in a global war on terrorism. Two terrorist regimes have been removed, but we still have terrorist enemies in Afghanistan and Iraq and across the globe who are seeking to harm our people. We can deal with them in one of two ways: we can find, capture, or kill them in Afghanistan, Iraq, or in other countries; or we can wait and end up having to deal with them here in the United States.[15]

General John Abizaid, Central Command's new head, echoed Rumsfeld's resolve, warning, "The global war on terrorism is going to be long; it's going to be hard; it's going to be difficult; and we're going to win."[16] When the Senate Foreign Relations Committee asked Deputy Defense Secretary Paul Wolfowitz how the U.S.-led coalition was going to address the insurgency, he answered in lofty terms rather than offering specific details. He intoned, "Our national sense of commitment and confidence must approximate what we demonstrated during the Berlin airlift: a sense that we could achieve the impossible, despite short-term constraints and severe conditions, risk, and consequences."[17]

EXCEPT for a handful of Arabs who joined Ansar al-Islam, an indigenous terror group encamped on the Iran-Iraq border and composed mostly of radical Kurds, al-Qaeda did not have a presence in Iraq before the war. However, jihadists from Syria, Egypt, Sudan, and other countries flocked to Iraq after Saddam's fall. Abu Musab al-Zarqawi was the most notorious. Zarqawi was an al-Qaeda associate who trained in Herat and fought with al-Qaeda in Afghanistan. Previously, he ran a terror group called al-Tawhid, whose goal was to depose Jordan's monarchy. It is believed that Zarqawi entered Iraq from Jordan and made his way across the western desert to Fallujah. Though former Ba'athists and al-Qaeda are ideologically incompatible, they forged cooperation against their common enemy, the United States. When U.S. forces engaged insurgents at Ar Rutbah in Western Iraq in July 2002, they found passports and identification at the scene, indicating that almost all the eighty fighters killed in the operation were non-Iraqi. Abizaid observed, "The terrorist problem is emerging as the number-one security threat."[18]

"Stability operations" did not mean that active combat was over. Field commanders stayed on the offensive. By the end of July, the coalition was conducting 2,000 patrols a day. More than 12,000 people had been taken into custody. The CPA announced Operation Victory Bounty to track down remnants of the Saddam Fedayeen. The walk-in traffic of people with suggestions, tips, and leads was overwhelming. The system paid off when an informant led U.S. forces to a safe house in Mosul where Qusay and Uday Hussein were ensconced. The Iraqi received a $30 million reward; he and his extended family were relocated and placed under protection.

By displaying the gruesome photos of Saddam's sons, the Pentagon hoped that news of their deaths would cause the violence to abate. It had killed or captured forty-two of the fifty-five "Most Wanted" senior leaders associated with Saddam's regime. But Saddam himself was still at large. Task Force 20 was established to coordinate intelligence in the hunt for Saddam Hussein.

Though it confiscated millions of dollars and large caches of weapons that would otherwise be used to ambush U.S. and British forces, the Defense Department knew that it was impossible to secure every convoy and protect every facility in a country the size of California. Field commanders understood that the best way to achieve a more secure environment was through the active engagement and support of the Iraqi people.

To change the face of occupation, the United States accelerated efforts to set up indigenous security forces. It initiated formation of an Iraqi national army and a civil defense corps in the hope that this would help with border security, site protection, and escorting convoys. Though more than 30,000 Iraqi police were hired, procurement problems delayed provision of their equipment. As insurgents targeted Iraq's cooperating with the U.S., poorly trained recruits were pushed onto the front lines like cannon fodder.

THE Congress wanted details about the Pentagon's plans to rotate forces and bring U.S. troops home. In July, the force level was about

160,000. This included 148,000 Americans and 12,000 troops from nineteen coalition countries. The U.S. Army's Third Infantry Division had been the point of the spear during the attack on Iraq and had remained in Baghdad to conduct stability operations. Though the Pentagon brass insisted that morale was high, many soldiers, exhausted by front-line duty in the oppressive summer heat, were angry about the mission's lack of focus. One member of the Third Infantry Division told ABC News, "If Donald Rumsfeld were here, I'd ask him for his resignation." He added, "I used to want to help these people, and now I really don't care about them anymore."[19]

The near total destruction of Iraqi security institutions forced U.S. troops to stay in Iraq for longer than expected. To maintain troop strength, the Defense Department relied on reserves who never imagined they would go overseas for more than a year. Senator Susan Collins, a Republican from Maine serving on the Armed Services Committee, participated in a congressional delegation to Iraq. A soldier from Bangor told her, "I'm proud of our mission. I helped free the Iraq people." But: "When do I get to go home? I can deal with another three months. I can deal with another six months, but I just need to know."[20]

General Abizaid wanted to reduce the U.S. troop presence. He understood that coalition patrols racing around in humvees exacerbated the resentment of Iraqis towards occupation. "There is a downside to having too many troops," Abizaid explained. "I have never been in favor of huge, ponderous forces, but light, agile, mobile forces that not only can deal with the problem in Iraq, but throughout the theater."[21] Abizaid maintained that the number of troops per square inch was not the issue. Capability matched to the mission was much more important; Abizaid took steps to replace heavily armored army units with lighter and more highly mechanized forces. He also expanded the use of private contractors.

At a hearing of the Senate Foreign Relations Committee, Paul Wolfowitz was grilled on the cost of the U.S. commitment in Iraq. When he insisted it was "unknowable," Senator Joe Biden shot back, "Give me a break, will you? When are you guys starting to be honest with us? Come on. This is ridiculous."[22]

In July 2003, the United States spent $3.9 billion on military operations in Iraq. Wolfowitz refused to speculate on the so-called burn rate—the number of troops over a projected period of time. All Wolfowitz would say is that the administration would seek a supplemental budget request. He tried to turn the tables by blaming the Congress for undermining U.S. efforts in Iraq. Wolfowitz charged that "Congress has [failed] to advance a predictable multi-year budget for operations in Iraq that would demonstrate American vision and commitment."[23] If the legislative branch understood the stakes, he emphasized, it would authorize a multi-year budget encompassing about $10 billion to rebuild Iraq's oil sector, $15 billion for water systems and a social safety net, and $20 billion to keep electricity production apace with demand. Regarding the U.S. commitment to Iraq, Rumsfeld insisted, "Is it an important thing to be doing? You bet. Is it tough? You bet. Are more people going to get killed? You bet. Does it cost money? You bet. Can we tell the world or anyone else exactly what it is going to cost or how long it's going to last? No."[24]

Members of Congress started to raise concerns about whether there were enough troops to do the job. They wanted to further internationalize security and give the United Nations a more important role in Iraq's reconstruction and political transition. Senator Carl Levin, a Democrat from Michigan, maintained, "We must succeed in this post-conflict stability effort. Part of that strategy, hopefully, will be an attempt to internationalize the security and nation-building efforts."[25] When Biden inquired about NATO's role, the administration pointed out that Spanish Guardia Civil and Italian Carabinieri had made commitments. U.S. officials suggested that more countries would come in when the security situation improved. Three pacing items would determine the number of U.S. troops: the level of violence; the capacity of Iraqi security personnel; and the involvement of multinational forces. Wolfowitz said that already troops from nineteen countries were on the ground, and that talks were under way with a dozen more. He also pointed out that two dozen countries had made contributions or had already spent funds on reconstruction.

That the United States had failed to secure international backing for waging the war made it even more difficult to arrange international cooperation in winning the peace. Wolfowitz recognized that "coalition efforts in Iraq must undergo further internationalization to be successful and affordable."[26] However, the Bush administration treated Iraq as though it were a prize to keep. Other than ceremonial roles, it refused to give other countries real decisionmaking authority in Iraq.

International skepticism also increased when no weapons of mass destruction (WMD) were found. Backing off his earlier assertion, "We know where they are,"[27] Rumsfeld revealed: "The coalition did not act in Iraq because we had discovered dramatic new evidence of Iraq's pursuit of weapons of mass murder. We acted because we saw the existing evidence in a new light, through the prism of the experience on September 11."[28]

E VEN when it became apparent that it lacked area and language expertise, the Office of the Secretary of Defense still refused to cooperate with the State Department. Of the 1,147 Americans employed by the CPA in July 2003, only 34 were Foreign Service Officers.[29] Ryan Crocker, who had a deep knowledge of Iraq and the region, briefly served as one of Bremer's deputies. However, Bremer resisted Crocker's advice and marginalized him within the CPA. Crocker went to the National Defense University, where he waited for more than a year before becoming U.S. ambassador to Pakistan. When Senator Carl Levin complained that Powell did not even appear in the CPA's organizational chart, Wolfowitz replied, "The Secretary of State has a great deal of input both through the NSC and at the working levels."[30] Bush dismissed charges that he had lost control of the Iraq policy amid staff infighting with the declaration, "The person who is in charge is me."[31] Whereas Powell recognized the need for UN nation-building expertise after the war, the Pentagon did not appreciate the need for a stronger international civilian component in postwar administration. The United Nations was no panacea for Iraq's problems. However, its imprimatur would have lent legitimacy to U.S. efforts. The Security Council had never defined a clear mandate for the United Nations to operate independently from the occupying powers. To many Iraqis, the UN was just a lackey of the United States.

To demonstrate its independence from the CPA, Sergio Vieira de Mello, the special representative of the UN's secretary general, insisted that U.S. forces take a low profile while protecting the UN headquarters in Baghdad. On August 19, 2002, a cement truck packed with explosives lumbered past the guard post, stopped under Sergio's corner office, and detonated, killing Sergio and twenty-one others. A few weeks before the attack, Wolfowitz had acknowledged that "Sergio de Mello has played an important role." However, Bremer refused to share responsibilities so that he could "preserve his authority to move the process forward as rapidly as possible, so that we can transfer authority not to some international agency, but to the Iraqi people themselves."[32]

In addition to involving the United Nations in Iraq's transition, other State Department suggestions were also discarded. The Future of Iraq Project had emphasized the importance of cooperation between Iraqi exiles and Iraqis from within Iraq. A State Department official remarked, "When we got to Baghdad the biggest surprise was that divisions between exiles and other Iraqis were much deeper than between Iraq's ethnic or religious groups."[33]

The CPA was discredited by its close association with Ahmad Chalabi. After entering Baghdad, Chalabi called a press conference to announce his arrival. Few reporters showed up. Iraqi bystanders were mostly curious about Chalabi and his entourage of staff and Free Iraqi Forces. As a senior U.S. official noted, "He was jeered more than cheered. Iraqis were shouting him down. It was embarrassing. We had to help bail him out."[34] Surveys of Iraqi public opinion at the time showed that Chalabi enjoyed even less public approval than Saddam. Chalabi's popular standing diminished even further when his militia set up roadblocks and extorted passenger tolls. One of Chalabi's aides declared himself mayor of Baghdad; Iraq National Congress (INC) loyalists sent out the word that Iraqis should report to the INC if they wanted to find jobs.

Despite Chalabi's assurances that the Shi'a would greet U.S. troops "with flowers," Ryan Crocker and other State Department officials knew that unleashing Shi'a passions would have unpredictable consequences. When Saddam's regime crumbled, Shi'a clerics stepped in to fill the void. Wary of exiles who presumed power in the new Iraq, they took over the management of basic services and established their authority over the Shi'a population. Using Ayatollah Khomeini's vitriolic language to describe the United States, Ayatollah al-Haeri, the radical cleric who was Moqtada al-Sadr's spiritual mentor and "source of emulation," issued a fatwa from Qum on April 8, 2003. He instructed Iraq's Shi'a clerics to "raise people's awareness of the Great Satan's plans and of the means to abort them." He also called on his Shi'a brethren to "seize as many positions as possible to impose a fait accompli for any coming government."[35]

Large amounts of cash were carried across the border from Iran and delivered to the Supreme Council for Islamic Revolution in Iraq (SCIRI). Though U.S. forces ordered SCIRI's Badr Brigade to disband soon after Saddam's fall on April 9, its militias soon appeared back on the streets; they insisted that they would take security into their own hands if the United States failed to be more assertive.

Some elements in Iran also supported Moqtada al-Sadr. U.S. soldiers seized coffers of Iranian currency during a raid on Sadr's offices. Suspicions were fueled that the Iranian Revolutionary Guard had joined Sadr's Mahdi Army when the loudspeaker at Kufa's main mosque appealed for blood donations in both Arabic and Farsi after a skirmish between U.S. forces and Sadr's militia.

AFTER the diplomatic debacle over the transit of U.S. troops, Turkey also tried to influence events in Iraq. In April 2003, a Turkish Red Crescent convoy was stopped at a checkpoint. Weapons and explosives were discovered in bags thought to contain humanitarian supplies. The shipment also contained banners and the flags of the Iraqi Turkmen Front (ITF). The "humanitarian workers" were actually Turkish Special Forces infiltrating northern Iraq to assist ITF militias. The United States deported eleven Turkish Special Forces to Turkey.

In another incident on July 4, U.S. troops detained thirty-two Turkish Special Forces on the grounds that they were conspiring to assassinate elected Kurdish officials in northern Iraq. Press reports of their handcuffed and hooded troops riled the Turkish public, already upset about the war and Turkey's subsequent exclusion from postwar arrangements. Hilmi Ozkok, the chief of the Turkish General Staff, maintained that the arrest was the "biggest crisis" ever between the two NATO allies. Hursit Tolon, a top general, called the incident "disgusting" and cancelled a trip to the United States.[36] Protesters burned flags outside the U.S. Embassy in Ankara; a bomb also exploded near the U.S. consulate in Istanbul.

Senator Biden warned, "I predict to you that Kirkuk is going to make Mitrovica look like a picnic."[37] I agreed fully with Biden's assessment. On March 24, 2003, I wrote to Zalmay Khalilzad: "A priority for Kirkuk is managing the spontaneous return of Internally Displaced Persons, including property adjudication. Without dialogue for resolving competing claims, Kirkuk could become the flash point for further conflict, which could exacerbate regional tensions and increase chances of Iraq's fragmentation."[38] Building on the Kurdish-Turkmen task force of the Democratic Principles Working Group, I proposed a consultative process with Kirkuk's ethnic, religious, and tribal leaders. The meeting would result in a coordinating committee serving as the nucleus for local government in Kirkuk.

I sent Khalilzad a follow-up memo proposing the establishment of a Kirkuk Property Claims and Compensation Commission. I argued that the early, peaceful, and orderly return of displaced persons would diminish prospects for conflict between the Kurds and Turkmen, as well as between the Kurdistan Democratic Party and the Patriotic Union of Kurdistan. It would also obviate widespread revenge-taking against Arabs who resettled in Kirkuk. The process would strengthen partnership between local actors while informing efforts in other parts of Iraq.

Though many Kurds had moved to Kirkuk after the first oil gusher in 1927, the 1947 census found that Kurds comprised only 25 percent of Kirkuk City and 53 percent of the province. In 1959, half of Kirkuk's population was Turkmen, the rest being Kurds, Arabs, Assyrians, and Armenians.[39] The 1974 Revolutionary Command Council decree renamed Kirkuk province as Ta'amim province and assigned Chamchamal, Kifri, and Kalar to Suleimania province and Tuz Hormatu to Salahuddin province. Kurds who fled during the 1980s and during the Anfal campaign are among the 800,000 Kurds, Turkmen, and Assyrians forcibly displaced during the government's Arabization campaign.[40] Compounding the tensions, Kirkuk's oil fields, with an estimated 10 billion barrels (1998), are one of the world's richest reserves. Kurdish political leaders insist upon Kirkuk as the capital of Iraqi Kurdistan. According to Barham Salih, "Kirkuk is a benchmark for how most Kurds would define their legitimacy in Iraq. We have a claim to Kirkuk rooted in history, geography and demographics."[41]

According to my plan, the Property Claims and Compensation Commission would work to ensure that all refugees and displaced persons had the right to enjoy full respect for human rights and fundamental freedoms; to return in safety, without risk of harassment, intimidation, persecution, or discrimination on account of their ethnic origin; to have restored to them property of which they were deprived; and to be compensated for property that cannot be restored. To these ends, the commission would consider claims for property that had been involuntarily transferred or for which the claimant did not currently have possession. It would develop a registration process for persons making claims or seeking compensation. It would determine the lawful property owner from available property records, and develop a system for evaluating claims where deeds and documentation had been deliberately destroyed. In addition, the commission would offer legal-aid services to persons pursuing claims or compensation and adjudicate claims for the return of the property or for compensation in lieu of return. I also had discussions with Norwegian officials about capitalizing "The Kirkuk Stabilization Fund," which would seek to create conditions for return by supporting community-building such as housing, health care, and job creation.

The State Department asked me to discuss the initiative with White House and Pentagon officials. I met Samantha Ravich at Cosi's coffee shop across from the Old Executive Office Building. She supported it and promised to speak with Pentagon officials. I tracked her effort by reaching out to an old friend in the Office of the Secretary of Defense responsible for Eurasia and the Caucasus.

The *New York Times* reported that "American officials have said a multiethnic commission will be formed to sort out the dizzying maze of property disputes."[42] On April 20, I was scheduled to board a military transport in Romania and then fly to northern Iraq. But when Marc Grossman sought to finalize arrangements, Douglas Feith shot down the initiative. My trip was canceled; I subsequently refused to work in Iraq under the auspices of the Defense Department.

Rumsfeld finally sent an assessment team to Kirkuk more than one month later. It was led by his old friend, William Eagleton, a former U.S. ambassador to Iraq. The group included members from Bosnia, Poland, and the Czech Republic who were supposed to be knowledgeable about refugee issues. After its report was submitted to the OSD, the Pentagon did nothing to establish a property claims and compensation system for almost a year.

M EANWHILE, conditions in Iraq were going from bad to worse. Bremer's seven-step plan never got off the ground. Because he was unable to establish security, plans for reconstruction and democratization stalled. The lack of progress worsened the disaffection of Iraqis. They, in turn, fueled the insurgency and contributed to heightened violence. Zarqawi's group emerged as the chief organizer of kidnappings, beheadings, and suicide bombings.

On August 7, a car bomb tore apart the Jordanian embassy, killing eleven people and wounding fifty. The UN headquarters was attacked on August 19. Ten days later, an explosion in Najaf killed scores, including SCIRI's Bakr al-Hakim. Later in the month, nineteen Italian Carabinieri were killed in a bombing. In the fall, violence continued to spread across the country. On October 14, a powerful car bomb blew up outside the Turkish Mission in Baghdad. Two weeks later, on the first day of the Islamic holy month of Ramadan, another car bomb exploded, killing forty people outside the International Committee of the Red Cross. In addition to the soft targets of the international community, insurgents were successfully killing coalition forces in ambushes and using remote detonation devices. With attacks on coalition forces averaging about thirty a day, postwar U.S. combat deaths in Iraq reached 117 on October 29, more than the number of troops who had died before the war officially ended.[43]

Bush was under fire at home. For the first time since 9/11, his popularity rating fell below 50 percent. Many Americans worried that U.S. policy in Iraq was rudderless and that Bush had lost control of his advisers, most particularly Rumsfeld. Senator Dick Lugar insisted that "the president has to be the president" and take control of his bickering cabinet. Bush should "take charge, settle this dispute," Senator Joe Biden admonished. "Let your secretary of defense know, 'This is my policy. Any one of you that divert from the policy is off the team.'" Resisting attempts to diminish the Pentagon's control in Iraq, Rumsfeld reacted angrily when he learned that the White House had established the "Iraq Stabilization Group" under the direction of Rice in October 2003.[44] The Stabilization Group was created to do what the National Security Adviser should have been doing all along: improve interagency coordination and restore civilian control over postwar reconstruction and transition efforts.

The American public was most concerned about the absence of an exit strategy. Bush insisted, "We've had a strategy from the beginning, Jerry Bremer is running the strategy and we are making very good progress about the establishment of a free Iraq. The definition of when we get out is 'when there is a free and peaceful Iraq based upon a constitution and elections,' and obviously we'd like that to happen as quickly as possible. But we are mindful of rushing the process, which would create the conditions for failure."[45]

On July 23, 2003, Bremer appointed the twenty-five-member Iraqi Governing Council. Establishing the council was the first step in the halting process of handing power back to Iraqis and of restoring Iraqi sovereignty.

— —

CHAPTER 16

SELF-RULE

IRAQ'S POLITICAL TRANSITION WAS MARRED BY CONFU-
sion and repeated course corrections. Delays and flip-flopping created
the impression that the Bush administration did not have a definite plan
for restoring sovereignty in Iraq. As support waned domestically, Iraqis
also lost confidence in the U.S. occupation. Essential services were spo-
radic, and security continued to worsen. Without a credible political
process to restore self-rule, Iraqis became embittered and turned against
Ambassador Bremer and the Coalition Provisional Authority (CPA).

The Pentagon earned high marks for the military campaign that defeated Saddam Hussein's forces. But when it came to civilian administration, Bremer was flying without instruments. Ahmad Chalabi's loyalists
blamed the State Department. They maintained that Iraq's problems
could have been avoided if only the United States had appointed a
government-in-exile and given them responsibility to run the country

I was not alone in emphasizing the importance of talking to Iraqis. Marc
Grossman, Ryan Crocker, and other State Department officials fully appreciated the need to establish a legitimate and broadly representative
transitional structure. We agreed that suspending consultations would
deprive Iraqis of their democratic rights, fuel simmering resentments, and
radicalize the country's Shi'a Muslim majority. I warned that failure to
involve Iraqis would lead to what the Bush administration feared most:
the emergence of an anti-American Islamic regime in Iraq.

State Department officials made these arguments at meetings of the
principals committee and their deputies. However, their Defense Department counterparts opposed almost all their advice. Proponents of
good government believe that the interagency process is a forum for

making your case and then, regardless of the outcome, U.S. officials should come together to support the president's decision. In principle, this is the way Washington should work. However, Colin Powell was unwilling to adopt the Pentagon's bureaucratic practices, and became increasingly marginalized.

At the Nasariyah meeting in April 2003, Jay Garner had announced plans for an enlarged national conference. When Bremer took over, he postponed the conference for a month and then canceled it. Bremer also reversed Garner's pledge to set up an interim Iraqi administration. Instead, he announced an advisory committee that would have only limited powers. Bremer's decision to suspend the handover of sovereignty riled Iraqis. Participants in the Democratic Principles Working Group felt betrayed; Ghassan Atiyyah, an at-large member of the group's coordinating committee, asked, "So this is liberation?"[1]

The CPA focused its efforts on establishing local government. Regarding local elections, Bremer advised caution: "I'm not opposed, but I want to do it in a way that takes care of our concerns. Elections that are held too early can be destructive. It's got to be done very carefully. In a situation like this, if you start holding elections, the people who are rejectionists tend to win."[2]

City council members were selected, not elected. Instead of "one person, one vote," the CPA tried to control the outcome by relying on handpicked local leaders to participate in neighborhood councils. In turn, the neighborhood councils selected district councils, which selected county councils, which selected a provincial council, which finally selected a governor. Many Iraqis objected to the system of indirect elections. Every decision had to be approved by U.S. military commanders, a situation that exacerbated the Iraqis' resentment. Making matters worse, former Ba'athists were sometimes appointed to important positions by accident. For example, a former colonel in the Republican Guard was designated head of the Fallujah Brigade, until it was discovered that he stood accused of committing war crimes against Marsh Arabs in 1991.

In instances when Iraqis tried to organize their own elections, the U.S. intervened. The Fourth Infantry Division's Major General Ray Odierno ordered a halt to local elections in favor of military-appointed city councils. As Sergeant Jeff Butler of the U.S. Army's 418th Civil Affairs Battalion in Samarra observed, "We would like to see some kind of democratic system, but for now, Iraqis need to be satisfied with 'baby steps.'"³ Denying Iraqis a direct role in selecting municipal officials angered aspiring leaders and ordinary citizens alike. Micromanaging self-rule arrangements made many Iraqis believe that the United States was insincere about promises of greater freedom and democracy.

Protests sometimes turned violent. After the CPA announced the formation of a Baghdad city council, Moqtada al-Sadr, the radical cleric who commanded the Mahdi Army, organized a rally of 10,000 Shi'a in Sadr City. They blocked the CPA-appointed municipal council from entering city hall and announced their own rival council. Despite protests in Sadr City, the CPA heralded its installation of grassroots democracy in towns and cities across the country. Some military commanders built confidence by dispensing small grants to neighborhood councils for sewerage and electricity projects. In flashpoints such as Kirkuk, Colonel Mayville of the 173rd Airborne Brigade helped keep things calm through extraordinary cooperation with the city's multi-ethnic municipal council.

D ESPITE progress at the grassroots level, Iraqis resented Bremer's unwillingness to share power with an Iraqi-led transitional authority in Baghdad. When Iraqis strongly objected, Bremer made several concessions, including renaming his advisory council the Iraqi Governing Council (IGC). Though the Governing Council fell far short of full sovereignty, it was a vast improvement over Bremer's original plan.

When it was announced on July 13, 2003, the Governing Council represented a breakthrough in Iraqi governance. Its ethnic, religious, and gender makeup was far more representative than that of any other body Iraqis had ever known. Its twenty-five members included thirteen Shi'a, four Arab Sunnis, six Kurds, one Turkmen, and one Assyrian Christian. Three of its members were women. For the first time in Iraqi history, the country's Shi'a majority had a leading voice in politics; Mohammed Bahr al-Ulum, an eighty-year-old moderate Shi'a cleric, was the most senior member. Other prominent members included Ahmad Chalabi; Ayad Allawi, head of the Iraqi National Accord; Abdul Aziz al-Hakim, the political leader of the Supreme Council for Islamic Revolution in Iraq (SCIRI) and brother of the highly revered Mohammed Bakr al-Hakim; Ibrahim Jafari, a medical doctor and spokesman of the Islamic Da'wa; and Mowaffak al-Rubaie, Da'wa's London representative and later Iraq's national security adviser. The most prominent Arab

Sunni representatives were Adnan Pachachi, who had served as foreign minister in the 1960s, and Ghazi al-Yawar, a leader of the powerful Shamar tribe from Mosul. Massoud Barzani and Jalal Talabani were also members.

Adopted on August 14, UN Security Council Resolution 1500 described the Governing Council as "broadly representative" and praised its formation as "an important step towards the formation by the people of Iraq of an internationally recognized, representative government."[4] Sergio Vieira de Mello described the council's establishment as a "defining moment" that moved Iraq "back where it rightfully belongs: at peace with itself and as a full participant in the community of nations."[5] Added Douglas Feith, "This month will be a political turning point for Iraq. We will see the beginnings of the process of creating Iraqi self-government after more than three decades of horrendous tyranny."[6]

Despite high praise from the international community, Bremer gave the Governing Council only limited powers. The council could name and dismiss interim ministers, propose a budget, appoint charges d'affaires to foreign capitals, and organize the drafting of Iraq's new constitution. However, foreign nationals appointed by the CPA as "shadow" ministers really ran the show. The Governing Council did not have authority over important issues such as the basing of U.S. troops, Iraq's oil sector, or foreign affairs. Sharif Ali refused to become a member when Bremer stipulated that the council was subject to the authority of the CPA. According to Ali, "This Council does not satisfy the minimal criteria of sovereignty and independence."[7]

The Governing Council had little standing with Iraqis, who saw it as an extension of the U.S. government and a rubber stamp for the CPA. Several council members had reputations as inefficient and corrupt self-promoters. Some Iraqis saw them as traitors and collaborators who were paid off by the United States. When Governing Council members could not agree on its leadership, Bremer appointed nine presidents rotating monthly in alphabetical order. With its headquarters in the heavily fortified Green Zone, the Governing Council was distant and incomprehensible to most Iraqis.

Illegitimacy was compounded by the lack of transparency. The Council failed to carry out the CPA's strategic public-diplomacy plan explaining its mandate and the involvement of Iraqis in its establishment. Credibility issues were exacerbated at the council's inaugural press conference.

Iraqis issued statements that were confused and contradictory; Ahmad Chalabi raised eyebrows by heaping praise on the Americans and highlighting his own role in liberating Iraq.

Bremer's decision to disband the armed forces and purge the Ba'ath Party had already convinced Iraq's Arab Sunnis that the CPA wanted to marginalize them. Concerns were heightened by the insufficient representation of Sunni Arabs on the Council, including the exclusion of former Ba'ath Party members, and the limited representation of tribal leaders, always a potent force in Iraqi society.

Prominent Shi'a clerics also rejected the Governing Council. Grand Ayatollah Ali al-Sistani maintained that only elections could determine Iraq's political leadership. During a Friday sermon at the Imam Ali mosque, Sistani called the council an illegal and "unelected body."[8] Foreign Minister Jack Straw of Britain tried to look on the bright side when thousands of Shi'a protesters protested on the streets of Najaf: "Iraqis are speaking out and demonstrating with a vigour not seen for decades," he said. "At the launch of the Governing Council last Sunday we saw many of the features of democracy. There was criticism, strong disagreement and compromise—all now possible in the new Iraq."[9]

To Iraqis, the council's most objectionable feature was its domination by exiles. During his visit to the Council on Foreign Relations with Aquila al-Hashimi, another council member, Adnan Pachachi, reacted sharply when I asked whether the preponderance of exiles undermined the body's credibility. Many Iraqis resented Pachachi and other exiles. Masooud Barzani and Jalal Talabani were among the few council members enjoying a bona fide constituency in Iraq. In addition, Ghazi al-Yawar was chosen by the paramount sheikh of the Shamar tribe, Iraq's largest with more than 2 million members.

When Bush administration officials promised democracy, Iraqis took them at their word. But instead of elections empowering Iraqis with responsibility for running their country, the Pentagon insisted on a new Iraqi constitution before Iraqis could go to the polls. As Bremer explained it:

Elections are the obvious solution to restoring sovereignty to the Iraqi people. But at the present, elections are simply not possible. There are no election rolls, no election law, no political party law, and no electoral districts. Electing a government without a permanent constitution defining and limiting government powers invites confusion and eventual abuse. . . . Writing a constitution, as we Americans know, is a solemn and important undertaking. It can not be done in days or weeks.[10]

After weeks of wrangling and delays, the Governing Council finally named twenty-five ministers on September 2, 2003. At the London Opposition Conference, I had told Hoshyar Zebari that he would become Iraq's next foreign minister; I was delighted when he was actually awarded the post. Representing Iraq at the Arab League summit was Zebari's first official duty, and it was indeed amazing to see a Kurd seated behind the "Iraq" placard in a hall full of Arabs.

Noting that every ministry was now run by an Iraqi appointed by other Iraqis, Bremer touted the formation of a technocratic government. He considered it an important step in the ongoing process of shifting authority to Iraqis. He also extolled progress when the Governing Council designated a preparatory committee to devise a process for preparing Iraq's permanent constitution.

Though Bremer heralded its achievement, the council's honeymoon was over before it had begun. Many Iraqis blamed it for the lack of security, the constant power outages, water shortages, as well as other problems plaguing the country. Bremer pressured members to perform, but, as criticisms mounted, the council became increasingly dysfunctional. Members bickered constantly. Most did not even show up for meetings. Relations between Bremer and the Governing Council went from bad to worse.

Although Bremer lauded the council in public, he lambasted its members in private. As a senior U.S. official complained, "There's not one of them who is a true democrat, who represents much more than his own group's narrow interests, who has any support except from his own people. They squabble with each other about everything—when they bother to show up at all—and they've made zero progress on the most important job, which is figuring out how to write a constitution and hold elections."[11]

It was easy for the CPA to blame the Governing Council for Iraq's problems—and for its own failings. With a few exceptions, I found that the council members were true patriots who had sacrificed to build a better Iraq. Some paid the ultimate price. Within weeks of her visit to my office in New York, Aquila al-Hashimi was assassinated in September

2003. Ezzedine Salim, while acting as president of the Governing Council, was killed in May 2004. Their murders were part of a burgeoning campaign by insurgents targeting police and other public officials cooperating with the coalition.

M IRRORING divisions in the Democratic Principles Working Group, the constitution preparatory committee also divided along ethnic and ideological lines. The large parties were unwilling to compromise; small groups refused to accept the will of the majority. Arab Shi'a favored an elected constitutional convention because the outcome would reflect their numerical advantage. However, Arab Sunnis and Kurds opposed a system granting power to the Shi'a. Fearing that a Shi'a-dominated body would impose a constitution that ignored federalism, Kurds rejected plans to elect the constitutional commission and demanded that one be appointed instead.

When the constitutional preparatory committee submitted its final report on September 30, 2003, it suggested three approaches to selecting Iraqi drafters of the constitution: direct appointment, partial elections, and general elections. The committee could not agree on any one of these options, so it punted responsibilities to the Governing Council. The episode was a microcosm of the profound differences that would keep Iraqis from achieving consensus on a vision for their country.

On September 30, Powell tried to speed up the process of restoring sovereignty, asserting that it would take only six months to adopt a permanent constitution. UN Security Council Resolution 1511 was adopted on October 16, 2003. Drafted by British and U.S. diplomats, it identified the coalition as Iraq's "occupying power," with the sole responsibility for security. Whereas it invited member states to assist in Iraq's reconstruction, it did not authorize a specific role for the United Nations in Iraq's political transition. Rather, it called on the Governing Council to provide a timetable and a program for the drafting of a new constitution and for holding elections. The report was due by December 15, 2003.

I N the fall of 2003, concerns intensified about the ability of the U.S.-led coalition to provide basic security. A series of deadly bombings rocked Baghdad when the Muslim holy month of Ramadan began in late October. A rocket attack barely missed Paul Wolfowitz's quarters at the al-Rashid Hotel on October 26. Conditions on the ground continued to deteriorate without a viable plan for the political transition and the inability to win Iraqi "hearts and minds" through demonstrable progress with reconstruction. The mission was far from accomplished. The United States was still at war in Iraq.

U.S. officials sought to minimize the problem by stating that the growing number of attacks was a measure of progress. The CPA tried to address the security situation by accelerating the creation of a new Iraqi army and police force. When the Bush administration called on other countries to send peacekeeping troops, many refused. They said there was no peace to keep.

Senator Joe Biden called on the Bush administration to involve NATO. But members of the North Atlantic Council, the alliance's political decisionmaking body, were still smarting from being taken for granted or treated as irrelevant in discussions at the United Nations. Botched diplomacy discouraged even such stalwart allies as Turkey.

Though U.S.-Turkish relations had hit a low point after Turkey rejected the passage of U.S. troops into northern Iraq in March 2003, both sides took a deep breath and decided to repair relations. In October, Turkey agreed to a request from the Pentagon that it deploy 10,000 peacekeeping troops in al-Anbar province, northwest of Baghdad. There was only one problem: Iraqis rejected the deployment of Turkish troops on their soil.

As the successor state to the Ottoman Empire, which ruled Iraq until 1917, Turkey was viewed with suspicion by Arabs and Kurds alike. In 1517, Arabs across the Middle East were outraged when the Muslim Caliphate was moved from Cairo to Constantinople and Sultan Selim I proclaimed himself the Prophet's sole representative and leader of Sunni Islam. Iraqi Shi'a resent the Turks for marginalizing them during Ottoman rule. Kurds also distrust Turkey because of its efforts to undermine progress in Iraqi Kurdistan. An October bomb attack on the Turkish embassy in Baghdad underscored the negative view of Iraqis to Ankara's deployment. When the Governing Council issued a unanimous statement rejecting the presence of Turkish troops, Marc Grossman went back to Ankara and said thanks but no thanks.

Isolated from the international community and with popular support quickly eroding in Iraq—only 14.8 percent of Iraqis viewed coalition forces as liberators as opposed to 43 percent six months earlier—Ambassador Bremer and General John Abizaid were summoned to Washington.[12] The Pentagon announced that the trip had been on the calendar for some time and was part of regular consultations. However, Bremer's rushed departure forced him to cancel a meeting with Prime Minister Leszek Miller of Poland, whose troops make up the third-largest contingent in Iraq. Underscoring the situation's volatility, a suicide bomber attacked the Italian base in Nasariyah as Bremer arrived in Washington.

Though Prime Minister Silvio Berlusconi of Italy dismissed calls to withdraw Italian forces, worldwide protests made it seem as though the U.S.-led coalition was crumbling. Just a week before, donors had pledged $37.5 billion in aid and credits at the Madrid Conference. However, escalating violence raised doubts in the international community abou whether these funds could actually be spent. Concerns were also mounting on Capitol Hill. With a vote pending in the U.S. Congress to authorize $87 billion for military operations and reconstruction, many U.S. legislators were demanding that Bush abandon his insistence on staying the course and make a course correction instead.

E VEN as Bremer blamed the Governing Council, Pentagon officials relentlessly continued to promote Ahmad Chalabi as Iraq's leader. To preserve Chalabi's role, a senior official insisted that "there is no other venue [than the IGC] where we can try and address all the competing demands of the different groups."[13] Dick Cheney, Donald Rumsfeld, and Condoleezza Rice attended Bremer's final meeting in the White House, but Colin Powell was conspicuously absent.

Bremer also had a rare one-on-one session with Bush, after which Bush announced, "We want the Iraqis to be more involved in the governance of their country. And so, Ambassador Bremer, with my instructions, is going back to talk to the Governing Council to develop a strategy."[14] Bremer left Washington on November 13. The White House expected him to take a couple of weeks to consult with Iraqis and come up with a new transitional plan and timetable. To the complete amazement of everyone in Washington working on Iraq, Bremer scheduled a press conference the day after his return to Baghdad and announced the "November 15 Agreement." Sharply changing course, he committed the Bush administration to create an interim government before the constitution had been completed. As a measure of just how far the administration had come, just a month earlier it had scoffed at a French proposal to do just that.

The agreement stipulated that, by February 28, the Governing Council would draft a basic law describing the structure of a transitional administration and codifying a bill of rights. By the end of March, the council would finalize a formal security arrangement with the coalition. By the end of May, Iraqis would select a transitional national assembly through a system of regional caucuses; by the end of June, the transitional assembly would appoint a government. By March 15, 2005, the transitional government would hold elections for delegates to a constitutional convention and, by the end of that year, national elections would be held in accordance with provisions of the constitution. Revealing Bremer's disaffection with the council, the agreement stipulated that the transitional assembly would not be an expansion of the Governing Council; council members would have no formal role in selecting members of the assembly and the council would dissolve upon the establishment of the assembly.

The November 15 Agreement satisfied no one. Worst of all, it put the United States on a collision course with Grand Ayatollah Ali al-Sistani. U.S. officials had failed to grasp Sistani's importance, not only vis-à-vis the political transition but also in controlling Moqtada al-Sadr.

WHEN a false rumor circulated that the United States was preparing a constitution to present de facto to the Iraqi people, Sistani insisted that he would support a constitution only if it was written by Iraqis chosen through a general election. As his June 28 fatwa declared, "There is no guarantee that the council would create a constitution conforming to the greater interests of the Iraqi people and expressing the national identity, whose basis is Islam, and its noble social values."[15]

Ensconced behind barricades in the Green Zone, U.S. officials did not appreciate the importance of Sistani's edict right away. Though the Shi'a had largely accepted the U.S.-led occupation, just a word from Sistani could cause a Shi'a revolt and lead to a dramatic deterioration of the situation. As Iraq's most senior Shi'a cleric, Sistani had the ability to disrupt U.S. plans simply by summoning his religious community to action.

The Bush administration sought an orderly political transition, one that it could control. It wanted a constitution that would be a model for democratizing the Arab world. Sistani's call for democratic elections was a serious challenge to Bush's vision for Iraq. Elections could lead to a constitution based on Shari'a law and so threaten the secularism of Iraqi governance. In addition, the U.S. worried that Islamicized Shi'a leaders in Iraq might forge an anti-U.S. partnership with the mullahs in Iran. Sistani also questioned the legitimacy of a security agreement between an unelected Iraqi government and the United States. "Is the political structure of Iraq going to be in the hands of one man?" Bremer complained.[16]

From the beginning, Bremer failed to reach out to Sistani. Instead, he tried to marginalize him by encouraging other Shi'a clerics, such as the Grand Ayatollah of Baghdad and Hussein al-Sadr, to support the CPA's plans. After Bakr al-Hakim was murdered on August 29, Bremer sought a meeting with Sistani; but he was rebuffed and forced to communicate through intermediaries who, in turn, used their ties with Sistani to enhance their own importance in the political process.

When Bremer returned from his consultations in Washington, Sistani dismissed the U.S. plan as "fundamentally unacceptable."[17] He also objected to the agreement's provision requiring an interim constitution by February 28. "No one has the right to appoint the members of the constitutional assembly," Sistani insisted. "We see no alternative but to go back to the people for choosing their representatives."[18]

At Bremer's meeting in the White House, it was decided that early elections were a recipe for civil war. If elections were held before political parties had time to establish themselves, well-organized Ba'athists and Islamic parties with ties to Iran would dominate the outcome. Sistani's demands were impractical: Iraq lacked a population census and an electoral law; it would take months to lay the infrastructure for a nationwide ballot, including an elections commission. A provisional government would have to come first.

The Shi'a feared that the U.S. would use the violence across the country as an excuse to postpone elections indefinitely. Many Shi'a thought the CPA was stalling to keep them from taking power. SCIRI's Aziz al-Hakim criticized Bremer, saying that, instead of finding excuses, he should just get on with the work of planning elections. A Shi'a Governing Council member protested, "We waited four months, thanks to Bremer. We could have organized this [transition] by now had we started when Sistani issued his fatwa. But the Americans were in denial."[19] Sistani's rejection of the transition plans threw the Governing Council into crisis. As most council members were Shi'a, they were bound to abide by Sistani's opinion.

T HE November 15 Agreement envisioned that the transitional assembly would be selected using a complicated system of indirect voting. Most Iraqis thought that it was decidedly undemocratic for U.S. officials and Governing Council members arbitrarily to choose from each of Iraq's eighteen provinces the political, religious, tribal, and other influential local figures who would then elect the country's 250-person national assembly. The plan virtually ensured that the United States and their favorites on the Governing Council would be able to shape future political developments in the country, the result being a government controlled by the United States.

Explaining the antipathy of Shi'a to the plan, Muhammed Hussein al-Hakim, the son of a senior ayatollah in Najaf, recalled, "We remember that under the British, the national assemblies were based on nominations. We never had proper representation in those parliaments."[20] Though a U.S. official called the caucus system a "holy writ,"[21] the plan was doomed from the outset. Bremer had difficulties even explaining the plan to Iraqis. There is no word for "caucus" in Arabic.

Though the Governing Council originally endorsed the November 15 Agreement, council members started having misgivings almost immediately. "The next day," said Allawi, "people woke up and thought this was done in too hasty a manner."[22] Recognizing that without the Governing Council he would be out of a job, Chalabi promoted the idea of turning the Governing Council into a senate, the new transitional assembly to resemble the U.S. House of Representatives. He gave a warning: "We will make a security agreement with the United States, but this will not be binding on the new guys. When the Governing Council is gone, there will be voices that want to cancel it." He even scolded Bremer: "The Governing Council is the force that opposed Saddam Hussein and, allied with the United States, overthrew him. Now the United States wants to overthrow us?"[23]

Sistani said he would abandon his demand for immediate elections only if the United Nations determined that the vote could not be conducted under current conditions. Drawing on ideas from the Democratic Principles Working Group, I went to the UN for a private meeting with the Department of Political Affairs to discuss ways of addressing the immediate need for a provisional government.

I suggested that a national assembly could be formed by joining Governing Council members with representatives from each of the eighteen governorates. Alternatively, a caretaker provisional government could be composed mainly of technocrats and professionals, including many of the current ministers. Another way would be to convene a national conference of delegates from across Iraqi society to establish an interim government. Alternatively, a smaller leadership roundtable of the main political, religious, and other groups could be convened to develop a consensus on an interim caretaker authority.

THE Governing Council had become an albatross. On December 1, Oxford Research released a nationwide survey that found nearly three-fourths of Iraqis had little or no confidence in a government led by the Governing Council.[24] Council members "have a fear of losing a grip on things," observed Ghazi al-Yawar. "They think they are entitled to a role because they believe they overthrew Saddam Hussein. It was the United States that overthrew Saddam while we were eating TV dinners."[25]

The CPA scrambled to carry out the November 15 Agreement. Bremer was concerned that plans to hand over sovereignty were falling behind schedule and asked Rumsfeld for another 1,000 staff. Adding election experts to help organize 108 caucuses nationwide and beefing up the CPA's public diplomacy and communications efforts would effectively double the CPA's size. But Rumsfeld resisted. He said that Bremer should be downsizing, not expanding. The CPA's staffing problems were compounded by Douglas Feith, who still blocked the assignment of those who did not meet the ideological litmus test.

Concerns were exacerbated when a top-secret CIA report was leaked; it warned that Iraqi insurgents were stepping up their attacks on coalition forces, as well as Iraqis collaborating with the occupation. It also warned that Iraq was on the verge of civil war. Saddam's capture in mid-December was the only good news coming from Iraq. Rumsfeld hoped the news would demoralize guerillas and former regime elements but, despite a brief lull, ambushes and suicide bombings continued unabated.

AFTER scorning the United Nations, Bush turned to the world body to help overcome the impasse with Sistani. Colin Powell noted: "One area where I think the UN can be helpful is in helping to bring all the parties together to support the 15 November plan."[26] The November 15 Agreement had anticipated no role for the United Nations.

Every now and then, I would also have a private meeting with UN Secretary General Kofi Annan to discuss the issues of the day. In my private capacity, I arranged a visit with Annan to discuss concerns about Iraq.[27]

Annan had been out with the flu. Though he usually sparkles with optimism, I found him tired, downbeat, and demoralized. The August 19 bombing of the UN headquarters in Baghdad had a devastating effect; Sergio Vieira de Mello, killed in that blast, was one of the UN's own. In addition, the Security Council's handling of the Iraq situation had been deeply humiliating for the entire UN system. More than Iraq, Annan was concerned that multilateralism might be mortally wounded unless the United Nations could play a role in Iraq's reconstruction.

Entreaties by the Bush administration put Annan in a profoundly uncomfortable position. He was determined not to send UN personnel into harm's way. However, he felt compelled to help overcome the impasse with Sistani. Failure to do so could spell Iraq's demise. Though Annan was wary of having the Iraq mess dumped on the UN, he did not want the United States to fail. A weakened America would weaken the United Nations. Annan was torn between his UN Charter responsibilities and the need to make sure that the United Nations did not become a rubber stamp for the Bush administration.

On January 19, 2004, Bremer and a delegation from the Governing Council had been to see Annan to request that the United Nations send representatives to help end the deadlock over how to transfer power to Iraqis. The Secretary General dispatched Lakhdar Brahimi, Algeria's former foreign minister and the UN's troubleshooter, to explore an acceptable plan for establishing an interim government and holding elections.

As an Arab nationalist, Brahimi was well suited to engage Iraq's Sunnis in the political process. However, his exceptional diplomatic skills would be challenged in Iraq. Although engaging Arab Sunnis had short-term benefits given the violence in the Sunni triangle, Brahimi would have to be very careful not to lose his objectivity. Even the suggestion of bias ran the risk of alienating Iraqi Kurds and radicalizing Iraq's Arab Shi'a.

After two hours of talks on February 12, Brahimi emerged from Sistani's home in an alley near the Imam Ali mosque in Najaf and announced, "Al-Sistani is insistent on holding the elections and we are with him on this 100 percent because elections are the best means to enable any people to set up a state that serves their interests."[28] He added, "We are in agreement with the Sayyid [al-Sistani] that these elections should be prepared well and should take place in the best possible conditions."[29] According to UN spokesman Ahmad Fawzi, "Brahimi explained in great detail to Sistani and his aides the process that is required to organize elections. You can't really start organizing them until you have a political consensus and a legal framework—not to mention security."[30]

On February 21, Annan briefed the Security Council on Brahimi's mission. Led by Carina Perelli, the UN Office of Electoral Assistance had toured the provinces and determined that elections could be organized by the end of the year if planning started immediately. Annan reported, "The United Nations would be willing to offer to help build consensus among Iraqis on the specific powers, structure, and composition of such a provisional governance body and the process through which it would be established."[31] Postponing the June 30 handover of sovereignty would be unwise, he continued. Iraqis were adamant about sticking to the deadline.

Sistani begrudgingly accepted the UN assessment. While dropping his demand for elections to be held before the United States handed over sovereignty on June 30, Sistani insisted on nationwide elections before the end of the year. He maintained, "The period in which an unelected government should take control of this country must be short and for a few months only."[32]

CHAPTER 17

––––

THE INTERIM
CONSTITUTION

AFTER RUNNING THE SISTANI GAUNTLET ON ELECTIONS,
U.S. officials took aim at the next milestone in Iraq's democratic
development. The November 15 Agreement required the Iraqi Governing Council to adopt an interim constitution by February 28, 2004.
However, progress was stalled. The ten-member drafting committee had
virtually suspended its work pending the UN's decision to send an assessment team and present its recommendation on elections.

Behind the scenes, Faisal al-Istrabadi, the legal adviser to Adnan
Pachachi, and Salem Chalabi, Ahmad's nephew, continued work on what
was called the "Pachachi draft." The document borrowed heavily from
Iraq's 1925 constitution as well as from the U.S. Constitution when it
came to the separation of powers. Both Salem and Faisal had been members of the Democratic Principles Working Group.

Like the Working Group, the Iraqi Governing Council did not agree
on various critical issues, such as the role of religion, women's rights,
ownership of natural resources, demilitarizing militia groups, and other
security matters, including measures to reform Iraq's security sector.
State Department lawyers tried to hammer out the differences. At a
meeting of the Governing Council, Ambassador Bremer went through
the tome paragraph by paragraph. A large oval table covered with a
patchy green felt cloth filled the conference room in the old Ministry of
Military Industrialization. The room was so tightly packed that there was
barely room for advisers and members of multiple entourages.

In the final stages of negotiation, a delegation of women visited the Governing Council to make their case for expanded women's rights, especially concerning family matters. Two months earlier, the Governing Council had adopted a law restricting women's freedoms. When the women's delegation visited on the morning of February 28, they wanted to make sure that the interim constitution fully guaranteed women's rights. Jalal Talabani spoke eloquently in support of their appeal. The women rejoiced by making the traditional high-pitched rhythmic wailing noise to signal their approval.

Ahmad Chalabi was not present at the time. However, Salem called to tell him what was going on. After getting off the phone, Salem went to each Shi'a member of the Governing Council and whispered in his ear. Suddenly and without notice, eleven of the Arab Shi'a Governing Council members stood up and, in protest, walked out of the room. Their walk-out threw the whole process into disarray.

The meeting reconvened after lunch and went until 5:00 A.M. of March 1. After a brief break, it resumed a few hours later. Marathon negotiations lasted another twenty hours. Bremer took a small group upstairs for private discussions. The Governing Council had just moved its offices into a new building resplendent with marble arches, fancy columns, and Saudi-gaudy designs.

The most contentious issue concerned the role of religion. Islamists had been pushing for a text affirming that Iraqi laws would be consistent with Islamic teachings. In defense of the country's religious diversity, secular members wanted Islam to be a source of legislation only. Enshrining Islam and transforming Iraq into an Islamic state was a deal-breaker for Bremer, who promised to use his veto to block a charter that established Shari'a law as the basis of Iraqi legislation. "Our position is clear," Bremer maintained. "It can't be law until I sign it."[1]

Shi'a council members had to choose between rejecting the interim constitution, thereby stopping the process of transferring power, or accepting the text and correcting it later. They decided that the priority was to form a body to which sovereignty could be transferred. As a compromise, the Transitional Administrative Law (TAL) recognized Islam as "a source of legislation"—rather than "the" only source of legal inspiration. A clause was added ensuring that no law would be promulgated, violating Muslim tenets.

Bremer and Governing Council members re-entered the room. After a brief debate, the entire Iraqi Governing Council agreed on a text. Everyone hugged and kissed. Many Iraqis made heart-wrenching statements about unity and their commitment to the Republic of Iraq.

The public announcement was originally envisioned for February 28; however, it was postponed to give the Iraqis time to negotiate. The announcement was further delayed by the need to respect the mandatory three-day mourning period after 271 people were killed by a carbomb in Karbala while celebrating the Shi'a holy day of Ashura. By March 5, Shi'a members of the council had become increasingly anxious, fearing they thought they had conceded too much, they asked for two additional days to visit Najaf and consult with Sistani.

To accommodate their concerns, Bremer rescheduled the signing ceremony for March 7. But at the last minute, the Shi'a did not show up. Bremer was furious.

The next day, council members finally assembled in the Convention Center, a large building opposite the Rashid Hotel in the heavily fortified Green Zone, to sign their names to the TAL. As the interim constitution governing Iraq until an elected assembly could approve a permanent charter, the Law was a historic document and it set a standard in the Arab world. It included a bill of rights guaranteeing freedom of speech and equal rights for all Iraqis regardless of ethnicity, sect, or gender; guaranteed minority and linguistic rights, as well as due process and an independent judiciary; repudiated the Ba'athists and put Iraqi armed forces under civilian control. It also targeted 25 percent female participation in the federal assembly. Direct elections were envisioned by the end of January 2005.

IRAQI Kurds played an important role during protracted negotiations over the interim constitution. The United States grew accustomed to taking the Kurds for granted. Whenever concessions were required, U.S. officials asked the Kurds to give way or enlisted their support in exacting concessions from others.

On January 2, 2004, Bremer visited Iraqi Kurdistan. He presented a list of demands ordering the Kurds to disband the peshmerga, abandon claims of oil in Kirkuk, and accede to the authority of the new Iraqi state in all matters. The Kurdish leadership sent Bremer packing. When Bremer returned a few days later, accompanied by the National Security Council's Ambassador Robert D. Blackwill, he was in a much more conciliatory mood. Instead of making specific demands, Bremer asked the

Kurds to be flexible in general and to avoid zero-sum situations that would alienate other Iraqis.

It was in the mutual interest of the Coalition Provisional Authority (CPA) and Iraqi Kurds to work together. The Kurds had proved themselves a loyal ally of the United States. They fought alongside U.S. forces in the Fourth Army Infantry Division and the 101st and 173rd Airborne Brigades. They were committed to democracy and secularism. Massoud Barzani and Jalal Talabani played a helpful role in the Governing Council. The United States had no better friends in Iraq than the Kurds.

The Kurds needed the United States as well. They counted on the Bush administration to make good on its promise to turn Iraq into a federal democracy. But the Kurds' close association with the United States also made them a target. On February 1, suicide bombers attacked the headquarters of the Kurdistan Democratic Party and the Patriotic Union of Kurdistan (PUK) in Erbil, killing 101 people, including my old friend Sami Abdul-Rahman.

The Kurds would not accept fewer freedoms than they enjoyed before the Iraq war. They used their ties with the CPA to leverage concessions during negotiations over the Transitional Administrative Law. As a result, the interim constitution met almost every Kurdish demand, and most important, it enshrined federalism as Iraq's future form of governance.

The Law stated: "The design of the federal system in Iraq shall be established in such a way as to prevent the concentration of power in the federal government that allowed the continuation of decades of tyranny and oppression under the previous regime."[2] It also recognized Kurdish cultural identity, made Kurdish an official language of the Iraqi state, and required the use of Kurdish in "federal institutions and agencies of the Kurdistan region."[3] In addition, it stated that the Kurdistan Regional Government (KRG) "shall retain regional control over police forces and internal security, and it will have the right to impose taxes and fees within the Kurdistan region."[4] When the Transitional Administrative Law was announced, tens of thousands of celebratory Kurds took to the streets in cities across Iraqi Kurdistan.

After concluding the marathon negotiations, Barham Salih said that it was "an important night" and the negotiations reflected "an exciting moment in history." He added, "This is the very first time in the contemporary history of the Middle East that such a wide range of opinions are engaged in a serious discussion about the future of their country."[5]

Brimming with satisfaction, Massoud Barzani recalled the sacrifice of the Kurdish people at the signing ceremony in the Green Zone: "The [interim] constitution will make some of the sadness go away. This is the first time we feel as Kurds that we are equal with others in this country, that we are not second-class citizens."[6]

Barzani and Talabani welcomed the interim constitution as a framework for guiding Iraq's transition to democracy. But despite its positive points, Kurds still viewed it as a compromise. Kurdish leaders made clear that they were prepared to surrender present powers only in exchange for protections in the future, including the right to approve the permanent constitution. They were wary that majority rule by Iraq's Arab Shi'a would become another form of tyranny by subjugating Kurdish interests.

JUST hours after the Transitional Administrative Law was announced, Shi'a political and religious leaders galvanized the Shi'a masses in protest. Breaking from the quietist tradition separating religion and politics, Sistani strongly objected to provisions he considered undemocratic. He was most concerned about the Law's failure to enshrine the role of Islam in legislation, particularly concerning family matters. Bremer and Shi'a Governing Council members had recently disagreed over family law provisions. In January 2004, the council adopted a bill applying Islamic law instead of civil statutes in domestic cases such as divorce and inheritance. Many Iraqi professional women protested, and Bremer refused to sign the legislation.

Sistani also complained that the Transitional Administrative Law fostered disunity by providing preferences to the Kurds. He specifically balked at provisions giving Kurds an effective veto over the adoption of Iraq's permanent constitution. In particular, Shi'a leaders cited Article 61C, which indicated that the permanent constitution would be adopted unless two-thirds of voters in three governorates voted against it. Kurds have demographic dominance in at least three of Iraq's eighteen governorates, so the provision amounted to an effective Kurdish veto. Sistani protested that the Law "places obstacles in the path of reaching a permanent constitution for the country that maintains its unity and the rights of sons of all sects and ethnic backgrounds."[7]

In addition, Iraqis across religious and ethnic lines were united in their objection to the process by which the Law was prepared and adopted.

They charged the CPA with inadequate consultation and lack of transparency. Peter Galbraith, a former U.S. ambassador to Croatia, advising the Kurds, pointed out that the document was drafted behind closed doors by CPA staff and select Governing Council members. No public hearings were held. There was no opportunity for public debate or popular ratification.

Kurds were outraged when Shi'a members of the Governing Council tried to walk away from the agreement. According to Mahmoud Othman, a Kurdish Governing Council member, "We have all agreed to a democratic Iraq. We have agreed to ballot boxes deciding everything. We have agreed that the people should choose everything. They have never said they wanted an Islamic law, Islamic state."[8]

In addition to the Shi'a, Iraqi Turkmen strongly opposed perceived inequities in the interim constitution. Songul Chapuk, the Turkmen representative on the Governing Council, demanded greater rights and representation for Iraqi Turkmen. Seeking recognition as an equal community in Iraq, Turkmen leaders announced a hunger strike. Wrapped in chains and duct tape, dozens of Turkmen staged a protest in Baghdad.[9]

DESPITE opposition from various Iraqi groups, U.S. officials heralded the Transitional Administrative Law as a major milestone. In addition to its legal merits, the interim constitution represented the last good chance to promote Chalabi as Iraq's leader.

The Law established an executive authority made up of a president and two vice presidents. It also created a prime minister's post that enjoyed strong powers. The Pentagon envisioned a Shi'a, an Arab Sunni, and a Kurd for the presidency council; Chalabi would become prime minister. By giving Chalabi executive and budget authority, his backers imagined he would win favor with the Iraqi people and emerge as the country's elected leader when national elections were held.

Chalabi promised to deliver on matters of concern to the Bush administration. He would steward Iraq's transformation into a liberal democracy. With Chalabi at the helm, Iraq would become an engine for reform across the Arab world. Chalabi would sign a "status of forces agreement" allowing U.S. troops to stay in Iraq. U.S. military bases in Iraq would serve as a launch point for the war on terror. But, after announcing the June 30 handover date, U.S. influence in Iraq immediately started waning.

Consistent with Iraq's future sovereign status, Bush announced that U.S. troops would be reduced from 138,000 to 100,000 by April 2004. He instructed U.S. commanders to draw up detailed proposals for immediate steps to consolidate U.S. forces so that they would become less vulnerable, including medium-term measures reducing the total number of troops. The goal was to have fewer than 50,000 U.S. troops in Iraq by mid-2005.[10]

Iraqis gave a mixed response to the announcement. A Gallup poll found that many people were frustrated: "Patience is wearing thin. But we found they did not want to have U.S. troops withdraw precipitously. They have two fears. One is that we are going to stay too long, and one is that we are going to leave too soon."[11]

The announcement also received a lukewarm response on Capitol Hill, where there was a growing concern that the United States did not have enough troops to stabilize Iraq. Senator John McCain insisted on least another U.S. division. Bush tried to reassure worried legislators: "We could have less troops in Iraq; we could have the same number of troops in Iraq; we could have more troops in Iraq." He added that the number would be whatever was "necessary to secure Iraq."[12] As Donald Rumsfeld explained, "It's important to recognize that numbers do not necessarily equate with capability. We're bringing in forces that are appropriate to deal with the evolving threats in Iraq today, including more mobile infantry elements. So while the number of U.S. forces may be level or decline slightly, this much is certain: The overall capability of the security forces in Iraq will increase."[13] Senator Joe Biden cautioned against handing over responsibility for security to Iraqi forces before they were ready, and warned that the premature transfer of security responsibilities was "another form of cutting and running."[14]

Other lawmakers were also critical of the November 15 Agreement. Critics believed that the administration had one eye on the U.S. presidential elections in setting an arbitrary deadline for handing over power to Iraqis. They expressed concern that the administration was feigning political progress to justify the premature withdrawal of U.S. troops.

THE biggest factor in determining the level of U.S. troops was the speed with which Iraqi security forces could be trained and deployed. Plans called for the transfer of control to Iraqi security forces to evolve at different rates across the country.

The Pentagon envisioned a 40,000-strong constabulary called the Iraqi Civil Defense Corps to patrol the streets and gather intelligence. It also rushed to field an Iraqi police force. About $1 billion was allocated to train and equip 85,000 police officers. Jordan and other neighboring states offered to help with training. The Bush administration wanted to stand up more than 200,000 Iraqi police officers, civil defense forces, border guards, soldiers, and facility-protection guards by the end of 2004.

The train-and-equip program was dogged by problems from the beginning. The procurement of equipment, such as heavy weapons, flak jackets, and radios, was delayed by bureaucrats in the U.S. government. Signaling the growing rift between Pentagon civilians and the U.S. military's top brass, General Richard Myers suggested that responsibility for the delays lay with the CPA. Many military professionals blamed Rumsfeld for not providing enough troops to stabilize Iraq after toppling Saddam Hussein, for not adequately equipping troops, for failing to anticipate and deal with the insurgency, and for mishandling the postwar reconstruction program.

Slow progress in building up Iraq's indigenous security forces forced the Bush administration to cancel its plan to reduce U.S. troop levels. Though sixteen of the twenty-six NATO members had sent forces as part of the U.S.-led coalition, the United States had hoped other countries would also contribute troops; but the administration dropped that idea when it could not raise interest.

Concerns about troop strength worsened when troop-contributing countries started to reconsider their involvement. Spain's newly elected Prime Minister Jose Luis Rodriguez Zapatero, who was voted into office after the Madrid terrorist bombings in March 2004, said that Iraq is "turning into a fiasco" and threatened to pull out the Spanish contingent of 1,300 troops.[15] Claiming that he was "misled" about Iraq's weapons of mass destruction, Poland's President Aleksander Kwasniewski suggested that Polish troops might leave months earlier than planned.[16] Iraq became a hot topic in the Ukranian election. NATO's Secretary General Jaap de Hoop Scheffer tried to shore up support: "It would be a very unwise decision by nations now to withdraw their forces from Iraq. I'd like to tell all NATO allies in Iraq and non-NATO allies, do not withdraw your forces now."[17]

Not only was the Pentagon forced to abandon plans for reducing force levels, it was hard pressed to maintain the current troop strength until the end of 2005. As a result, the U.S. Army extended the tour of 20,000 troops in the First Armored Division past their original deployment schedule of one year. U.S. troops were diverted from other security operations, including a 4,000-member brigade from the Second Infantry based in South Korea.

Senator Jack Reed, a Democrat from Rhode Island, criticized the rotation plan as "another ad hoc effort to cobble together units to send to Iraq."[18] The continued uncertainty about the number of troops in Iraq brought new charges of poor postwar planning. "There wasn't a serious plan," said Senator Russell D. Feingold, a Democrat from Wisconsin. "And I think at this point, we're paying a serious price for it."[19] According to General Anthony Zinni (Ret.), "In the lead-up to the Iraq war and its later conduct, I saw at a minimum true dereliction, negligence and irresponsibility, and at worst, lying, incompetence and corruption."[20]

Commanders braced for increased attacks by insurgents as the deadline approached for handing over sovereignty to Iraqis on June 30. Undeterred by questions about whether a caretaker government could control the country, the Bush administration pushed ahead with its plan to hand over security and pull back forces from major cities. Once again, the United States was forced to change course when violence broke out in Fallujah and spread like wildfire throughout the Sunni triangle.

CHAPTER 18

FIGHTING ON
TWO FRONTS

FOUR U.S. CONTRACTORS WERE AMBUSHED AND KILLED in Fallujah on March 31, 2004. In an outburst of anti-U.S. rage, the bodies were burned, ripped from their vehicles, and dragged through the streets by a frenzied mob: "Death to America!" the crowd chanted. "Death to occupation! Yes to Islam!"[1] The mob suspended two of the charred and mangled corpses from a bridge over the Euphrates River. The gruesome spectacle outraged Americans.

The victims worked for a firm called Blackwater Security Consulting. Consistent with the Pentagon's policy to "outsource" security services, up to 20,000 private security personnel were working in Iraq.[2] "We will respond. It's going to be deliberate, it will be precise and it will be overwhelming," said Brigadier General Mark Kimmit, the U.S. Army's deputy operations director in Iraq. He warned, "We will pacify Fallujah."[3]

Fallujah is a medium-sized city surrounded by date trees and located on a scenic bend of the Euphrates. It has a population of about 300,000. Though it was never a Ba'athist stronghold, Fallujah became a hotbed of anti-U.S. resistance. Two weeks after Saddam Hussein fell, the U.S. Army's First Infantry Division turned one of Fallujah's schoolhouses into a barracks. Local residents protested and a confrontation ensued; U.S. troops fired on the crowd, killing seventeen people. The incident catalyzed a conflict that engulfed the entire Sunni triangle, which includes Baghdad, Ramadi, Baquba, and Tikrit and covers an area about the size of England.

The United States responded by launching operation "Desert Scorpion." In addition to attacking insurgents and extremists, the multifaceted

strategy sought to strengthen ties with local sheikhs, expand the local police force, and fund infrastructure projects to build bonds with local
Iraqis. When the First Marine Expeditionary Force took over from the
army in mid-March 2004, its spokesman emphasized, "We wanted to
knock on doors, not knock down doors."[4]

The nuanced approach changed after the Blackwater contractors were
murdered. U.S. commanders met Fallujah's clerics and demanded that
they condemn the killings. At Friday prayers, the clerics pointed out that
Islam forbade the desecration of dead bodies—but they refused to condemn the killing of Americans.

On April 4, U.S. troops moved against the insurgents in Fallujah. The
marines erected earth barricades and cordoned off the city. Block-by-
block they fought, searching for insurgent leaders, including those responsible for the Blackwater incident.

Fallujah is a twisted mix of narrow streets, back alleys, and boulevards.
The insurgents had fortified their positions and fashioned a tunnel network between buildings so they could fire from one building and then
flee to another. Careful not to hit civilian targets, the U.S. military forces
responded with Cobra helicopters and laser-guided bombs. General John
Abizaid called the Fallujah insurgents "brutal and determined."[5] The insurgency included diehard Ba'athists, foreign fighters, and common criminals. Though they lacked a unified command, the insurgents showed
surprising tenacity and skill in joining the battle.

U.S. commanders were fully aware of the political costs of taking Fallujah by force. An assault could spark uprisings elsewhere in Iraq. In addition, urban combat would take a heavy toll on U.S. forces as well as on
Iraqi civilians. Undeterred, President Bush expressed optimism in his
weekly radio address: "This week in Iraq, our coalition forces have faced
challenges, and taken the fight to the enemy. And our offensive will continue in the weeks ahead."[6]

IRAQI Governing Council members strongly protested the U.S. offensive in Fallujah. Adnan Pachachi condemned the siege as "illegal, fero-
cious and completely unacceptable." The interior and human rights
ministers resigned. The communications minister asserted, "It's as if the
U.S. Army is out of control. Iraqis can no longer be seen siding with the
Americans."[7]

Warning that U.S. operations were eroding civilian immunity not just
in practice but in principle, Governing Council members tried to nego-

tiate a humanitarian pause to the fighting. The Fallujah Muslim Scholars' Council, the Iraqi Islamic Party, and the mayor of Fallujah participated in a seven-man leadership council that met with the Governing Council's delegation. After ten days of fighting, the United States and Iraqi insurgents agreed to a ceasefire to allow the delivery of food and medicine for the wounded.

In exchange, U.S. commanders demanded that the insurgents disarm. When Iraqis refused to put down their weapons, General Kimmit bluntly warned, "Our patience is not eternal."[8] Bush also dug in his heels: "The U.S. will never be run out of Iraq by a bunch of thugs and killers," he insisted.[9] Fighting resumed. Across the country, coalition forces braced for reprisals in the event of an all-out offensive against Fallujah.

In a last-ditch effort, negotiations focused on disarming the insurgents in exchange for the withdrawal of U.S. troops. But who would provide security in Fallujah if not the U.S. Marines? Iraqi security forces had proved to be a big disappointment. When the fighting started, some disappeared; others went over and joined ranks with the insurgents. In explaining their refusal to fight alongside U.S. marines in Fallujah, Iraqi soldiers said they were trained to fight external threats, not other Iraqis.

There seemed to be no alternative to a full frontal assault until the CIA approached U.S. field commanders and suggested that ex-Ba'athists take over security in the city. The agency proposed that Jassim Mohammed Saleh, a former head of the Iraqi Army's Thirty-Eighth Infantry Division, assume command of a nine hundred man Fallujah Brigade; General Abizaid accepted "the opportunity . . . to build an Iraqi security force from former elements of the army that will work under the command of coalition forces." At the time, Senator Joe Biden commended the decision: "We have to give the deal a chance to work," he said. "If it doesn't then we may well have to use force, but that should be our last option. We don't want to generate more Fallujahs."

SALEH'S appointment was ultimately withdrawn when it surfaced that he had committed atrocities against the Kurds and Shi'a in the early 1990s. However, the Fallujah Brigade marked a change in the U.S. approach to de-Ba'athification. Ambassador Bremer announced that the United States would begin reinstating "honorable men" who had previously served in the Iraqi armed forces.[10] After a vetting process, he also pledged to rehire university professors and teachers "who were Ba'athists in name only."[11] Though Dan Senor, the spokesman for the Coalition Provisional Authority (CPA), called it a "technical correction in the implementation of procedures," it represented a major shift in U.S. policy.[12]

The decision also signified a break between the CPA and Ahmad Chalabi; Bremer had been trying to rein in Chalabi, who headed up the Governing Council's de-Ba'athification efforts. "I've told him they've got to stop this overzealous approach if we're going to allow this to continue,"[13] Bremer said. U.S. officials now faced a conundrum: Backing Chalabi alienated other Iraqis, potentially undermining Iraq's transition. However, dumping Chalabi could antagonize him to the point where he would expose details embarrassing to administration officials.

In April 2004, one of the most deadly months for Americans in Iraq, 134 U.S. soldiers died. To Iraqis, Fallujah was the "mother of all battles" and a rallying point for Iraqi resistance to the occupation. Fighting spread across the Sunni triangle and as far away as Qusaybah, near the Syrian border, two hundred miles northwest.

U.S. officials tried to explain the negative turn of events. "I'm not a psychiatrist, but I think [Iraqis] feel somewhat guilty that they were not able to liberate themselves. So there is a lot of perverse resentment," Bremer reflected. "The only thing worse than being occupied is being an occupier."[14]

Resentment was not exclusive to the Sunni triangle. Though southern Iraq had been relatively peaceful, the United States found itself fighting an insurgency on two fronts when the radical Shi'a cleric, Moqtada al-Sadr, called for a nationwide jihad against the United States and coalition forces.

SOON after the overthrow of Saddam Hussein, Moqtada al-Sadr had filled the power vacuum using his family's network of foundations to provide food and other essential services to Iraqis. After Saddam's statue fell in Firdos Square, Sadr's followers did everything from protecting the mosques to acting as traffic police and picking up the garbage. Despite his youth and inexperience, Sadr gained support from seminary students and the masses of impoverished Shi'a.

Ayatollah Kadhem al-Husseini al-Haeri, who was born in Karbala and moved to Qum, Iran, in 1973, has had the greatest influence over the young Sadr. In April 2003, al-Haeri announced: "Moqtada al-Sadr is our deputy and representative in all fatwa affairs."[15] Emboldened by al-Haeri's support, Sadr established the Mahdi Army as his personal militia. Aspiring to leadership, Sadr took matters into his own hands in eliminating rivals and enhancing his personal power. Iraqis suspected Sadr of arranging the assassination of Ayatollah Abdul Majid al-Khoei, who was slain at the gate of the Imam Ali mosque in Najaf on April 10, 2003. In addition Sadr may also have been involved in an attack on August 24 that seriously wounded Ayatollah Mohammed Saeed al-Hakim. Sadr's opponents also suspected that he was behind the August 29 car bombing in Najaf that killed Ayatollah Mohammed Bakr al-Hakim, head of the Supreme Council for Islamic Revolution in Iraq (SCIRI).

For many years, the Sadr family and Ayatollah Ali al-Sistani had vied for control of the Shi'a community *(Hawza)* in Najaf. Shi'a Muslims recognize four grand ayatollahs; Sistani is most revered as the "object of emulation" *(Marja al-taqlid)*. Devotees contributed millions of dollars to Sistani, money that he used for social work and, consequently, to broaden his base of followers.

Unlike Sistani, who urged moderation, Sadr defiantly called for an end to the U.S.-led occupation. He tried to install his cadres in the city hall of Sadr City, a Baghdad district. The CPA responded by evicting them and putting Sadr on notice. Bremer had planned to arrest Sadr in October 2003. Sistani intervened: He sent Bremer a message (via Mowaffak al-Rubaie) warning that Sadr's arrest would only enhance the young rabble rouser's stature.

Sadr's importance waned as Sistani emerged as the primary powerbroker over elections and the interim constitution. However, Sadr seized on the events in Fallujah to reassert himself in Iraqi politics: He proclaimed common cause with his Sunni brethren in resisting occupation and fighting the American infidels. According to a member of Sadr's Mahdi Army, "We have orders from our leader to fight as one to help the Sunnis. We want to increase the fighting, increase the killing and drive the Americans out. To do this, we must combine forces."[16]

Bremer set the stage for Sadr's insurrection by issuing a decree closing Sadr's newspaper for inciting hatred against Americans. When Iraq's interior minister issued an arrest warrant for a senior Sadr aid in connection with the killing of Ayatollah al-Khoei in Najaf the previous year, Sadr ordered his Mahdi Army into battle. SCIRI's Hamid al-Bayati bemoaned the arrest. "It is very bad timing, even if the basis is right," he complained. "I don't know why they decided to act now."[17]

Within hours of Sadr's sermon calling on his followers to "terrorize
your enemy," the Mahdi Army took control in Sadr City, Amara, Kufa,
and parts of Najaf. Sadr's black-clad militia overran Iraqi police, occupied government buildings, and set up heavily armed checkpoints in and
out of the cities. Militia members also attacked a Spanish garrison on the
road between Najaf and Kufa.

The United States crossed a watershed by announcing its intention to
"kill or capture" Sadr.[18] Bremer called Sadr an "outlaw": "We will not tolerate this," he emphasized. "We will reassert the law and order that people expect."[19] Sadr, in turn, responded defiantly: "I have the honor to be
termed an outlaw by the occupation."[20] If U.S. forces moved against holy
sites in Najaf or Karbala, he warned, "we will be human time bombs
which would explode in their faces."[21]

Sadr took refuge in the grand mosque of Kufa. But after hearing reports that Apache helicopters had strafed targets in Sadr City, Sadr
shifted his sanctuary to an office in a more densely populated area near
the gold-domed Imam Ali Shrine in Najaf.

U.S. commanders were cautious about moving against Sadr. Instead,
they tried to marginalize him by recruiting other Shi'a clerics. While de-
nouncing "provocation by U.S. troops," Sistani also called for a peaceful
solution to the problem.[22] Shi'a community and religious leaders sent a
message to the Mahdi Army: "It's your responsibility to keep Najaf safe,
so don't cause any bloodshed. If you reject our advice and decide to
fight, then go outside the city, where there are no people and no buildings. Don't make innocents suffer the outcome of your wrongful decision."[23] General Kimmit assured the citizens of Najaf that "the target
[was] Moqtada al-Sadr and his militia." He added: "We have very great
respect for the shrines of the Shi'a, for the religion."[24]

In the middle of the crisis, Iran sent a delegation to gain "a better understanding of [what was] going on."[25] But the Bush administration kept
the Iranian mediation effort at arm's length. To reports that Iranian
sources were giving Sadr $5 million every month,[26] Donald Rumsfeld
retorted, "We know the Iranians have been meddling." In response to
Rumsfeld's criticisms, Iranian President Mohammad Khatami blamed
the United States for mismanaging the crisis, maintaining that America's
"iron fist policy" had undermined peace efforts.[27]

Ratcheting up the pressure, U.S. commanders used warplanes, attack
helicopters, and armored units on the Mahdi Army. Bush intoned: "The

violence we have seen is a power grab by these extreme and ruthless elements. It's not a civil war. It's not a popular uprising. Most of Iraq is relatively stable. Most Iraqis, by far, reject violence."[28] Echoing the president, Rumsfeld described the fighting in Iraq as the work of "thugs, gangs and terrorists."[29] "We're facing a test of wills," he admonished. "We will meet the test."[30]

Despite the bravado, U.S. officials did not come to grips with the nature of the opposition. They refused to acknowledge the broad base of support for the insurgency among Iraqis. In April 2004, Central Command (CENTCOM) believed the rebellion was the work of a small minority that included no more than 5,000 Ba'athists and foreign fighters. But Jack Straw, Britain's foreign minister, understood the severity of the situation: "It is plainly the fact today that there are large numbers of people, and they are people on the ground, Iraqis and not foreign fighters, who are engaged in this insurgency." Straw added a warning: "The lid of the pressure cooker has come off."[31]

After weeks of bluster and violence, Sadr finally offered to dismantle his militia if the United States would withdraw from Najaf and suspend the warrant for his arrest. U.S. officials took him at his word. However, the Mahdi Army simply dissolved into the population only to renew the insurrection a hundred days later. Falling out with Sadr and other radical Shi'a was a big blow to U.S. plans. Save for Iraqi Kurdistan, the split left no safe haven anywhere in Iraq.

THE Bush administration planned to start reducing the number of U.S. troops during the spring of 2004. To this end, the plan also called for building up Iraqi security forces and expanding the number of troops from coalition countries. By year's end, CENTCOM counted on 200,000 Iraqis serving in police and civil-defense units, border patrol, the new national army, and facility-protection units. However, the Iraqi army and police proved woefully inadequate in confronting the insurgency. According to General Abizaid, their failure "was a great disappointment." [32]

Multinational forces were mostly stationed in the south, which had been relatively stable. But as the insurgency spread, it also became clear that some of them were not up to the task. Ukrainian troops withdrew under pressure in Kut; Bulgaria asked the United States to reinforce its 450 soldiers in Karbala. Spain, Honduras, and the Dominican Republic announced that they were withdrawing forces from Iraq. In response,

Bush accused Spain's new prime minister of giving "false comfort to terrorists and enemies of freedom in Iraq."[33] On April 9, Bush called the
leaders of Poland, Italy, and El Salvador to shore up support; Prime Minister Silvio Berlusconi of Italy assured him, "It is unthinkable to flee the
mission we have started. We would leave the country in chaos."[34]

The Pentagon had drawn up contingency plans in the event the situation deteriorated badly. Reversing the trend of troop reductions,
Rumsfeld announced that the United States would add two additional
combat brigades consisting of 20,000 troops. On April 15, Rumsfeld
indicated that the troops would be required to extend their rotation
for another three months. U.S. forces were already frustrated by the
on-again, off-again actions in Fallujah and Najaf; with summer temper-
atures soaring to 120 degrees, Rumsfeld's announcement had a devastating effect on morale.

So did the steady drip of casualties. Ambushes, roadside improvised
explosive devices, attacks using rocket-propelled grenades, and suicide
car bombings were killing and maiming more and more soldiers. As a result, the United States was forced to close the stretch of road connect-
ing Baghdad and Hilla, sixty miles to the south. U.S. forces also lost
control of the 375-mile highway running from Baghdad to Jordan via
Fallujah. The stretch between the Baghdad airport and the city became
known as the "highway of death." Supplies of fuel and food started to
run short. Water rationing was required and troops were given ready-to-
eat combat rations.

Insurgents adopted a new tactic to undermine the resolve of the
United States and its allies. In April, they kidnapped forty foreign
hostages from twelve countries. A masked man appeared on al-Jazeera,
the Arab news network based in Qatar, warning, "If America doesn't lift
its blockade of Fallujah, their heads will be cut off."[35] Web sites showed
the gruesome beheadings of hostages from Bulgaria, Italy, and South
Korea, as well as U.S. businessman Nicholas Berg.

As the hostage-taking escalated, France and Germany warned their
citizens to leave; Russia withdrew six hundred workers. Those who
stayed behind were restricted to protected work sites. Brown & Root, a
division of Halliburton, suspended all convoys into Iraq after an ambush
on a fuel convoy near Abu Ghraib on April 9. By mid-April, General
Electric and Siemens also suspended operations on about two dozen
power plants. Motorola personnel sought refuge at the airport. Bechtel
also curtailed employee travel. Iraq's trade fair was postponed and

moved from Baghdad to Suleimania. An oil conference scheduled for Basra was indefinitely postponed.

A FEW months after Saddam was removed from power, Rumsfeld touted the vast number of reconstruction projects. "They have touched the lives of millions of Iraqis," he said. "They've seen progress. They've seen things happen."[36] Despite Rumsfeld's assertions, reconstruction efforts had been seriously marred from the beginning.

The Pentagon anticipated that it would soon be able to bring Iraq's oil production up to prewar levels (2.5 to 3 million barrels per day) and that oil revenues would cover the costs of reconstruction. However, Iraq's oil sector was far more decrepit than had been anticipated. Sabotage of the electricity facilities compounded production problems. Insurgents also attacked pipelines transporting oil to refineries as well as export markets. By January 2004, insurgents launched eighty-five attacks on Iraq's oil infrastructure.[37]

The reconstruction price tag was much more than the U.S. Congress had expected. The Bush administration initially submitted to Congress an $87 billion budget supplemental; it included $21 billion for reconstruction that would augment the Iraqi Assistance Fund. This fund had been established with Iraqi assets and the UN Oil for Food Program escrow, as well as with $37.5 billion in pledges made at the October donors' conference in Madrid. The administration provided few details on how the money would be spent; Senator Robert C. Byrd, a Democrat from West Virginia, angrily responded, "Congress is not an ATM. We have to be able to explain this enormous bill to the American people."[38]

Six months after the supplemental was approved, less than $1 billion had actually been spent on reconstruction. In addition to the security crisis, there were several other reasons why spending had become bogged down. Only companies from countries in the U.S.-led coalition were allowed to bid. Iraq's $125 billion debt burden was crippling. Foreign direct investment was negligible. The Pentagon's contracting process vacillated between large sole-source contracts and dysfunctional procurement procedures. The Army Inspector General blew the whistle on Halliburton. Responding to questions by the Senate Armed Services Committee about why Iraqi security services had not been supplied adequate equipment, Wolfowitz explained, "We have red tape and bureaucracy that's gotten in the way."[39]

Despite serious problems, Bremer accentuated the positive. "As I drove in from the airport, Baghdad was on fire, literally," he reflected. "There was no traffic in the streets. There was not a single policeman on duty anywhere in the country. There was no electricity anywhere in the country. There was no economic activity anywhere. When I look at where we have arrived from where we started, it is an astonishing record."[40]

Nothing undermined Bremer's claims and America's credibility more than the Abu Ghraib prisoner-abuse scandal. On April 30, photos surfaced documenting the physical and sexual abuse of Iraqi prisoners held in Abu Ghraib. The notorious prison had been used by the Ba'athist regime to torture and execute political prisoners. International public opinion was outraged by images of hooded Iraqis, prisoners on dog leashes, and pyramids of naked detainees. The Bush administration's virtuous claim that it had invaded Iraq to liberate the Iraqi people from Saddam's abuses was put to shame. The Arab world was incensed. A comic in *al-Hayat*, a leading Arabic-language newspaper, depicted the gates of Abu Ghraib with a sign that read "Under New Management."

By the end of April 2004, conditions were going from bad to worse. Security, reconstruction, and the political process were intertwined. Reconstruction efforts had failed to keep pace with Iraq's requirements. Job shortages had increased the number of malcontents, who, in turn, were recruited by the insurgency. The security crisis eroded confidence in the CPA, undermined the political transition, and widened the gap between the expectations of Iraqis and the ability of the United States to improve conditions.

As concerns mounted over the feasibility of handing over sovereignty to Iraqis by June 30, Bush was adamant about sticking to the deadline. "Were the coalition to step back from the June 30 pledge," he said, "many Iraqis would question our intentions and feel their hopes betrayed."[41]

CHAPTER 19

THE HANDOVER

IN MARCH 2004, BUSH TURNED TO THE UNITED NATIONS to bail out the United States from its failed efforts to steward Iraq's political transition. UN officials greeted the request with a mixture of vindication and apprehension. In 2003, the Bush administration had consistently disparaged the world body. But after a year of missteps, the United States was desperate to secure an international stamp of approval on its plan to establish an interim government in Iraq. The United Nations had become indispensable.

President Bush's request came at a difficult time for the United Nations. Corruption and kickbacks were uncovered in the UN Oil for Food Program. An internal investigation determined that lapses in the UN's own security management had led to the bombing of the UN headquarters in Baghdad on August 19, 2003. Some of Kofi Annan's senior advisers strongly disapproved of the UN's further involvement in Iraq. Despite reservations, Annan acceded and sent Lakhdar Brahimi to Iraq from April 4 to 15, 2004. Annan concluded that failure to facilitate the timely handover of sovereignty would lead to even more violence. "The date [of June 30] has been there for some time," he reasoned. "It has been embraced by the Iraqis themselves, who are anxious to see the end of occupation as soon as possible, and I believe it is going to be difficult to pull it back."[1] Brahimi was given a straightforward task: Determine to whom the Coalition Provisional Authority (CPA) would yield power on June 30.

Over eleven days, Brahimi visited Baghdad, Basra, and Mosul, where he and his small team of advisers met Iraqi politicians, civic and religious leaders, women's groups, academics, intellectuals, artists, businessmen, and merchants. This time, Grand Ayatollah Ali al-Sistani declined to receive him when Brahimi refused to pass judgment on the interim constitution. Likewise, the Muslim Scholars Association canceled its meeting when he would not denounce the U.S. siege of Fallujah. Brahimi decided against a visit to Iraqi Kurdistan, thereby upsetting the Kurds.

Brahimi presented his much anticipated report to the UN Security Council on April 28. His proposal built on previous recommendations of the CPA. Brahimi suggested replacing the Governing Council with a transitional government made up of "men and women known for their honesty, integrity, and competence."[2] Personnel would be selected by the United Nations, after consultations with the United States, as well as by Iraqis. He envisioned that the caretaker government would be led by a prime minister. A president would serve as the head of state and there would be two vice presidents. The government would be staffed by technocrats, not politicians, and none of the interim leaders would stand for elections in the future. Brahimi suggested reversing de-Ba'athification, pointing out, "It is difficult to understand that thousands upon thousands of professionals who are sorely needed have been dismissed within the de-Ba'athification process."[3]

According to Brahimi, the caretaker government's responsibilities would be limited to basic day-to-day affairs and preparing the country for elections. It should not make decisions binding Iraq's future elected government. Brahimi proposed the creation of a consultative assembly elected by delegates to a national conference of 1,000 Iraqis. The conference would serve as a forum to discuss challenges facing the country, build consensus, and foster cooperation. Rather than the United Nations, it would be organized by a preparatory committee made up of Iraqis. Brahimi also indicated that, if asked, the United Nations would work with Iraqis to help draft the constitution and organize national elections.

Annan endorsed the Brahimi plan. "There will not be a fully representative government until there are free and fair elections, which we all hope will happen in January 2005," said Annan. "Somehow we have to get from here to there, and I think that the kind of caretaker government [Brahimi] has proposed is the way forward."[4]

BRAHIMI ran into trouble when, in response to a question on a French radio program, he said, "The great poison in the region is this Israeli policy of domination and the suffering imposed on the Palestinians" as well as the "equally unjust support of the United States for this policy."[5] Annan asserted that the remarks were Brahimi's personal views in his attempt to distance the United Nations.

Brahimi's comment appeared to be gratuitous. However, it was a move by Brahimi to solidify support and separate himself from the policies of the Bush administration. By siding with the Palestinians, Brahimi earned favor from the Arab world and was commended by several European countries. He also burnished his credentials with some Iraqis who likened the Iraqi insurgency to the Palestinians' Intifada.

Neo-cons and surrogates for Bush's reelection campaign attacked Brahimi; despite criticism, the Bush administration had no choice but to stand by him. John Negroponte, the U.S. permanent representative to the United Nations and ambassador-designate to Iraq, emphasized that cooperating with the United Nations was in America's "strategic interest."[6]

Washington waited anxiously for Brahimi to come up with a list of officeholders for the interim government. Asked to whom the United States would hand over sovereignty on June 30, Bush replied, "You'll find that out soon."[7] According to Colin Powell, "We've been in daily contact with Ambassador Brahimi, and he's quite skilled at these kinds of things."[8] The UN spokesman said, "Mr. Brahimi is going flat out, trying to develop consensus among a broad cross-section of Iraqi leadership. And of course the closer you get to your goal, the tougher the bargaining becomes."[9]

On May 28, 2004, the Governing Council announced that Ayad Allawi had been selected as prime minister. Ghazi al-Yawar would be Iraq's interim president; Ibrahim al-Jaffari and Roj Nuri Shaways would serve as vice presidents.

WHEN U.S. officials suggested that the interim government would only have "partial sovereignty," the international community clamored for a UN Security Council resolution spelling out its responsibilities. On the Sunday before the vote, I met Foreign Minister Hoshyar Zebari at the Waldorf Astoria Hotel. He and his delegation were staying in Negroponte's suite on the thirty-eighth floor of the Waldorf Towers. Zebari and I went to Sir Harry's, a bar off the main lobby, and talked for several hours.

Zebari was caught between two worlds. As Iraq's foreign minister, he was charged with negotiating a resolution strengthening Iraq's national sovereignty. But as a Kurd, he also felt compelled to safeguard Kurdish interests. In a letter to Allawi, Sistani had called the interim constitution "undemocratic" and warned of "serious consequences" if it was endorsed by the UN Security Council. The draft resolution, which was prepared by Britain and the United Nations, made no mention of the Transitional Administrative Law on which the Kurds had pinned their hopes. In a letter to Bush, Massoud Barzani and Jalal Talabani wrote: "If the Transitional Administrative Law is abrogated, we will have no choice but to refrain from participating in the central government and its institutions, not to take part in the national elections, and to bar representatives of the central government from Kurdistan."[10]

UN Security Council Resolution 1546 was approved unanimously on June 8. It represented an important milestone for Iraq, the region, and the international community. The resolution endorsed the formation of an interim government until an elected transitional government could take office. It also stipulated that the CPA would cease to exist and that the occupation would end when the interim government assumed power. It required elections by December 31, 2004, if possible, and no later than January 31, 2005. The transitional national assembly was given responsibility to draft the constitution and organize elections to be held by December 31, 2005. According to the resolution, which did not mention the Transitional Administrative Law, the Iraqi people should freely determine their own political future and exercise full control over their financial and natural resources.

The resolution also outlined the UN's role during the transition phase, authorized a U.S.-led multinational force to help stabilize the country, and defined the relationship between the United Nations, the United States, and the new Iraqi authorities. Specifically, the UN was authorized to advise and support the interim government, the transitional national assembly, and the elections commission. It was invited to assist the organization of the national conference and the drafting of a national constitution. In addition, the resolution affirmed the UN's role in coordinating humanitarian and reconstruction assistance, promoting the rule of law, and advising on the national census.

Though a multinational force was authorized, France proposed a time limit lest sovereignty have no real meaning. It was agreed that the force could remain in Iraq only with the consent of the Iraqi government and that its mandate would be reviewed within one year. The resolution also called for a dedicated protection force assigned to the UN mission.

The Bush administration relinquished many responsibilities to the United Nations. However, there was no denying that the United States retained enormous influence in Iraq. The U.S. was in charge of Iraq's military and security affairs. America's "super-embassy" controlled $8 billion in reconstruction aid. As U.S. ambassador to Iraq, Negroponte reported to the secretary of state. The State Department assumed responsibility for most nation-building functions, with the exception of military operations.

Until the Bush administration negotiated a "status of forces" agreement with the new Iraqi government, it was unclear just how much control it would have over 150,000 U.S. and coalition troops still stationed in Iraq. U.S. officials believed it is unlikely that the new government would ask foreign forces to leave, but they agreed that U.S. forces would go if asked. The deployment of coalition troops required the Iraqi government's consent: "If there's a political decision as to whether you go into a place like Fallujah in a particular way, that has to be done with the consent of the Iraqi government," Powell said. However, "U.S. forces remain under U.S. command, and will do what is necessary to protect themselves."[11]

Security was still the top concern. "Security affects everything. Security affects the process we are in," Annan maintained. "It affects elections. It affects reconstruction and recovery. It affects the lives of ordinary Iraqis—their daily lives—and so it is absolutely important that everything is done to improve the security environment."[12] He also expressed hope that the handover of sovereignty would reduce the level of violence across the country. If what we are witnessing is a resistance against the occupation, and the occupation were to end, I hope some would be dissuaded not to continue fighting because, in a way, they would have achieved their objectives."[13]

NOT all Iraqis welcomed the UN resolution. The Kurds were furious because it did not mention the interim constitution. The omission added to their long list of grievances. At Bremer's request, the Kurds had relinquished hundreds of millions of dollars in UN Oil for Food Program funds intended for projects in Kurdistan. They wanted a Kurd to be designated president or prime minister, but were given only one of the vice-presidential slots. From the prewar period through combat operations to the postwar phase, the Iraqi Kurds had bent over backwards to accommodate the United States. Barzani and Talabani felt they had received little in return.

The Bush administration knew that excluding the Transitional Administrative Law from Resolution 1546 would render the interim constitution legally inoperative. Laws adopted during occupation do not survive unless they are upheld by the sovereign successor state. At the Waldorf, Zebari complained, "The United States has lowered the bar when it comes to democracy in Iraq. Its current policies are unduly influenced by former Ba'athists, Arab nationalists, and Shi'a clerics."[14] Najmaldin Karim likened the abrogation of the interim constitution to the most tragic events in Kurdish history—America's betrayals in 1975 and 1991.

Ahmad Chalabi was also dismayed. Not only was he excluded from a leadership position in the interim government but the Bush administration took steps to distance the United States from the man whom the Pentagon once envisioned as the new ruler of Iraq.

Amid allegations that Chalabi had provided faulty intelligence in the run-up to the war, the Pentagon discontinued its monthly payment of $347,000 to the Iraq National Congress (INC). When the CPA alleged that Chalabi had passed classified information to Iran on U.S. decoding and communications capabilities, an Iraqi judge issued an arrest warrant for Arras Habib, the INC's intelligence chief. Iraqi police, backed by U.S. troops, broke down the door of Chalabi's house in Baghdad, arresting fifteen people and carting away computers and thousands of documents. In another raid on an INC office, fifty computers were confiscated.

Chalabi claimed that the charges were intended to disgrace him and silence his criticism of the CPA: "They are charges put out by George Tenet and the CIA to discredit us."[15] The INC's Francis Brooke called the accusations "disgusting nonsense" that shows "how decrepit" our intelligence services had become.[16] Chalabi wailed, "Let my people go. Let my people be free. We are grateful to President Bush for liberating Iraq, but it is time for the Iraqi people to run their own affairs."[17] Senator Joe Biden commented, "I predict to you Mr. Chalabi will not go quietly into the night."[18] Sure enough, Chalabi used the raid to his advantage, carrying favor with Sistani, forging a political partnership with Sadr, and re-positioning himself as an opponent of the U.S. occupation and a champion of the Shi'a.

AYAD Allawi's first days as prime minister were marred by miscalculations and missteps. Allawi upset the Shi'a by suggesting that elections might have to be postponed. He angered the Kurds by refusing to support the Transitional Administrative Law beyond the date of Iraq's elections. He angered many Iraqis by proffering some form of emergency rule restricting basic freedoms. He even managed to anger the United States by offering an amnesty to guerrilla fighters in exchange for laying down their arms.

Allawi talked tough about cracking down on insurgents, even as security conditions continued to deteriorate. "I warn the forces of terror once again," Allawi said. "We will not forget who stood with us and against us in our national crisis. I say that we, with God's will and the support of our people, will be ready for them, that we will hunt them down to face justice and give them their just punishment."[19] Allawi vowed to crack down even if that meant sacrificing Iraq's newfound freedoms.

THOUGH Ambassador Bremer was scheduled to turn over formal sovereignty to Iraq's new leaders on June 30, 2004, Zebari raised the first suspicions that that handover could come early during his address to the NATO summit a few days before the deadline. "We are very pleased, we are confident, and we are ready to take up our responsibility—even before 30 June," Zebari announced.[20]

Zebari had leaked the CPA's best-kept secret. Only six of Bremer's advisers knew that the handover would occur ahead of time. To foil the timing of terrorist attacks that might be in the works, U.S. and Iraqi officials decided to move up the date and hold the ceremony in near secrecy.

On June 28, 2004, at 10:26 A.M., Ambassador L. Paul Bremer III rose from a gilded sofa at CPA headquarters in the heavily fortified Green Zone. Instead of the Stars and Stripes, an Iraqi flag was raised over the sprawling compound. He addressed an audience of no more than two dozen people: "Anybody who has any doubt about whether Iraq is a better place today than it was fourteen months ago should go down to see the mass graves in Hilla. Anybody who has seen those things that I have will know that Iraq is a much better place."[21] Bremer handed Allawi a leatherbound note from President Bush; it said that the CPA was dissolved and the interim government was officially in charge. The ceremony lasted less than thirty minutes. Then Bremer flew by helicopter to Baghdad International Airport, boarded a C–130 military transport, and left the country.

Following the handover, an Iraqi judge administered the oath of office for Ayad Allawi, Ghazi al-Yawar, and other members of the new government. "This is a historic day, a happy day, a day that all Iraqis have been looking forward to," Ghazi al-Yawar said. "This is the time when we take the country back into the international community."[22] A few hours later, Negroponte arrived in Baghdad and presented his credentials, re-establishing U.S. diplomatic ties with Iraq for the first time since the invasion of Kuwait in 1990.

IRAQIS barely celebrated the handover to an unelected government. They viewed the secret ceremony as a sign of weakness. Iraqis were well aware that they were still reliant on the United States and other countries for their security. The country still faced enormous challenges.

In contrast, Bush was in a celebratory mood: "After decades of brutal rule by a terror regime, the Iraqi people have their country back," he happily proclaimed.

This is a day of great hope for Iraqis, and a day that terrorist enemies hoped never to see. The terrorists are doing all they can to stop the rise of a free Iraq. But their bombs and attacks have not prevented Iraqi sovereignty, and they will not prevent Iraqi democracy. Iraqi sovereignty is a tribute to the will of the Iraqi people and the courage of Iraqi leaders. This day also marks a proud moral achievement for members of our coalition. We pledged to end a dangerous regime, to free the oppressed, and to restore sovereignty. We have kept our word. Fifteen months ago, we faced the threat of a dictator with a history of using weapons of mass destruction; today the dictator is a threat to no one from the cell he now occupies. Fifteen months ago, the regime in Baghdad was the most aggressive in the Middle East, and a constant source of fear and alarm for Iraq's neighbors; today Iraq threatens no other country and its democratic progress will be an example to the broader Middle East. In Iraq, we're serving the cause of liberty, and liberty is always worth fighting for. . . . In Iraq, we're serving the cause of peace, by promoting progress and hope in the Middle East, and as the alternative to stagnation and hatred and violence for export. In Iraq, we're serving the cause of our own security, striking the terrorists where we find them, instead of waiting for them to strike us at home. For all these reasons, we accepted a difficult task in Iraq. And for all these reasons, we will finish that task.[23]

Meanwhile, Allawi focused on the monumental task of laying out the agenda of Iraq's new government:

Our government's policies will be based on four interrelated objectives. First and foremost, our priority is to establish security, without which little other progress can be made in the long-overdue reconstruction of the country. This requires the rapid rebuilding of Iraq's key institutions for law enforcement, including the army, police, border control, and intelligence services. The process is already under way, with a multifaceted, integrated plan that encompasses establishment of five divisions in the new Iraqi Army, unifying the command-and-control structure of the various security forces, building counterterrorism intelligence capabilities, establishing a ministerial national security council, and assembling a framework for the disbanding of militias and their reintegration into the nation's security forces.

Throughout this process the government will make a clear distinction between those Iraqis who have acted against the occupation out of a sense of desperation and those foreign terrorist fundamentalists and criminals whose sole objective is to kill and maim innocent people and to see Iraq fail. Our objective will be to reach out to the former group in a national reconciliation effort and invite them to join us in a fresh start to build our country's future together, while at the same time isolating and defeating the latter group. In this regard we are drawing up plans to provide amnesty to Iraqis who supported the so-called resistance without committing crimes, while isolating the hard-core elements of terrorists and criminals and undercutting their base of support. The honor of decent Iraqi ex-officials including military and police should be restored, excluding of course those who committed heinous crimes against the nation.

The second key element of our policy will address the dire economic situation. The immediate priorities must be reduction of the high rate of unemployment and restoration of essential basic services throughout the country. Promises must be translated into tangible results in order to address the crisis of credibility and win back the trust and loyalty of the Iraqi people. This will require absorbing a high number of skilled and unskilled workers in reconstruction projects and activities that will follow the restoration of sovereignty. The main focus of these works will be rehabilitating the infrastructure, including transportation, electricity and water networks, health services, and education. In addition, we must restore and build up the nation's oil production and revenue.

Third, the sovereign Iraqi government will secure the development of and support for a strong and independent judicial system, well trained and well funded, in order to ensure the rule of law, protection of property rights and respect for human rights. One important area will be anti-corruption laws and regulations. These steps are not only a vital prerequisite for security and economic progress but also a cornerstone for the future free and democratic Iraq that we aim to build.

The fourth objective of our government's policy will be to continue and accelerate the nation's political process and march toward democracy. Our aim is to cement national unity and promote a spirit of reconciliation by ensuring that all voices and groups are heard, and to prepare the country for free and fair elections through an agreed constitution. Ballots must replace bullets as the determinant of political authority in Iraq. Nation-building is the key.[24]

The Bush administration's plan came full circle with the handover of sovereignty on June 28, 2004. After a year of failed occupation, the administration finally focused on giving power to Iraqis and establishing self-rule. It was a year behind schedule, but Iraqis hoped it was not too late to salvage their dreams of democracy.

EPILOGUE

George W. Bush gambled his presidency on the Iraq War—and won. By conflating Iraq and Afghanistan, Bush convinced voters that Iraq was the central front in the war on terror. Americans were reluctant to change Commanders-in-Chief while the country was at war. Flush with victory in the U.S. presidential election, Bush pressed ahead with his plans in Iraq.

U.S. officials maintained that Iraq's first multiparty elections since 1954 would be a watershed in the country's history. On January 30, 2005, Iraqis would choose a 275-person provisional assembly and local provincial councils. The assembly would elect a president and two deputy presidents who, in turn, would appoint a prime minister and other cabinet ministers. The government would designate a constitutional committee to draft Iraq's permanent constitution for approval by the assembly and then ratification in a national referendum. Another round of elections would be held by December 15 to choose a permanent government for a five-year term. The United States hoped that legitimate elections would motivate Iraqis to stand up to insurgents and more effectively defend their national institutions.

But meanwhile Iraq was wracked with violence. The National Intelligence Estimate of August 2004 described three potential scenarios for the near future of Iraq ranging from "tenuous stability"—in the best case—to civil war. Three months later, the CIA station chief in Baghdad warned that conditions were deteriorating and that security would get worse. The Bush administration warned that Iraq's progress towards democracy would prompt insurgents to intensify their attacks. It concluded that elections could not occur until Baghdad and the provinces of al-Anbar, Nineveh and Salahuddin were brought under control.

——

Fallujah and other parts of the Sunni triangle had fallen under a Taliban-like rule. The Mujahadeen Council joined forces with former Ba'athists, tribal militias, and foreign fighters calling themselves the Black Banners who were linked to Abu Musab al-Zarqawi. Iraqis working with the occupying forces were assassinated, intimidated, or forced to repudiate the coalition: The Fallujah National Guard battalion chief was beheaded. The governor of al-Anbar province resigned after his three sons were kidnapped. Ramadi's police chief was coerced into cooperating with the insurgents.

On November 8—less than a week after Bush was re-elected—the First Marine Expeditionary Force launched an all-out assault on Fallujah. U.S. troops moved across Highway 10 in the first wave of a fierce fight to retake the city. Over three weeks, fifty-two American soldiers died and 425 were wounded; 2,085 Iraqi insurgents were killed and 1,600 taken prisoner.

U.S. commanders were convinced that most Fallujans were tired of bloodshed and would return to their homes as soon as the terrorists were driven out and services restored. Learning from past mistakes, they developed a detailed post-combat plan for rebuilding Fallujah. Portable generators and water tanks were moved into place. To prevent looting, heads of household were issued identification badges. Both U.S. and Iraqi troops were trained on how to deal with theft. No cars were allowed into the city. Almost as soon as the fighting stopped, homes were bull-dozed and rebuilding began. Iraqis who lost relatives were given "condolence payments" of $25,000. Reconstruction contracts were given to Iraqi contractors and Fallujah residents were given hiring preferences. Within a couple of months, a $35 million wastewater treatment plant, four new schools, and several health clinics had been built.

Despite these efforts, only a trickle of people returned to Fallujah. Insurgents infiltrated back into the city, taking relief supplies from the U.S. troops by day and attacking them at night. U.S. forces stayed on the offensive in Fallujah, as well as in Ramadi and Samarra. They also launched a new sweep focusing on Jabella, west of the Euphrates and south of Baghdad in an area U.S. commanders called the "triangle of death." Another front was opened in Mosul, the largest city in Nineveh province.

——

Ayad Allawi portrayed Iraq's spiral of deadly violence as a conflict between Iraqi people and terrorists who sought to derail Iraq's progress.

After taking office on June 28, he tried to establish the Iraqi government's authority through a combination of carrots and sticks: He instituted a state of emergency, restored the death penalty, and announced an amnesty for relatively minor crimes associated with the insurgency.

Allawi's decision to allow U.S. forces into Fallujah discredited him with many Arab Sunnis. Closely aligning himself with Bush's policies also undermined Allawi. In October, Allawi addressed a joint session of the U.S. Congress; his remarks sounded like they were written by Bush's speechwriter. In fact, the text was reviewed by former staff of the Coalition Provisional Authority.

Disgruntled Iraqis criticized Allawi for everything wrong in Iraq. He was blamed for shortages of water, electricity and fuel. Most of all, Iraqis were deeply frustrated by the escalating security crisis. Those participating in Iraq's security services encountered a ruthless campaign of fear, intimidation and murder.

Leaflets warned that Iraqis cooperating with the occupation would be beheaded. Hundreds of security recruits were assassinated. Car bombings targeted applicants at police stations. During the Spring of 2004, the Karbala Iraqi Civil Defense Corps (ICDC) disappeared entirely and half of Baghdad's ICDC either quit or sided with insurgents. Corruption, desertion and infiltration became increasingly widespread. The situation was not much improved six months later. Several Iraqi National Guard battalions and nearly the entire Mosul police force deserted during the insurgent uprising in November. Except for the Kurds, Iraqis refused to fight other Iraqis especially when ordered by Americans.

— —

When General David Petraeus assumed responsibility for training of Iraqi security forces, he emphasized the chain of command as well as field training. His approach was based on the realization that Iraqis needed to be in charge of the Iraqi army and government. General Petraeus also sought to foster allegiance to the state that would transcend tribal and religious loyalties.

Commanders tried to leave a lighter footprint by reducing the presence of American forces on the streets and at checkpoints. U.S. troops still bore the brunt in combat operations, but only Iraqi personnel were allowed to enter the major mosques of Najaf and Fallujah. As Iraqis started patrolling on their own, U.S. forces were assigned to ministries, police stations and army units as mentors.

Allawi estimated it would take 275,000 trained Iraqi troops to protect polling stations on January 30. In her confirmation hearing as U.S. secretary of state, Condoleezza Rice asserted that 120,000 Iraqis were ready for the role. Senator Joe Biden had just returned from Iraq. "Malarkey," he retorted. Only 4,000 Iraqis were up to the job.[1]

With elections in limbo and violence on the rise, the United States increased its force level from 138,000 to 150,000. Not only did the Pentagon deploy new troops; it delayed the departure of soldiers from Iraq. In December 2004 the mix of troops was evenly divided between active-duty soldiers and reservists. With the active-duty share expected to increase, the Pentagon was forced to consider new arrangements governing the length and frequency of Army National Guard and Army Reserve deployments.

Soldiers complained about their extended tours of duty. They also objected to going into combat without the proper equipment. At Camp Buehring in Kuwait on December 7, Specialist Thomas Wilson of Tennessee told Rumsfeld that reservists were digging through local landfills looking for "hillbilly armor" to bolt onto their vehicles. Roadside improvised explosive devices were responsible for two-thirds of U.S. fatalities in Iraq.

— —

After assuring Grand Ayatollah Ali al-Sistani that elections would be held by January 2005, Ambassador Bremer sought advice about conducting the ballot from the UN Office of Electoral Assistance. UN experts indicated that it would not be possible to conduct a nationwide census or draw district lines given the U.S.-imposed deadline. As one of his last decrees, Bremer decided that the vote for a national assembly would be based on party lists rather than on a more representative system (in which candidates represent specific districts). Bremer also acquiesced to the demands of exile politicians by deciding to give Iraqis outside of Iraq the right to vote.

Bremer's list system precluded the possibility of postponing elections in parts of Iraq gripped by violence. It also undermined minority representation, worsening the fears of disenfranchisement among Arab Sunnis who believed that the system favored Shi'a parties with national organizations. Adnan Pachachi and other Arab Sunni politicians warned that violence would limit turnout thus raising doubts about the election's legitimacy. The Muslim Scholars Association, which represented 3,000 mosques, announced a boycott; the Iraqi Islamic Party threatened to join. Pachachi proposed postponing the vote. Other remedies were considered to address the anxieties of Arab Sunnis, such as adding seats to the 275-member assembly to ensure greater Arab Sunni participation. Guaranteeing cabinet positions and a number of seats for Arab Sunnis on the constitutional committee was also proposed.

Shi'a groups protested. They asserted that postponement would "lead to more security and political problems that will help the terrorist forces continue their planning and that could result in more delays."[2] The Bush administration also rejected delay. Putting off the election would damage America's plans for Iraq's democratization. It would delay plans for writing Iraq's constitution and holding Iraq's presidential elections. Postponement would be an admission of failure. Elections were critical to Bush's success strategy and timetable for drawing down U.S. troops from Iraq.

After hyping Iraq's elections, U.S. officials confronted the reality of a Sunni boycott and systematically tried to lower expectations. Preparing the American public for more casualties, Bush warned that violence would continue even after Iraqis went to the polls. Zarqawi "declared an all-out war on this evil principle of democracy and those who follow this wrong ideology" and threatened to wash the streets of Baghdad in the blood of voters.[3]

Zarqawi also described elections as a "wicked plot to install Shiites in power." [4] Overcoming divisions among Shi'a, Sistani endorsed the United Iraqi Alliance, a unified slate of Shi'a parties including the Supreme Council for Islamic Revolution in Iraq and the Da'wa Party. Its platform emphasized unity, sovereignty and respect for Iraq's Islamic identity. After centuries of disenfranchisement, Iraq's Arab Shi'a were poised to take power.

———

U.S. relations with Iraq's neighbors continued to worsen. The administration accused Tehran of infiltrating Iraq with agents and money to subvert the political process. America's unwillingness to participate in the European nonproliferation initiative left Tehran convinced that the United States was bent on confrontation. Cooperation with the People's Mujahadeen to identify targets for potential U.S. air strikes against Iran's nuclear facilities further poisoned relations.

Turkey was also incensed. When Iraqi Kurds threatened to boycott elections in protest of the slow progress in restoring the rights of displaced Kurds from Kirkuk and other areas south of the 36th parallel, the Iraqi Electoral Commission extended the voter registration period allowing an additional 75,000 Kurds to add their names to Kirkuk's voter rolls. The move was a big step towards including Kirkuk in the province of Kurdistan.

Turkish military officials indicated that they were ready to intervene in the event of post-election clashes between Kurds and Turkmen. Calls for intervention intensified when General John Abizaid refused to take action against Turkey's nemesis, the Kurdistan Worker's Party, indicating that U.S. forces were too tied up fighting the insurgency. Turks were also anguished by kidnappings and killings of Turkish truck drivers and workers in Iraq.

U.S.-Syrian relations also worsened. The Bush administration blamed Damascus for failing to crack down on Iraqis who were using Syria as a command center to provide financial and logistical support to insurgents in Iraq. As a state sponsor of terrorism, Syria was already subject to limited U.S. economic sanctions. The administration sought new measures including steps by the Treasury Department to isolate Syria's banking system. After Iraq, Syrians believed that Bush wanted regime change in Syria.

— —

Though the Bush administration relied on the United Nations to give its stamp of legitimacy to Iraq's elections, it was growing increasingly distrustful of the world body and Secretary General Kofi Annan. Absent a dedicated protection force for UN personnel, Annan sent only a handful of UN electoral experts to Iraq. During an interview with the BBC, he asserted that the Iraq War was "illegal."[5] Annan wrote a letter to Allawi, Bush and Tony Blair on October 31, 2004 discouraging the use of force against insurgents in Fallujah and warning that military action would further alienate Arab Sunnis who already felt left out of the political process. (The letter was leaked to the press.) At the same time, Annan was facing criticism related to the corrupted UN Oil for Food Program, which had allowed huge kickbacks to Saddam Hussein. But instead of demanding Annan's immediate resignation over the scandal, Washington waited for former Federal Reserve chairman Paul A. Volker to conduct his investigation. A diminished secretary general would be easier to mold in service of U.S. interests.

On November 23, 2004—eighteen months after the war started – the Bush administration finally agreed to a regional conference on developments in Iraq. Foreign ministers from twenty countries, including

Britain, France, China and Russia, gathered with the heads of the UN, the European Commission, the Arab League and the Organization of the Islamic Conference. Emotions were raw in the wake of the Fallujah offensive. Though France and the Arab League demanded a timetable for withdrawing U.S. troops, delegates ultimately succeeded in hammering out consensus to support Iraq's political transition and calling upon the international community to assist with economic reconstruction. In addition, NATO begrudgingly decided to expand its training of Iraqi security forces increasing the number of non-U.S. trainers to 166.

— —

U.S. senators sought accountability for postwar problems in Iraq; Donald Rumsfeld was accused of a broad pattern of arrogance, misjudgments, and passing the buck. According to Senator Susan Collins: "I think there are increasing concerns about the secretary's leadership of the war, the repeated failures to predict the strengths of the insurgency, the lack of essential safety equipment for our troops, the reluctance to expand the number of troops. All of these are factors that are causing people to raise more questions about the secretary."[6] Despite the clamor in some circles on Capitol Hill and the media, Bush's public support for Rumsfeld never wavered. When Rumsfeld offered his resignation over prisoner abuses at Abu Ghraib, Bush publicly supported the defense secretary.

The architects of U.S. policy in Iraq were promoted in Bush's second term; Condoleezza Rice became U.S. secretary of state and Alberto R. Gonzalez, who influenced policy on the treatment of prisoners at Abu Ghraib and Guantanamo, became the attorney general.

On December 15, 2004, Bush presented the Presidential Medal of Freedom to General Tommy R. Franks, George J. Tenet and L. Paul Bremer III. Critics raised questions about the recipients. Franks deployed too few troops and failed to develop a plan for post-combat stability operations. Tenet allowed bogus intelligence to influence U.S. policy when he claimed that the existence of WMD in Iraq was a "slam dunk." Bremer's decrees and misjudgments helped fuel the insurgency and create the reconstruction fiasco. There was no award for Colin Powell, but he bought himself a new silver Corvette after leaving office.

A few days after Bush's second-term inauguration, Douglas Feith preempted demands for his removal by resigning as undersecretary of defense. He said that he was leaving government to spend more time with his family.

The same week Bush decorated Franks, Tenet, and Bremer, the United States discontinued its search for WMD. Without fanfare or notification, the Iraq Survey Group was formally disbanded and sent home. They never found illicit weapons. Saddam perpetuated the belief that he possessed WMD in order to portray an image of invincibility and keep dissent at bay. One can only wonder whether Iraqis might have been emboldened to overthrow the Ba'ath regime had UN weapons inspections run their course.

— —

Iraq had elections on January 30, 2005. The vote was a truly historic event. Jubilant Iraqis demonstrated great courage in going to the polls amidst threats of violence. The Iraqi Electoral Commission indicated that 8.5 million Iraqis, a turnout of 58 percent, went to the polls. Their reasons for voting were twofold: Iraqis were determined to exercise their democratic rights; many turned out because they saw elections as the best way to end the occupation.

As expected, Iraqi Shi'a and Kurds voted in large numbers. Sistani's United Iraqi Alliance won a slight majority of seats in the assembly. Iraqi Kurds were the big winners. With the second largest block of seats, the Kurds are playing a role as power-broker between Shi'a factions.

Arab Sunnis did not go to the polls; most were too scared or chose not to vote. Despite their paltry representation in the assembly, it is a hopeful sign that Arab Sunnis are participating in the constitutional committee and have accepted leadership positions in various ministries.

It is important to maintain perspective. Democracy involves much more than elections. It is about the distribution of power and systems of governance that enable representative rule.

— —

At every critical juncture in Iraq's political transition—establishment of the Iraqi Governing Council, the November 15 Agreement, adoption of the Transitional Administrative Law, the hand-over of sovereignty to an interim authority on June 28—the Bush administration claimed that Iraq was turning the corner. True to course, U.S. officials were exuberant about Iraq's elections of January 30. Alas, not much has changed. Violence continues unabated; the insurgency rages on. Democracy can only thrive in a stable and secure environment. The elections may prove to be yet another false horizon.

The real fight for power in Iraq will be over the permanent constitution. After decades of subjugation, some Shi'a seek dominance and the adoption of Shari'a law. The Kurds are adamant about secularism and federalism; Arab Sunnis demand decentralization and minority rights.

In accordance with Article 61(c) of the Transitional Administrative Law, both Kurds and Arab Sunnis are prepared to exercise a veto of the permanent constitution if their core concerns are not adequately addressed. Negotiations on the constitution are sure to sharpen differences. Not everyone will be satisfied with the outcome. Compromise and consent will be needed. Failure to harmonize competing claims could result in civil war and Iraq's bloody breakup.

If that were to happen, the United States would have to salvage what it could. If Iraq is dominated by religious extremists or slips into Taliban-like conditions and becomes a haven for terrorist recruitment, the United States would have to withdraw its forces to Iraqi Kurdistan. From there, it could still nurture Kurdistan's democratic development and derive benefit from Kirkuk's vast oil fields. It would be wrong to betray the Kurds again. The Bush administration must not abandon the Kurds to angry Iraqis and aggressive neighbors with whom it has so far failed to work effectively.

— —

Iraq today is facing many of the same challenges it faced emerging from colonial rule. In 1920, Iraqi tribes launched a rebellion against British occupation. Demonstrations started in the mosques of Baghdad and then spread to Karbala when a leading Shi'a cleric denounced British occupation. An increasingly brutal and well-organized insurgency attacked railway and telegraph lines to disrupt communications. Civilians were besieged and taken hostage, bodies mutilated. Britain suppressed the rebellion using harsh measures, but its occupation became untenable. Though Iraq achieved independence in 1932, British troops stayed until 1955.

Fast forward to today: Is Iraq really lost? To be sure, the ideal of a Jeffersonian style liberal democracy in Iraq perished almost immediately after U.S. forces tore down Saddam's statue in Firdos Square on April 9, 2003. The failure to implement a postwar plan brought unnecessary hardship to the Iraqi people. Delays in handing over sovereignty fueled the insurgency and embittered Iraqis.

By the date of Iraq's elections, 1,432 Americans had been killed and 10,662 wounded.[7] Estimates vary widely on the tens of thousands of Iraqis killed and injured. Including the 2005 fiscal year, military operations and reconstruction in Iraq are estimated to cost the United States $230 billion.[8]

As of this writing, Iraq's future remains uncertain. The January 30 elections could give rise to a legitimate government that enables the recruitment of an army that is able and willing to defend the country and its institutions. Iraqis were hopeful on election-day; their country might yet emerge stable, whole and free.

The United States will not occupy Iraq indefinitely. However, its exit strategy must be based on a sustainable outcome—not an arbitrary timetable. For the foreseeable future, or until the Iraqi government seeks its departure, the United States must remain engaged. The responsibility of Iraq's emerging democratic leaders does not obviate America's responsibility to assist with security and reconstruction.

Progress is in the interests of both Iraq and the United States; Iraq's future will shape U.S. foreign policy for decades to come. Despite delays and the Bush administration's mishandling of Iraq's political transition, Iraqis might yet succeed in fashioning their country into a federal democratic republic that acts as a catalyst for reform in the Middle East, as well as a bulwark against terrorism in the Muslim world.

David L. Phillips
New York City
February 22, 2005

ADDENDUM:

LESSONS IN NATION-BUILDING

Iraq will not be the last case in which the United States intervenes militarily to protect its security interests, remove weapons of mass destruction (WMD), or prevent genocide. The U.S. experience in Iraq offers important lessons about intervention and nation-building.

U.S. INTERESTS

Why should the United States care about rogue regimes or failed states? Simply put, unstable regimes are a threat to U.S. interests. Terror groups and criminal networks find haven in weak or failed states. They exploit porous borders to move people, money, weapons, and drugs. Human security is affected when government institutions are unable to meet basic needs or provide essential services. Poverty, disease, and humanitarian emergencies have transnational implications. Not only are conflict prevention and nation-building investments in U.S. security, they are also consistent with American ideals.

THE END-STATE

Clarity of purpose is critical. What was the reason for intervention? Was it to stop aggression, to prevent ethnic cleansing, to eradicate weapons of mass destruction, or to create a liberal democracy? Goals must be based on a realistic assessment of what can be achieved. Without a clear vision of the end-state, government agencies and international organizations will not know what to do.

Governments always feel pressure to complete the mission and execute an exit strategy. Self-imposed deadlines can be avoided by measuring progress in milestones; however, setting goals and moving quickly to achieve them does not obviate the need to sustain activities. Success is contingent upon the level of commitment as measured in time, manpower, and money—and only success can win "hearts and minds."

INTERNATIONAL COOPERATION

Burden-sharing and unity of command are the twin pillars of successful nation-building. Governments, regional organizations, multilateral bodies, international financial institutions, and nongovernmental organizations must define their respective responsibilities to develop a shared understanding, reduce redundancy, and maximize resources.

The United Nations is typically the vehicle through which the international community organizes collective action. Encompassing various aspects of nation-building—from peace and security to humanitarian relief and reconstruction—the UN has undertaken forty-one missions since 1990. Authorization under Chapter VII of the UN Charter enhances local and international legitimacy, enshrines political and security arrangements, and gives nation-building a clear mandate.

A holistic approach includes humanitarian relief, transitional security, rule of law, infrastructure reconstruction, economic development, and the political transition. During the immediate post-conflict period, activities focus on humanitarian assistance and quick-impact projects to jump-start the economy. Once conditions have stabilized, reconstruction emphasizes rebuilding physical infrastructure and creating conditions for investment and long-term economic development. The political transition involves elections at the local and national levels, adopting a permanent constitution, building democratic institutions across the country, and restoring full sovereignty.

Coordination is essential. Agencies should focus on areas of expertise. For example, the UN High Commissioner for Refugees (UNHCR) is best suited to assist the return of displaced persons. The European Union (EU) is experienced in economic development. Bretton Woods institutions—the World Bank and International Monetary Fund (IMF)—help broaden the donor base and contribute to economic restructuring. The Organization for Security and Cooperation in Europe (OSCE) has the skills needed to organize elections and promote civil society. Peacekeeping and police operations should provide protection to the field personnel of these various organizations.

Institutions must be adequately resourced to be effective. The political commitment and resources of G-8 and other countries can be leveraged through a Peace Implementation Council (PIC). The PIC encourages consensus among donors, concerned countries, and neighboring states. It also serves as a consultative framework to keep neighbors abreast of plans and to involve them in activities. For example, managing refugee flows requires a common approach to opening borders, as well as assistance and protection in accordance with international humanitarian law. Neighbors have legitimate concerns when a failed state exists on their borders, but they must not meddle in the internal affairs of other countries, nor must they unilaterally deploy troops across frontiers.

Burden-sharing is not a one-way street. If PIC members contribute to nation-building, they are also entitled to a reasonable share of the decisionmaking. It is also reasonable for them to expect a level playing field when it comes to reconstruction opportunities. The United States should not be concerned about losing control of the nation-building process. It retains influence by virtue of its leadership within the institutional hierarchies of international organizations. At the same time, U.S. interests are served by diffusing responsibility, thereby reducing costs and obligations. Efficiencies are to be encouraged, but nation-building cannot be done on the cheap. There is no such thing as "nation-building light."

A fast-moving emergency necessitates a rapid response. Though lag time will inevitably result, it can be reduced by integrating lessons learned and best practices from previous nation-building experiences. A standby response corps, a database of nation-building experts, and a standing crisis-response fund can help prevent delays.

The United States needs to bridge the gap during the early stages of a crisis or when negotiations become bogged down at the UN Security Council. To create a secure environment for nation-building, the military needs a clear mission and adequate resources for addressing security and related challenges. The military must pivot quickly from combat operations to civilian administration. To this end, civilian planning and civil-military relations should be integrated into all phases of planning and post-conflict stability operations.

SECURITY

Nation-building is impossible without adequate security. The economy cannot revive when conflict is widespread. Looting destroys infrastructure and productive capacity. The transport of goods becomes immobilized. Foreign investment is deterred. Violence also undermines the political transition by making people too frightened to participate in the political process.

Measures are needed to fill the power vacuum and prevent looting, chaos, and general malfeasance. Essential infrastructure and institutions must be identified in advance and protected. Forces should be deployed to seal borders and prevent infiltration by terror groups or criminal gangs. The recurrence of conflict can also be prevented by separating former combatants, demarcating a zone of separation, and sequestering heavy weapons into designated cantonment areas under international control.

There is a big difference between fighting a war and winning the peace. A mechanized attack using precision weaponry can overwhelm the enemy, but it may not involve enough troops to prevent looting when existing structures crumble. After fighting and winning a war, stability operations emphasize the need to create conditions for the provision of essential services and humanitarian relief. Different tasks require different capabilities.

Because security and nation-building are interconnected, civilian and security structures should overlap to prevent important tasks from slipping through the cracks. Incorporating civilian affairs into troop deployments builds bonds between peacekeepers and affected populations. Provincial reconstruction teams should include civilian and military personnel. Commanders must also focus on security for the local population, not just force protection.

In addition to conventional peacekeeping, recurring conflict can be prevented by dismantling indigenous security structures. Though individuals who committed atrocities must not be allowed to reemerge, not all former members of the security services are guilty of war crimes. A process is needed to demobilize the armed forces formally so that, after vetting, some personnel can be incorporated into a reconstituted military.

Despite the importance of coordination between civilian and military authorities, there is still need for a clear differentiation of their respective responsibilities at different stages of the conflict cycle. Though the military may take the lead at the outset, including efforts to meet the humanitarian needs of vulnerable populations, the U.S. Department of Defense should not control indefinitely the political and economic dimensions of post-conflict transition. Troops can help create conditions for registering voters and conducting elections. However, the Pentagon lacks expertise to do basic nation-building, such as organizing elections and drafting a constitution.

It is optimum for the UN Security Council (UNSC) to authorize peacekeeping. When the UNSC is unable to act, NATO should take the lead. A U.S.-led coalition of the willing is the last resort. Regardless, a readily deployable, well-trained cadre of security personnel is essential.

CONSTABULARY FORCES

To make sure that the military is not saddled with the full panoply of peacekeeping responsibilities, the peacekeeping timetable should be coordinated with efforts to stand-up civilian police capabilities. Constabulary forces, such as U.S. Civilian Police (CivPol), Italy's Carabinieri, Spain's Guardia Civil, and France's Gendarmerie, can serve as a bridge between the deployment of military forces and the establishment of competent domestic police and law-enforcement structures.

As they meet the immediate requirements of local law enforcement, constabulary forces can also train and mentor local law-enforcement officers. In 2003, the G-8 summit agreed to build a global constabulary capacity with a police training center in Italy. The Initiative is worth while and should be supported. More than infrastructure protection, counterterrorism, and fighting organized crime, training of constabularies should include internationally recognized standards of human rights and democratic policing.

A plan is also needed for dealing with local militias so that spoilers are not able to disrupt progress. After disbanding, local militias could be trained as a national guard to participate in disaster-response, search-and-rescue, and de-mining efforts. Militias are always reluctant to disarm until they believe they are safe and that other militias are being treated comparably. To promote disarmament, innovative weapons-buy-back programs not only reduce the potential for violence but also inject funds into the local economy. While maintaining unity of command, different countries should assume distinct roles: creating the army, training police, strengthening the justice sector, supporting disarmament, and combating transnational crime. The United Nations can help in areas where it has expertise such as disarming, demobilizing, and reintegrating combatants and militia groups.

HUMANITARIAN ACTION

The most urgent requirement is providing protection and assistance to vulnerable populations; this is especially true during the first days of conflict when most civilian casualties occur. Before conflict escalates, the United States and the international community can prepare by working with NGOs and UN agencies to acquire food, potable water, and shelter materials. So that resources and expertise can be dispatched immediately and with minimum bureaucratic constraints, U.S. bodies such as the Office of Foreign Disaster Assistance (OFDA) and the Food for Peace Program should incorporate surge capacity into their contingency planning. As evidenced by the tsunami response in South Asia, the military's logistical capabilities make it the most efficient first responder during a fast-moving humanitarian crisis. However, military systems and personnel are not trained or equipped to engage in the transition from relief to rehabilitation and then to reconstruction.

The military's involvement in humanitarian operations raises other issues. The International Committee of the Red Cross (ICRC) and humanitarian NGOs do not want to be stigmatized as instruments of a foreign power. The kidnapping and killing of aid workers is a side effect when the distinction between military operatives and civilian aid workers is blurred. Donor countries are often reluctant to support humanitarian activities controlled by the U.S. military.

Integrating U.S. and UN humanitarian agencies into all aspects of planning and service delivery helps ensure a smooth segue from combat operations to multilateral post-conflict reconstruction. The United Nations Humanitarian Coordinator can play a pivotal role complementing aid efforts and making the most of scarce resources. The humanitarian coordinator assists UN agencies such as the High Commissioner for Refugees (UNHCR), the World Food Programme (WFP), and the UN Development Programme's Bureau of Crisis Prevention and Recovery (BCPR). Coordination should also involve U.S. bodies—the Office of Transitional Initiatives (OTI) and the Disaster Assistance Relief Team (DART). A stand-by crisis-response fund can help cushion the lag between the onset of a crisis and the international donor's conference, as well as the gap between making pledges and delivering resources.

Humanitarian assistance is not just about providing food, blankets, and potable water. Vulnerable populations need to feel they are able to restore some modicum of control over their lives. To empower victims and avoid long-term dependency, aid agencies should develop a partnership with beneficiaries. Reconciliation can also be advanced by incorporating peace-building strategies into phases of humanitarian action.

Once population flows and emergency conditions stabilize, foreign aid is still needed to move from relief to development. War-torn countries lack resources and, therefore, need funds to pay government salaries, support civilian administration, and provide essential services such as health care. Requirements are endless. For example, assistance is needed to repair damaged infrastructure such as the electricity system that powers water and sewerage systems.

Anti-personnel land mines are another tragic legacy of conflict, maiming victims for years after the fighting has stopped. Land mine centers raise awareness, conduct de-mining, and provide prosthetics and counseling to traumatized victims. Training former members of the armed forces in land mine clearance provides them with employment and should be incorporated into an overall strategy for security-sector reform.

A system is also needed to manage the early, orderly, and peaceful return of displaced persons and so avoid violence and acts of revenge. A property claims and compensation commission can help identify rightful owners. In situations where the property has been destroyed or cannot be reclaimed, the commission may also provide compensation. Managing the return of displaced persons should also be linked to employment-generation, family unification, and other efforts to improve social and economic conditions.

ECONOMY

Achieving peace and prosperity can be undermined by economic stagnation causing anger and exacerbating conditions of insecurity. Such frustrations can be mitigated by quick-impact projects that provide short-term employment (e.g. clearing mines, rubble, and debris). Such projects not only compensate people for their work, but also help restore self-respect. Whereas stopgap employment meets immediate needs, it is no substitute for a real job or a genuine long-term commercial opportunity. Integrating UNDP and World Bank development planning with humanitarian assistance and quick-impact projects helps maximize opportunities for sustainable economic development.

Though economic reconstruction is easier in countries with a modern economy, it still takes a long time to address poverty and other root causes of conflict. Contracts to rebuild utilities, roads, and bridges should give preferences to local firms and contractors that meet local hiring quotas. Assistance must not focus exclusively on big-ticket projects lest money not find its way into the local economy.

The transition from relief to development can start with donor funds, but to be sustainable it needs foreign direct investment (FDI). Privatization of former state-owned industries also stimulates jobs and develops a tax base. Because FDI occurs when there are viable industries, consumer countries can help by extending duty-free and quota-free arrangements. When FDI occurs in the extractive industries, multinational corporations should publish their earnings to ensure transparent revenue-sharing. In addition, a percentage of revenues should be deposited into a trust fund for local communities. To guard against corruption, donors and local authorities should set up a review board to oversee spending from FDI.

Steps are also needed to reduce the debt burden. To this end, the World Bank should avoid making loans that poor countries can not repay. Concessional grants are preferred. In addition, creditors should convene at the earliest possible time to reconfigure repayment schedules and consider maximum possible debt forgiveness. Debt relief helps reduce poverty and allows the government to spend more on social services and essential infrastructure.

Privatization is needed, but not right away. Premature privatization can result in the transfer of assets to politically connected individuals and corruption that undermines the rule of law and erodes public confidence in the government. Before selling off state-owned assets, steps should be taken to build them up so they are not undervalued. Building assets and preserving human capital can also be enhanced through tax breaks and other concessions that encourage participation by the country's diaspora, including investment.

Priority should be placed on developing a strong private banking system with stringent licensing procedures, capital requirements, and close oversight by the central government authorities. To stabilize currency values and build confidence, the central bank could temporarily anchor the local currency to the most trusted and widely used foreign currency.

Post-conflict countries typically have little or no tax revenues as a result of the almost total collapse of their national economies, as well as governance short-comings. Inability to control national frontiers contributes to smuggling that further deprives the government of customs revenues and gives rise to organized criminal networks. Border control and customs collection are priorities.

POLITICAL TRANSITION

Democracy is often synonymous with elections, but elections are not an end unto themselves. Free and fair elections are the best way to involve all stakeholders and eliminate zero-sum demands. However, early elections run the risk of restoring to power the same leaders who fomented conflict in the first place. Should elections entrench spoilers, elections can impede democratization. Early elections are often driven by the international community's desire to meet deadlines and address their domestic constituencies.

Elections must be carefully organized. A population census is needed. An election law and legislation governing political parties must be prepared. Voter education and candidate training are necessary. An electoral commission must also be established. While proceeding carefully, authorities should avoid delays lest they generate resentment among the local population. Only a credible political process can offer an alternative to violence as a means for achieving political objectives.

The UN Office for Electoral Assistance and the Organization for Security and Cooperation in Europe (OSCE), have developed a system for organizing elections in post-conflict countries. They have experience developing electoral laws and physical infrastructure for conducting the ballot. Eligible candidates, excluding persons who committed war crimes, are certified. And security is enhanced so that voters can go to the polls free from fear. If all goes well, international observers confirm that elections were free and fair. Whereas national elections are a milestone in nation-building, it is better to build democratic institutions, strengthen civil society, and start with local elections.

At the central government level, a national constitution is needed to define checks and balances; these, in turn, enhance accountability and minimize corruption. In addition, the constitution should codify the rights and responsibilities of citizens. It is never advisable to impose a constitution that does not enjoy popular support. Making a constitution requires a transparent and participatory process. After the constitution is drafted, it should be debated, disseminated, and ultimately ratified in a popular referendum. Just as establishing a government-in-exile raises questions of legitimacy, constitution-making must be a local process.

Though the international community can support nation-building by, for example, placing expatriate staff as advisers within government ministries, it must never supplant local participation. To develop a capable technocracy, recruitment and promotion systems must be based on merit, not loyalty. Quotas are one way to ensure representative government; however, they also run the risk of entrenching existing ethnic and religious divisions. Another problem is dealing with former officials who were associated with the previous regime. Lustration laws can help weed out war criminals by removing offenders from their posts and keeping them from serving in government or running for public office. Moreover, a transitional justice strategy is needed to promote the rule of law and guide the democratization process.

TRANSITIONAL JUSTICE

Transitional justice seeks to prosecute those who have committed atrocities, to deter future crimes, and to create conditions of peace through reconciliation. It involves the dismantling of state structures responsible for human rights abuses while retaining those that can play a constructive role in creating conditions for national reconciliation. The goal is to hold accountable the perpetrators of human rights violations so that victims believe that justice prevails. A delicate balance exists between truth and reconciliation. Amnesty can not replace accountability. Nor can truth-telling be a substitute for justice.

Rather than wielding a blunt instrument, transitional justice uses precise techniques targeting individuals. Holding individuals accountable not only obviates collective guilt but also prevents a witch hunt and the continued cycle of violence. An interim criminal-justice system made up of international lawyers, judges, and penal experts is needed to fill the gap until indigenous capabilities can be reconstituted. However, the interim system is just a stopgap measure and it must not replace efforts by local actors.

NGOs and civil society also play a key role. Civil society is virtually nonexistent in countries emerging from a long period of authoritarian rule. To become effective participants in the democratic process, NGOs need training in organizational development and advocacy. Training should focus on negotiation, consensus, and team-building skills. It should also address interaction with government bodies, political parties, and the media, as well as methods and tools of effective advocacy.

Many opportunities exist for NGOs to help shape policies and programs. For example, NGOs can work with the Education Ministry to eliminate negative stereotyping in academic curricula and to develop educational materials that incorporate conflict resolution. NGOs may also participate in public-opinion research, including polling and focus groups to set priorities and help guide political-participation strategies.

Female participation maximizes the potential of women as peacemakers. Policies and programs promoting gender equity include access to education by young girls. Policies should also involve fostering the awareness and understanding of women's rights. In addition, the role of women is enhanced through vocational-skills training and support in generating income, including access to credit. Gender equity should be a part of all development and governance activities.

Women are an important pillar of civil society that helps keep governments accountable. Civil society monitors government and exposes corruption and other abuses of power. Efforts to enforce transparency are enhanced through access to information at Internet cafés and by way of other information technology. Although the media can be effective in strengthening democracy and creating a climate for reconciliation, it should not be allowed to spread vitriol or to undermine national progress by propagating ethnic divisions.

PUBLIC DIPLOMACY

Public diplomacy utilizes radio, satellite, Internet, and local television stations, as well as regional and national newspapers, to provide information on security, services, and other issues with direct bearing on citizens' day-to-day lives. International efforts in assisting nation-building should also use public diplomacy to justify aims and explain plans to the affected population and the governments of neighboring states. To avoid the impression that public diplomacy is another form of propaganda, an advisory council of local experts could be established to evaluate the effectiveness of public-diplomacy efforts and recommend measures enhancing local media and investments in media infrastructure. Even if stakeholders disapprove of nation-building activities, it is better that they know about them instead of being taken by surprise. It is easier to create a positive impression during the early stages of a mission than to correct negative impressions that become ingrained over time.

U.S. COORDINATING STRUCTURE

After Afghanistan and Iraq, the Bush administration recognized that it lacked an interagency focal point to manage the complex political, economic, and military dimensions of post-conflict transitions. The State Department's Office for the Coordinator of Reconstruction and Stabilization (S/CRS) was established in July 2004. S/CRS brings together working-level officials from the State Department, Department of Defense, U.S. Agency for International Development, Central Intelligence Agency, Joint Forces Command, the Army Corps of Engineers, and the Treasury Department. Coordination is commendable. However, S/CRS has no decision-making authority. It is just another layer of the government's bureaucracy that lacks the capability to put war-torn countries on the path to sustainable peace.

A presidential directive should create a nation-building directorate within the White House's National Security Council. The directorate would provide coherence and avoid overlapping efforts while strengthening and permanently institutionalizing the U.S. response to post-conflict emergencies. The directorate would:

- Manage resources and develop policy options for the president.
- Overcome interagency infighting that can cause mission paralysis.
- Track weak or failed states and monitor the nation-building efforts.
- Foster cooperation with international partners and NGOs.
- Apply lessons learned and best practices.

FINAL THOUGHTS

Iraq is the seventh major U.S.-led reconstruction effort in a decade.* If the idea was to create a model democracy in the heart of the Arab world, Iraq was not the place to start.

---

*They are Somalia, Liberia, Haiti, Bosnia, Kosovo, Afghanistan, and Iraq.

Iraqis lack a sense of national identity. They are deeply divided along ethnic and sectarian lines. There is no tradition of participation in politics. Leadership has always been about power and force. Iraq's infrastructure was badly degraded by years of sanctions, war, and neglect. Sanctions led to corruption and the emergence of a pervasive black-market economy that destroyed the middle class. Iraq's neighbors were obstructionist and wary of democratization.

Problems were compounded by the lack of international cooperation and the failure to share responsibility for nation-building with Iraqis and the international community. Many countries were alienated when the United States rushed to war, almost unilaterally and under false pretenses. Reconstructing Iraq would have been hard to begin with; however, mistakes made it even harder.

There is an adage that goes "When you're digging a hole, stop digging." For too long, the Bush administration did not admit its failures and change course.

Alliances are assets, not inconveniences. Partnerships are needed to meet daunting challenges in Iraq and around the world. Though the United States is the world's wealthiest and most powerful nation, it cannot address global challenges alone. The United States must learn from its mistakes in Iraq so that it does not repeat them elsewhere.

Appendix A:

Acronyms

ACDA . . . . . . .Arms Control and Disarmament Agency
AID . . . . .U.S. Agency for International Development
AIPAC . . . . . . .American Israel Public Affairs Committee
AKP . . . . .Justice and Development Party in Turkey
BPRM . . . . . . .State Department's Bureau of Population, Refugees,
                   and Migration
CENTCOM . .Central Command
CIA . . . . .Central Intelligence Agency
CPA . . . . .Coalition Provisional Authority
DART . . . . . . .Disaster Assistance Relief Team
DCM . . . . . . .Deputy Chief of Mission
DFI . . . . .Development Fund for Iraq
DIA . . . . .Defense Intelligence Agency
DOD . . . . . . .Department of Defense
DPD . . . . .Defense Policy Board
EU . . . . .European Union
FDI . . . . .Foreign Direct Investment
FIF . . . . .Free Iraqi Forces
GAO . . . . . . .Government Accounting Office
IAEA . . . . . . .International Atomic Energy Agency
ICDC . . . . . . .Iraqi Civil Defense Corps
ICRC . . . . . . .International Committee of the Red Cross
ID . . . . .Infantry Division
IDPs . . . . . . .Internally Displaced Persons
IG . . . . .Inspector General
IGC . . . . .Iraqi Governing Council
IIA . . . . .Interim Iraqi Administration
ILAC . . . . . . .Iraqi Liberation Action Committee
IMF . . . . .International Monetary Fund

INA . . . . .Iraqi Naitonal Accord
INC . . . . .Iraq National Congress
INR . . . . .State Department's Bureau of Intelligence and Research
IRC . . . . .International Rescue Committee
ITF . . . . .Iraqi Turkmen Front
JINSA . . . . . .Jewish Institute for National Security Affairs
KDP . . . . . . .Kurdistan Democratic Party
KNC . . . . . . .Kurdish National Congress of North America
KRG . . . . . . .Kurdistan Regional Government
LPG . . . . . . .Liquefied Petroleum Gas
MEK . . . . . . .Mujahadeen e-Khalkq
NATO . . . . . .North Atlantic Treaty Organization
NDU . . . . . . .National Defense University
NEA . . . . . . .State Department's Bureau for Near Eastern Affairs
NGA . . . . . . .State Department's Office of Northern Gulf Affairs
NGO . . . . . .Non-Governmental Organization
NIE . . . . .National Intelligence Estimate
NSC . . . . . . .National Security Council
OFAC . . . . . .Treasury Department's Office of Foreign Assets Control
ORHA . . . . . .Office for Reconstruction and Humanitarian Assistance
OSCE . . . . . .Organization for Security and Cooperation in Europe
OSD . . . . . . .Office of the Secretary of Defense
OSP . . . . . . .Office of Special Plans
OTI . . . . .Office of Transitional Initiatives
OVP . . . . . . .Office of the Vice President
PIC . . . . .Peace Implementation Council
PKK . . . . . . .Kurdistan Worker's Party
PNAC . . . . . .Project for the New American Century
PUK . . . . . . .Patriotic Union of Kurdistan
QIZ . . . . .Qualified Industrial Zone
RCC . . . . . . .Revolutionary Command Council
RPGs . . . . . . .Rocket-Propelled Grenades
SCIRI . . . . . .Supreme Council for Islamic Revolution in Iraq
S/CRS . . . . . .State Department Office for the Coordinator of
                 Reconstruction and Stabilization
TAL . . . . . . .Transitional Administrative Law
TGNA . . . . . .Turkish Grand National Assembly
TGS . . . . . . .Turkish General Staff
UN . . . . .United Nations
UNDP . . . . . .United Nations Development Programme
UNHCR . . . . .United Nations High Commissioner for Refugees
UNSC . . . . . .United Nations Security Council
WFP . . . . . . .World Food Programme
WMD . . . . . .Weapons of Mass Destruction

APPENDIX B:

TIMELINE OF MAJOR EVENTS

2002

JANUARY 29: President George W. Bush delivers his "axis of evil" speech to the U.S. Congress.

JULY 5: The author crosses the Tigris River to meet with Iraqis and discuss power-sharing constitutional arrangements.

AUGUST 8: Iraqi opposition leaders meet senior U.S. officials and agree to organize a political conference to plan Iraq's transition.

AUGUST 21: Bush and his national security advisers gather in Crawford to discuss regime change in Iraq.

AUGUST 26: Cheney addresses the Veterans of Foreign Wars Association Convention: "There is no doubt that Saddam Hussein now has weapons of mass destruction."

SEPTEMBER 3-5. The Future of Iraq Project's Democratic Principles Working Group holds its first meeting and establishes task forces.

SEPTEMBER 12: Bush addresses the United Nations General Assembly and challenges the world body to enforce Iraq's disarmament obligations.

SEPTEMBER 20: The National Security Strategy codifies the Doctrine of Preemption.

OCTOBER 1: The National Intelligence Estimate releases warnings that, left unchecked, Iraq could develop a nuclear device during this decade.

OCTOBER 4: The Democratic Principles Working Group's coordinating committee meets in Washington, D.C., to review progress of the task forces.

OCTOBER 7: Bush gives a speech at the Cincinnati Museum Center asserting that Iraq is reconstituting its nuclear program and alleging ties between al-Qaeda and Iraq.

OCTOBER 8–10: The Democratic Principles Working Group meets at Wilton Park in Surrey, U.K.

NOVEMBER 8: The United Nations Security Council unanimously adopts UNSC Resolution 1441, giving Iraq its last chance to disarm.

DECEMBER 14–17: The Iraqi Opposition Conference is held in London.

2003

JANUARY 21: The White House assigns responsibility for postwar reconstruction to the Office of the Secretary of Defense (OSD), which establishes the Office for Reconstruction and Humanitarian Assistance (ORHA).

FEBRUARY 4: Powell and Yasar Yakis, Turkey's foreign minister, discuss U.S. aid to Turkey.

FEBRUARY 5: Powell briefs the United Nations Security Council on Iraq's weapons of mass destruction (WMD).

FEBRUARY 6: Khalilzad meets Turkish officials, Kurdish representatives, and the Iraqi Turkmen Front in Ankara.

FEBRUARY 11: Marc Grossman and Douglas Feith testify on postwar plans before the Senate Foreign Relations Committee.

FEBRUARY 21–22: ORHA conducts a rehearsal of the postwar mission at the National Defense University.

FEBRUARY 24: The United States, Britain, and Spain introduce a UN resolution authorizing the use of force but it fails to garner support.

MARCH 1: Turkey's Grand National Assembly fails to approve the transit of the U.S. Army's Fourth Infantry Division through Turkey into northern Iraq.

MARCH 10: Recep Tayyip Erdogan meets Bush in the Oval Office to discuss the war in Iraq.

MARCH 17: Bush delivers an ultimatum to Saddam Hussein to leave the country within forty-eight hours or face an attack.

MARCH 19: The U.S. and U.K. launch "shock and awe" with a decapitation strike targeting Saddam Hussein at Dora Farms.

MARCH 20: The ground invasion begins.

MARCH 26: U.S. forces launch operations in northern Iraq.

MARCH 30: Donald Rumsfeld is criticized for not deploying enough ground troops.

APRIL 1: Jessica Lynch is rescued.

APRIL 5: U.S. forces enter Baghdad.

APRIL 6: Iraqi political leader Ahmad Chalabi and his Free Iraqi Forces are airlifted to Nasariyah. British troops take control of Basra.

APRIL 9: Baghdad falls and U.S. Marines help pull down the statue of Saddam Hussein in Firdos Square.

APRIL 14: The Pentagon declares an end to major combat operations after U.S. forces take control of Tikrit.

APRIL 15: Iraqis meet in Nasariyah to discuss the political transition.

APRIL 20: Gen. Jay Garner enters Baghdad.

MAY 1: Bush announces "mission accomplished" and the end of major combat operations.

MAY 11: Ambassador L. Paul Bremer III takes over from Garner.

MAY 16: Bremer issues a decree disestablishing the Ba'ath Party.

MAY 20: Chalabi moves into the Baghdad Hunting Club, establishing INC offices in Baghdad.

MAY 22: The UN Security Council lifts economic sanctions against Iraq.

MAY 23: Bremer issues a decree disbanding the Iraqi armed forces.

JULY 4: Turkish Special Forces are detained, hooded, and expelled for plotting to assassinate Kurdish officials in northern Iraq.

JULY 7: The Bush administration withdraws its claim that Iraq was trying to buy uranium from Africa.

JULY 13: The twenty-five-member Iraqi Governing Council is established.

JULY 16: Gen. John Abizaid calls attacks on coalition troops a "guerrilla-type campaign" and says troops may be deployed for up to one year.

JULY 22: Uday and Qusay Hussein are killed by U.S. forces in Mosul.

AUGUST 7: A large car bomb explodes near the Jordanian Embassy, killing eleven people and wounding fifty.

AUGUST 14: The UN Security Council approves resolution 1500 endorsing the Iraqi Governing Council.

AUGUST 19: The UN's Baghdad office is bombed, killing Sergio Vieira de Mello and twenty-one others.

AUGUST 21: Ali Hassan al-Majid ("Chemical Ali") is captured.

AUGUST 29: Bombing in Najaf kills eighty-three people, including SCIRI's Mohammed Bakr al-Hakim.

SEPTEMBER 2: The Iraqi Governing Council names twenty-five ministers responsible for day-to-day affairs.

SEPTEMBER 7: Bush requests $87 billion to cover additional military and reconstruction costs.

OCTOBER 5: The Iraqi Stabilization Group is established by Condoleezza Rice to coordinate reconstruction and transition activities.

OCTOBER 14: A car bomb explodes outside the Turkish Mission in Baghdad.

OCTOBER 16: The UN Security Council unanimously approves a resolution endorsing an international force under U.S. authority and calling on the Governing Council to submit to the UN a timetable/plan for drafting the constitution and holding elections by December 15, 2003.

OCTOBER 23: Cpl. Charles A. Graner Jr. photographs Pfc. Lyndie England holding a leash around the neck of a naked Iraqi and other prisoner abuse at Abu Ghraib.

OCTOBER 23–24: $37.5 billion in aid and credits is pledged at the Madrid donors' conference.

OCTOBER 26: Insurgents launch a rocket attack targeting Paul Wolfowitz at the al-Rashid Hotel.

OCTOBER 29: U.S. combat deaths in Iraq reach 117, more than died before combat was declared over.

NOVEMBER 1: A truck bomb explodes at the Italian Carabinieri headquarters in Nassiriyah, killing fourteen people.

NOVEMBER 2: Sixteen U.S. soldiers die when insurgents shoot down a Chinook transport helicopter near Fallujah.

NOVEMBER 15: The CPA and Iraqi Governing Council sign an agreement to draft an interim constitution by February 28 and transfer power by July 1.

NOVEMBER 27: President Bush visits Baghdad for Thanksgiving.

DECEMBER 13: Saddam Hussein captured near Tikrit

2004

JANUARY 4: Osama bin Laden says the U.S. war in Iraq is the beginning of the "occupation" of Gulf States for oil and calls for an expanded "holy war" in the Middle East.

JANUARY 11: Grand Ayatollah Ali al-Sistani rejects the U.S. proposal for indirect caucus-style elections.

JANUARY 14: Lt. Gen. Ricardo S. Sanchez begins a criminal investigation over incidents at Abu Ghraib.

JANUARY 15: Shi'a demonstrate, demanding direct elections.

JANUARY 17: The number of U.S. soldiers killed in Iraq since the start of the war reaches five hundred.

JANUARY 19: The United States asks the United Nations to resolve the impasse over elections.

JANUARY 28: David Kay testifies that no WMD have been found in Iraq and that prewar intelligence was "almost all wrong."

FEBRUARY 1: In Erbil, a double suicide attack on the KDP and PUK kills 101 Kurds.

FEBRUARY 8: Japanese troops arrive in Iraq for their first overseas deployment since World War II.

FEBRUARY 12: UN Envoy Lakhdar Brahimi visits Iraq to assess the feasibility of direct elections and meets with Sistani.

FEBRUARY 21: UN Secretary General Kofi Annan tells the Security Council that "elections cannot be held before the end of June (but) that the June 30 date for the handover of sovereignty must be respected."

FEBRUARY 23: Brahimi issues a report concluding that the earliest that credible, direct elections could be held would be late 2004 or early 2005.

FEBRUARY 26: Sistani drops demand for national elections by June 30 but insists they be held by end of 2004.

MARCH 2: In Karbala and Baghdad, 271 Shi'a celebrating the holy festival of Ashura are killed.

MARCH 8: The Iraqi Governing Council adopts the Transitional Administrative Law.

MARCH 21: Six U.S. soldiers are charged and eleven suspended for indecency and assaulting Iraqi prisoners at Abu Ghraib.

MARCH 31: Iraqis in Fallujah ambush and mutilate the bodies of four American contractors.

APRIL 4: Attacks against coalition forces are launched in Kufa, Karbala, Najaf, al-Kut, and Sadr City.

APRIL 5: U.S. officials issue an arrest warrant for Moqtada al-Sadr; U.S. forces attack Fallujah.

APRIL 11: A ceasefire is announced for Fallujah after two members of the Iraqi Governing Council resign in protest of U.S. military actions.

APRIL 14: U.S. accepts Brahimi's proposals for a caretaker government to replace the Iraqi Governing Council on June 30.

APRIL 22: Bremer announces that some Ba'ath Party officials will be allowed to resume their positions.

APRIL 28: Brahimi reports to the UN Security Council that by the end of May he will select a transitional government serving until elections in late 2004 or early 2005.

APRIL 30: Physical and sexual abuse of Iraqi prisoners at Abu Ghraib is reported in the U.S. media. Security responsibilities for Fallujah are transferred to the Fallujah Brigade.

MAY 5: Bush appears on two Arab television stations to condemn prisoner abuse at Abu Ghraib.

MAY 11: A video on the Internet shows Nick Berg being beheaded.

MAY 17: Ezzedine Salim, head of the Iraqi Governing Council, is killed in a car bombing.

MAY 20: Iraqi police raid Chalabi's home, confiscating files and computer equipment.

MAY 27: U.S. forces and the Mahdi Army reach a truce after seven weeks of fighting in Najaf.

MAY 28: Iraq's interim administration is announced; Ghazi al-Yawar is president and Ayad Allawi is prime minister.

JUNE 1: The Iraqi Governing Council dissolves itself immediately rather than wait for the official handover of sovereignty on June 30.

JUNE 8: The UN Security Council unanimously passes resolution 1546 endorsing the Iraqi interim administration and authorizing a U.S.-led multinational force to remain in Iraq through January 2006.

JUNE 16: The 9/11 Commission states that there is "no credible evidence that Iraq and al-Qaeda cooperated on attacks against the United States."

JUNE 28: The CPA transfers power back to Iraqis two days ahead of schedule.

Appendix C:

Personalities

Gen. John Abizaid: Head of Central Command for the Department of Defense (2003–present).

Morton I. Abramowitz: Senior Fellow at the Century Foundation, former President of the Carnegie Endowment, former U.S. Ambassador to Turkey, and former Assistant Secretary of State.

Fouad Ajami: Majid Khadduri Associate Professor and Director of Middle East Studies at Johns Hopkins University; Contributing Editor, *U.S. News and World Report*; and Consultant for CBS News.

Sharif Ali: Head of London-based Iraqi opposition faction; first cousin of King Faisal II, who was deposed and killed in a 1958 coup.

Ayad Allawi: Head of the Iraqi National Accord; interim Prime Minister of Iraq (2004–2005).

Kofi Annan: United Nations Secretary General (1997–present).

Richard L. Armitage: Deputy Secretary of State (2001–2005), former President of Armitage Associates L.C. (1993–2001).

Mohammed Atta: Leader of the 9/11 terror attacks

Ghassan Attiyah: Iraqi Sunni Arab who participated in the Democratic Principles Working Group of the Future of Iraq Project.

Jose Maria Aznar: Prime Minister of Spain (1996–2004).

Egeman Bagis: Foreign Policy Adviser to Turkey's Prime Minister Erdogan, Deputy in the Turkish Parliament, and Chair of the Parliament's Turkey-U.S. Friendship Caucus.

James A. Baker III: Senior Partner at Baker Botts, LLP; White House Chief of Staff (1992–1993); Secretary of State (1989–1992); Secretary of the Treasury (1985–1988); and White House Chief of Staff (1981–1985).

Mula Mustafa Barzani: Kurdish leader (1904–1979).

Massoud Barzani: Leader of the Kurdistan Democratic Party (KDP) and son of Mula Mustafa Barzani.

Nechervan Barzani: KDP Prime Minister and nephew of Massoud Barzani.

Maj. Gen. John R. S. Batiste: Commander of the U.S. Army's 1st Infantry Division.

Hamid al-Bayati: Deputy Foreign Minister of Iraq (2003–present) and former SCIRI representative in London.

Silvio Berlusconi: Prime Minister of Italy (2001–present).

Joseph R. Biden, Jr.: Democratic Senator from Delaware (1972–present).

Robert D. Blackwill: President of Barbour Griffith & Rogers, International who spent 22 years in the foreign service with posts in Nairobi, London, and Tel Aviv before joining the National Security Council and working on Iraq.

Tony Blair: British Prime Minister (1997–present).

Barbara K. Bodine: Responsible for ORHA's central sector, including Baghdad; former U.S. Ambassador to Yemen.

John R. Bolton: Undersecretary of State of Arms Control and International Security Affairs (2001–present); Senior Vice President of the American Enterprise Institute (1999–2001); Assistant Secretary of State for International Organization Affairs (1989–1993); and former Assistant Attorney General, Department of Justice (1985–1989).

Barbara Boxer: Democratic Senator from California (1992–present).

Lakhdar Brahimi: Special Adviser to the UN Secretary General (2004–present), former Special Representative of the Secretary General for Afghanistan and Head of the United Nations Assistance Mission in Afghanistan (2001–2004).

L. Paul Bremer III: Civilian Administrator of Iraq (2003–2004), Chairman and CEO of Marsh Crisis Consulting (2000–2003), Managing Director of Kissinger Associates (1989–2000), Ambassador-at-Large for Counterterrorism (1986–1989), and Ambassador to the Netherlands (1983–1986).

Francis Brooke: Assistant to Ahmad Chalabi and Director of the Iraq Liberation Action Committee.

Sam Brownback: Republican Senator from Kansas (1996–present).

George H. W. Bush: 41st President of the United States of America.

George W. Bush: 43rd President of the United States of America.

Sgt. Jeff Butler: Member of the U.S. Army's 418th Civil Affairs Battalion.

Robert C. Byrd: Democratic Senator from West Virginia (1959–present).

Andrew Card: White House Chief of Staff (2001–present).

Tim Carney: Appointed to ORHA by Paul Wolfowitz.

Ilnur Cevik: Editor of the *Turkish Daily News*.

Lincoln D. Chaffee: Republican Senator from Rhode Island (1999–present).

Ahmad Chalabi: Chairman of the Iraqi National Congress (1992–present).

Salem Chalabi: Member of the Future of Iraq Project's Democratic Principles Working Group, and nephew of Ahmad Chalabi.

Dick Cheney: Vice President (2001–present) and U.S. Defense Secretary (1989–1993).

Jacques Chirac: President of France (1995–present).

Richard A. Clarke: Special Advisor (2001–2003) and National Coordinator for Security, Infrastructure Protection, and Counterterrorism (1998–2000) in the National Security Council; Assistant Secretary of State for Politico-Military Affairs (1989–1992).

William J. Clinton: 42nd President of the United States of America.

Susan Collins: Republican Senator from Maine (1996–present).

Ryan C. Crocker: Ambassador to Pakistan (2004–present), Deputy Assistant Secretary of State for Near Eastern Affairs (2001–2003); Ambassador to Syria (1998–2001), to Kuwait (1994–1997), and to Lebanon (1990–1993); Director of Governance, CPA (May–August 2003).

Ivo H. Daalder: Special Adviser on National Security at Center for American Progress and Senior Fellow in Foreign Policy Studies at the Brookings Institution, where he holds the Sydney Stein Jr. Chair in International Security.

Alfonse D'Amato: Republican Senator from New York (1981–1998).

Kassim Daoud: Member of the Iraqi Democratic Movement, Iraq's National Security Adviser (2004–present).

Charles A. Deulfer: Chief U.S. Weapons Inspector (2004–present).

Lawrence DiRita: Acting Secretary of Defense for Public Affairs and Special Assistant to the Secretary of Defense (2001–present).

James Dobbins: Former Foreign Senior Officer and Acting Assistant Secretary of State for European and Canadian Affairs who supervised postwar operations in Haiti, Somalia, Bosnia, and Kosovo.

Christopher J. Dodd: Democratic Senator from Connecticut (1980–present).

William Eagleton: Public Affairs Officer in Kirkuk (1954–1955); Chief of the U.S. Interests Section in Baghdad (1980–1984).

Tayyip Recep Erdogan: Prime Minister of Turkey (2003–present).

Maj. Mohammed Faour: Former member of Iraq's Special Forces, member of the Future of Iraq Project's Defense Working Group.

Ahmad Fawzi: Director of the News and Media Division in the United Nations Department of Public Information (2003–present), UN spokesman for Lakhdar Brahimi.

Col. Scott R. Feil, U.S. Army (Ret.): Works in the Operational Evaluation Division at the Institute for Defense Analyses and as executive director of the Association of the United States Army's Program on the Role of American Military Power and codirector of the Post-Conflict Reconstruction Project.

Russell D. Feingold: Democratic Senator from Wisconsin (1993–present).

Douglas H. Feith: Undersecretary of Defense for Policy (2001–present), Managing Attorney of the law firm of Feith & Zell, P.C.

Gen. Tommy R. Franks: Head of Central Command for the Department of Defense (2000–2003).

Louise Frechette: Deputy Secretary General of the UN (1998–present), Canada's Deputy Minister of Defense (1995–1998).

Peter W. Galbraith: Served as the first U.S. ambassador to Croatia and with the UN in East Timor. As a staff member of the Senate Foreign Relations Committee in the 1980s, he documented and called attention to Iraq's "Anfal" campaign against the Kurds.

Gen. Jay M. Garner: Director of the Office for Reconstruction and Humanitarian Assistance in Iraq (January–May 2003), former President of SY Technology.

Marc Grossman: Undersecretary of State for Political Affairs (2001–2005), Assistant Secretary of State for European and Canadian Affairs (1997–1998), and U.S. Ambassador to Turkey (1995–1997).

Kadhem al-Husseini al-Haeri: Grand Ayatollah based in Qum who mentored Moqtada al-Sadr.

Chuck Hagel: Republican Senator from Nebraska (1996–present).

Adnan Ihsan al-Haideri: Informant provided by the INC.

Abdul Aziz al-Hakim: Leader of the Supreme Council for Islamic Revolution in Iraq (SCIRI), former member of the Iraqi Governing Council, and brother of Bakr al-Hakim.

Bakr al-Hakim: Head of the Supreme Council for Islamic Revolution in Iraq who was assassinated in August 2003.

Brig. Gen. Carter F. Ham: Commander of the northern sector of Iraq (2004–2005).

Khidir Hamza: Informant provided by the INC who claimed involvement in Iraq's nuclear program.

John Hannah: Deputy Assistant to the Vice President for National Security Affairs.

Aquila al-Hashimi: Member of the Iraqi Governing Council who was assassinated in September 2003.

Jesse Helms: Republican Senator from North Carolina (1972–2000).

Jim Hoagland: Columnist for the *Washington Post* and a two-time Pulitzer Prize recipient.

Col. Paul F. Hughes: Adviser to ORHA; Army Senior Military Fellow in the Institute for National Strategic Studies, National Defense University.

Qusay Hussein: Son of Saddam who oversaw all Iraqi intelligence and security services, the Republican Guard, and the Special Republican Guard; killed in July 2003.

Uday Hussein: Son of Saddam who ran Iraq's Olympic Committee and owned the *Babil* daily paper, the weekly *Rafidayn*, and the Al-Shabab TV Station; killed in July 2003.

Faisal al-Istrabadi: Professor of constitutional law at DePaul University who went to Iraq to join the constitutional drafting committee and then became Iraq's deputy permanent representative to the United Nations (2004–present).

Gen. Sir Michael Jackson: Commander of the British armed forces.

Ibrahim al-Jaffari: One of the two Vice Presidents in Iraq's interim government, main spokesman for the Islamic Da'wa Party in Iraq, and brother-in-law of the Shi'a Grand Ayatollah Ali al-Sistani.

Major Jeff Jurgensen: Public Affairs Officer for ORHA.

Najmaldin Karim: Neurosurgeon, former Chairman of the Kurdish National Congress of America and Chairman of the Washington Kurdish Institute.

Nancy Kassebaum: Republican Senator from Kansas (1979–1997).

David Kay: IAEA/UNSCOM Chief Nuclear Weapons Inspector.

Orhan Ketene: Washington representative of the Iraqi Turkmen Front.

Sabah Khalifa: Informant provided by the INC who claimed that Iraq's security services were receiving WMD and anthrax training.

Zalmay Khalilzad: U.S. Ambassador to Afghanistan (2003–present); former Senior Director for Islamic Outreach and Southwest Asia Initiatives and for Southwest Asia, Near East, and North African Affairs at the NSC (2001–2003); Special Presidential Envoy and Ambassador-at-Large for Free Iraqis (2002–2003).

Ayatollah Ali Khamenei: Supreme Leader of Iran (1989–present).

Mohammad Khatami: President of the Islamic Republic of Iran (1997–present).

Ayatollah Ruhollah Khomeini: Grand Ayatollah who led the Iranian Revolution in 1979.

Sayyid Hussein Khomeini: Grandson of Ayatollah Khomeini.

Abdul Majid al-Khoei: Ayatollah who returned to Iraq from exile in London and was assassinated at the Imam Ali mosque in April 2003.

Brig. Gen. Mark Kimmit: Deputy Director of Planning for the U.S. Central Command (2004–present), U.S. Army's Deputy Director for Operations and U.S. military spokesman in Iraq (2003–2004).

Henry Kissinger: Founder of Kissinger Associates, Secretary of State (1973–1977), and National Security Adviser (1969–1973).

Jim Kolbe: Republican House member from Arizona (1984–present).

Aleksander Kwasniewski: President of Poland (1995–present).

Laith Kubba: Senior Program Officer, Middle East and North Africa, at the National Endowment for Democracy; one of the founders of the Iraqi National Congress.

Osama bin Laden: Head of al-Qaeda.

Yael Lempert: Foreign Service Officer who worked on the Future of Iraq Project and with the CPA.

Carl M. Levin: Democratic Senator from Michigan (1978–present)

Bernard Lewis: Cleveland E. Dodge Professor of Near Eastern Studies, Emeritus, at Princeton University.

I. Lewis "Scooter" Libby: Chief of Staff to the Vice President (2001–present).

James M. Lindsay: Vice President and Director of the Studies Department at the Council on Foreign Relations (2003–present).

Lewis W. Lucke: USAID Iraq Mission Director, former ORHA Reconstruction Coordinator.

Richard G. Lugar: Republican Senator from Indiana (1976–present).

William J. Luti: Deputy Undersecretary of Defense for Near Eastern and South Asian Affairs (2002–present); Special Adviser to the Vice President for National Security Affairs in the Middle East (2001); Commander, USS *Guam* (1997–1998).

Ali Hassan al-Majid: Cousin of Saddam Hussein, Iraq's Minister of Defense under Saddam, Secretary General of the Ba'ath Party's Northern Bureau; also known as "Chemical Ali."

Kanan Makiya: Brandeis University Professor, Director of Harvard University's Iraq Research and Documentation project, and author of *Republic of Fear*.

F. Michael Malouf: Worked for Richard Perle in the Pentagon (1980s).

Favad Ma'soum: London representative of the Patriotic Union of Kurdistan.

John McCain: Republican Senator from Arizona (1986–present).

Mikael McKowan: State Department Desk Officer for Iraq (2002–2004).

Sergio Vieira de Mello: United Nations High Commissioner for Human Rights who served as Special Representative of the UN Secretary General in Iraq, where he was killed in August 2003; former Undersecretary General for Humanitarian Affairs and Emergency Relief Coordinator; UN Assistant High Commissioner for Refugees; Special Representative of the Secretary General in Kosovo; and UN Transitional Administrator in East Timor.

Leszek Miller: Prime Minister of Poland (2001–2004).

Judith Miller: Senior Correspondent for the *New York Times*.

Michael H. Mobbs: Former Civil Administration Coordinator for ORHA and Special Advisor to the Undersecretary of Defense for Policy.

Maj. Gen. W. Bruce Moore: Former Regional Coordinator for North Iraq for ORHA.

Gen. Richard B. Myers: Chairman of the Joint Chiefs of Staff (2001–present).

Behzad Nabavi: Deputy Speaker of Iran's Majlis (parliament).

John Negroponte: National Director of Intelligence (2005–present), U.S. Ambassador to Iraq (2004–2005) and U.S. Permanent Representative to the United Nations (2001–2004).

Maj. Gen. Ray Odierno: Commander of the U.S. Army's 4th Infantry Division (2003–2004).

Paul O'Neill: Treasury Secretary (2001–2003).

Meghan O'Sullivan: Member of the CPA staff who became Rice's Principal Adviser on Iraq.

Mahmoud Othman: Member of the IGC and an independent Kurd.

Turgut Ozal: Prime Minister of Turkey (1983–1989) and President of Turkey (1989–1993).

Gen. Hilmi Ozkok: Chief of the General Staff of the Turkish Army.

Adnan Pachachi: Iraqi Foreign Minister and Ambassador to the UN before the Ba'athists seized power in 1968.

David Pearce: Chief of Mission and Consul General at the U.S. Consulate General in Jerusalem (2003–present); Director of the State Department's Office of Northern Gulf Affairs, in the Bureau of Near East Affairs, with responsibility for Iraq and Iran (2001–2003); Deputy Chief of Mission, U.S. Embassy, Damascus (1997–2001).

Richard N. Perle: Member (1987–2004) and Chairman (2001–2003), of the Defense Policy Board Advisory Committee, Assistant Secretary of Defense (1981–1987).

Colin L. Powell: Secretary of State (2001–2005) and Chairman of the Joint Chiefs of Staff (1989–1993).

Entifadh Qanbar: Spokesman of the Iraqi National Congress.

Abu Zeinab al-Qurairy: Informant provided by the INC who claimed to witness terrorist training at Salman Park.

Rend al-Rahim: Director of the Iraq Foundation and Iraq's Ambassador to the United States (2003–present).

Sami Abdul Rahman: KDP official who was assassinated in February 2004.

Samantha Ravich: Vice President for Proliferation Studies at the Long Term Strategy Project and former Special Adviser on National Security Affairs to the Vice President (2001–2003).

Jack Reed: Democratic Senator from Rhode Island (1996–present).

Condoleezza Rice: Secretary of State (2005–present) and National Security Adviser (2001–2005).

Jay Rockefeller IV: Democratic Senator from West Virginia (1984–present).

Claudia Rossett: Columnist for the *Opinion Journal*, previously with the *Wall Street Journal*.

Mowaffak al-Rubaie: Da'wa's London Representative and Iraq's National Security Adviser (2003–2004).

Trudi Rubin: Senior Correspondent for the *Philadelphia Enquirer*.

Donald H. Rumsfeld: Secretary of Defense (2001–present), and (1975–1977), former White House Chief of Staff (1974–1975), U.S. Ambassador to NATO (1973–1974), and U.S. Congressman (1962–1969).

Moqtada al-Sadr: Radical cleric who commands the Mahdi Army; son of the Grand Ayatollah Mohammed Sadiq Sadr who was assassinated in 1999.

Abdul Aziz Said: Professor and Mohammed Said Farsi Chair of Islamic Peace at American University and the Founding Director of the Center for Global Peace and the International Peace and Conflict Resolution Program at American University.

Jassim Mohammed Saleh: Former Head of the Iraqi Army's 38th Infantry Division who led the Fallujah Brigade.

Barham Salih: Deputy Prime Minister of Iraq (2004–2005), PUK official and Prime Minister of Kurdistan Regional Government (2001–2004).

Ezzedine Salim: Member of the Iraqi Governing Council who was assassinated in May 2004.

Jaap de Hoop Scheffer: NATO Secretary General (2004–present).

Brent Scowcroft: U.S. National Security Adviser to Presidents Ford and Bush.

Dan Senor: Senior Advisor to the CPA Administrator.

General Eric Shinseki: U.S. Army chief of staff (1999–2003).

Ali al-Sistani: Grand Ayatollah and the leading Shi'a cleric in Iraq.

Michael Scott Speicher: Navy pilot missing in action after his plane was shot down during the Gulf War.

Jack Straw: British Secretary of State for Foreign and Commonwealth Affairs (2001–present).

Jalal Talabani: Leader of the Patriotic Union of Kurdistan (PUK).

Qubad Talabani: Washington representative of the PUK and son of Jalal Talabani.

George J. Tenet: Director of the CIA (1997–2004).

Harry S. Truman: 33rd President of the United States of America.

Muhammed Bahr al-Ulum: Shi'a leader and member of the Iraqi Governing Council.

Francesc Vandrell: UN Assistant Secretary General for Political Affairs who led the "Geneva process."

Dominique de Villepin: France's Interior Minister (2004–present) and Foreign Minister (2002–2004).

George V. Voinovich: Republican Senator from Ohio (1999–present).

Edward "Ned" Walker: President of the Middle East Institute; former U.S. Ambassador to the United Arab Emirates (1989–1992), Egypt (1994–1997), and Israel (1997–1999).

Roger "Buck" Walters: Retired General assigned responsibility for ORHA's southern sector.

George F. Ward: Former Marine and Ambassador to Namibia who directed ORHA's humanitarian efforts.

Thomas Warrick: Director of the Future of Iraq Project.

Paul D. Wolfowitz: Deputy Secretary of Defense (2001–present).

R. James Woolsey: Distinguished Advisor to the Foundation for the Defense of Democracies (2002–present); Director of the CIA (1993–1995).

David Wurmser: Principal Deputy Assistant for National Security Affairs in the Office of the Vice President (2003–present).

Yasar Yakis: Foreign Minister of Turkey (2003–present).

Ghazi Ajil al-Yawar: Leader of the Shamar tribe and President of Iraq (2004–2005).

Albert Yelda: Assyrian representative and Iraq's Ambassador to the Vatican (2003–present).

Ramzi Yousef: Mastermind of the 1993 World Trade Center bombing.

Jose Luis Rodriguez Zapatero: Prime Minister of Spain (2004–present).

Javad Zarif: Ambassador and the Permanent Representative of the Islamic Republic of Iran to the United Nations (2003–present); Iran's Deputy Foreign Minister for Legal and International Affairs (1992–2003).

Abu Musab al-Zarqawi: Al-Qaeda associate who established the al-Tawhid to overthrow the Jordanian monarchy and founded al Qaeda in Iraq.

Hoshyar Zebari: KDP London representative who became Iraq's Foreign Minister (2003–present).

Gen. Anthony Zinni: Former Commander in Chief of the U.S. Central Command (1997–2000).

Mustafa Ziya: Ankara Representative of the Iraqi Turkmen Front.

Ugur Ziyal: Turkey's Undersecretary of Foreign Affairs.

NOTES

INTRODUCTION

1. Carole O'Leary, "The Kurds of Iraq; Recent History, Future Projects," *Middle East Review of International Affairs Journal*, Volume 6, Number 4, December 2002.

2. Interview by the author with Najmaldin Karim. June 25, 2004.

3. John Hernden, "A Huge Postwar Force Seen," *Los Angeles Times*, February 26, 2003.

4. Sam Tanennhaus, *Vanity Fair*, June 2003. Transcript available at http://www.defenselink.mil/transcripts/2003/tr20030509-depsecdef0223.html.

CHAPTER 1

1. Governor George W. Bush, "A Distinctly American Internationalism," Ronald Reagan Library, November 19, 1999.

2. Condoleezza Rice, "Promoting the National Interest," *Foreign Affairs*, Jan.–Feb. 2000, 47–48.

3. Public Papers of the Presidents of the United States: Harry S. Truman, 1947 (Washington, D.C.: Government Printing Office, 1963): 178–179.

4. Michael Gordon, "Bush Would Stop U.S. Peacekeeping in Balkan Fights," *New York Times*, October 21, 2000, A1.

5. George W. Bush, interview by George F. Will, *This Week*, ABC, January 23, 2000.

6. Jeffrey A. Kluger, "A Climate of Despair," *Time*, April 9, 2001.

7. Colin Powell, press briefing, February 23, 2001.

8. George W. Bush, remarks made on September 26, 2002.

9. SR 23, "Authorization for the Use of Military Force," September 14, 2001.

10. *Le Monde* (Paris), September 12, 2001.

11. George W. Bush, remarks made at the Warsaw Conference on Combating Terrorism, November 6, 2001.

12. George W. Bush, remarks made at the United States Military Academy, West Point, New York, June 1, 2002.

13. George W. Bush, remarks made at the National Day of Prayer and Remembrance, September 14, 2001.

14. George W. Bush, address to a joint session of the Congress, January 2002.

15. George W. Bush, State of the Union Address, January 28, 2003.

16. Dan Balz, Bob Woodward, and Jeff Himmelman, "Afghan Campaign's Blueprint Emerges," *Washington Post*, January 29, 2002, A11.

17. Richard A. Clarke, interview by Leslie Stahl, *60 Minutes*, CBS, March 21, 2004.

18. Ibid.

19. Bart Gellman, "A Strategy's Curious Evolution," *Washington Post*, December 30, 2001, A16.

20. Bob Woodward, *Bush at War* (Simon & Schuster, 2003), 98.

21. George W. Bush, State of the Union Address, January 29, 2002.

22. Woodward, *Bush at War*, 99.

23. George W. Bush, news conference, October 11, 2001.

24. George W. Bush, remarks made when welcoming aid workers from Afghanistan, November 26, 2001.

25. Michael Elliott and James Carney, "First Stop Iraq," *Time*, March 23, 2003, 173.

26. Condoleezza Rice, interview by Bob Schiffer, *Face the Nation*, CBS, February 17, 2002.

27. Richard Cheney, remarks to the Veterans of Foreign Wars Convention in Nashville, Tennessee, August 26, 2002.

28. Colin Powell, testimony to the Senate Budget Committee, February 12, 2002.

29. Javad Zarif, interview by author at the Iranian Mission to the United Nations in New York, August 4, 2004.

30. David Kay, testimony to the Senate Armed Services Committee, January 28, 2004.

31. George W. Bush, remarks made about Iraq, Cincinnati, Ohio, October 7, 2002.

CHAPTER 2

1. Directive SF/4008, June 20, 1987, clause 4.

2. Ibid., clause 5.

3. Najmaldin Karim, telephone interview by author, Bethesda, Maryland, June 25, 2004.

4. Peter W. Galbraith, "How to Get Out of Iraq," *New York Review of Books*, vol. 51, no. 8, May 13, 2004.

5. Claudia Rossett, "The Real World," *Wall Street Journal*, September 4, 2002.

6. Asla Aydintasbas, *Salon.com*, September 6, 2002.

7. KDP draft constitution, May 2002.

CHAPTER 3

1. Meeting with Deputy Assistant Secretary of State for Near Eastern Affairs Ryan Crocker, U.S. Department of State, July 15, 2002.

2. Interview with Laith Kubba by author. Washington, D.C., September 28, 2004.

3. Ibid.

4. Marc Grossman, testimony to Senate Foreign Relations Committee, February 11, 2003.

5. Ibid.

6. Ibid.

7. Ibid.

CHAPTER 4

1. Eric Schmitt and David E. Sanger, "Bush Has Received Pentagon Option on Attacking Iraq," *New York Times*, September 21, 2002, A1–11.

2. Richard Cheney, speech to the Veterans of Foreign Wars Association, August 26, 2002.

CHAPTER 5

1. George Packer, "Dreaming of Democracy," *New York Times Magazine*, March 3, 2003.

2. Final Statement of the Meetings of the Iraqi National Congress National Assembly in Salahuddin, October 31, 1992.

3. Meeting Notes, Cobham, Surrey, U.K., September 3–5, 2002.

4. "Iraq's Mr. Cellophane," *Newsweek*, December 29–January 5, 2003–2004.

5. Faisal al-Istrabadi, email, August 29, 2002.

6. Kassim Daoud, email, August 26, 2002.

7. Albert Yelda, email, August 30, 2002.

CHAPTER 6

1. George W. Bush, address to the United Nations General Assembly, September 12, 2002.

2. Ibid.

3. United Nations Security Council resolution 1441, adopted November 8, 2002.

4. Ivo H. Daalder and James M. Lindsay, *America Unbound* (The Brookings Institution, 2003), 141.

5. Bryan Burrough, "The Path to War," *Vanity Fair*, May 2004.

6. Ibid.

7. Ibid.

8. Jonathan S. Landay, Warren P. Strobel, and John Walcott, "Doubts Cast on Efforts to Link Saddam and Al-Qaeda," Knight Ridder/Tribune News Service, March 3, 2004.

9. FAQs, "Was the War Inevitable?" April 22, 2004. http://nths.newtrier. k12.il.us/academics/faculty/khall/IraqSitesArts/IraqNew802/IraqFAQWar Inevitable.htm

10. David E. Sanger, "A Seat of Honor Lost to Open Political Warfare," *New York Times*, May 21, 2004, A1.

11. The Iraq Liberation Act (Public Law 105–338), adopted October 1998.

12. United Nations Development Programme, Arab Development Report, 2001.

13. George W. Bush, remarks at the 20th Anniversary of the National Endowment for Democracy, Washington, D.C.

14. Richard Cheney, speech to the Council on Foreign Relations, November 15, 2001.

15. *Time*, January 29, 2004.

16. Jane Mayer, "The Manipulator," *New Yorker*, June 7, 2004.

17. Nicholas Lehman, "After Iraq," *New Yorker*, February 17 and 24, 2003, 72.

18. David Rieff, *New York Times Magazine*, November 2, 2003.

19. *Wolf Blitzer Reports*, CNN, July 14, 2004.

20. Richard Perle, remarks to the Foreign Policy Research Institute, November 14, 2001.

21. Ibid.

22. Jonathan S. Landay, Warren P. Strobel, and John Walcott, "Faulty Intelligence Continues to Plague U.S. Efforts in Iraq," Knight Ridder/Tribune News Service, March 20, 2004.

23. Bruce B. Auster, Mark Mazetti, and Edward T. Pound, "Truth and Consequences," *U.S. News and World Report*, June 9, 2003, 14.

24. Jonathan S. Landay, Warren P. Strobel, and Joseph L. Galloway, "Iraq Intelligence Efforts Led by Cheney Magnified Errors," Knight Ridder/Tribune News Service, February 3, 2004.

25. Burrough, "Path to War."

26. Jonathan S. Landay, Joseph Walcott, and Joseph L. Galloway, "Rumsfeld Advisor Who Vocally Endorsed Saddam's Ouster Resigns," Knight Ridder/Tribune News Service, February 26, 2004.

27. David Rieff, "How to Plan a Mess," *New York Times Magazine*, November 2, 2003.

28. Ibid.

29. Bill Keller, "The World According to Powell," *New York Times*, November 25, 2001.

30. Philip Shenon, "Former Iraq Arms Inspector Faults Prewar Intelligence," *New York Times*, August 19, 2004, A20.

31. Jonathan S. Landay, Warren P. Strobel, and John Walcott, "Doubts Cast on Efforts to Link Saddam and Al-Qaeda," Knight Ridder/Tribune News Service, March 3, 2004.

Chapter 7

1. *Morning Edition*, National Public Radio, May 21, 2004.

2. Evan Thomas and Mark Hosenball, "The Rise and Fall of Chalabi: Bush's Mr. Wrong," *Newsweek*, May 31, 2004, 22.

3. Jane Mayer, "The Manipulator," *New Yorker*, June 7, 2004, 58.

4. Ibid., 64.

5. Dexter Filkins and Ian Fisher, "Iraqis and GIs Raid the Offices of an Ex-Favorite," *New York Times*, May 21, 2004, A1.

6. Mayer, "The Manipulator," 64.

7. Thomas and Hosenball, "Rise and Fall of Chalabi," 22.

8. Jonathan S. Landay and Warren P. Strobel, "Iraqi Exile Group May Have Violated Rules Barring It from Lobbying," Knight Rider/Tribune News Service, April 23, 2004.

9. Ibid.

10. Jonathan Landay and Tish Wells, "Iraqi Exiles Gave False Information to Media," *Miami Herald*, March 16, 2004.

11. Jonathan S. Landay and Tish Wells, "Iraqi Exile Group Fed False Information to the Media," Knight Ridder/Tribune News Service, March 16, 2004.

12. Thomas and Hosenball, "Rise and Fall of Chalabi," 22.

13. Ibid.

14. David E. Sanger, "Friend to Foe: Chalabi's Slide from U.S. Favor," *International Herald Tribune*, May 22, 2004, 1.

15. David E. Sanger, "A Seat of Honor Lost to Open Political Warfare," *New York Times*, May 21, 2004, A1.

16. Daniel Okrent, "Weapons of Mass Destruction? Or Mass Distraction?" *New York Times*, May 30, 2004

17. Pew Charitable Research public opinion survey, October 2001.

18. Mayer, "The Manipulator."

19. Landay and Strobel, "Iraqi Exile Group May Have Violated Rules."

20. Mayer, "The Manipulator," 71.

21. Sanger, "Seat of Honor Lost."

Chapter 8

1. Key Judgments of the National Intelligence Estimate, October 1, 2002.

2. George W. Bush, remarks made at the Cincinnati Museum Center, October 7, 2002.

3. *Report on the Transition to Democracy in Iraq*, adopted by the Coordinating Committee of the Democratic Principles Working Group, October 4, 2002, 4.

4. Ibid., 17.

5. Ibid., 5.

6. Ibid., 17.

7. Kanan Makiya, conversation with author, Wilton Park, Surrey, U.K., October 10, 2001.

8. *Report on the Transition to Democracy in Iraq*, 5.

CHAPTER 9

1. Judith Miller and Lowell Bergman, "Iraq Opposition Is Pursuing Ties with Iran," *New York Times*, December 13, 2002, A1.

2. "Iran Contra Figure Named to Senior Post in White House," *Washington Post*, December 3, 2002, A2.

3. "President Bush's Favorite Muslim," Jim Reed, CBC Newsworld International, March 17, 2003.

4. Peter Slevin and Daniel Williams, "Key Exiles Agree U.S. Should Not Run Postwar Iraq," *Washington Post*, December 15, 2002, A39.

5. Daniel Williams and Peter Slevin, "Leagues Apart, Iraqi Exiles Convene in London," *Washington Post*, December 13, 2002, A50.

6. Craig S. Smith, "Threats and Responses: The Opposition," *New York Times*, December 14, 2002, A14.

7. Williams and Slevin, "Leagues Apart."

8. Smith, "Threats and Responses: The Opposition."

9. Williams and Slevin, "Leagues Apart."

10. Meeting notes, August 15, 2001.

11. Ibid.

12. Slevin and Williams, "Key Exiles Agree."

13. Meeting notes, August 15, 2001.

14. Ibid.

15. Smith, "Threats and Responses: The Opposition."

16. Meeting notes, August 15, 2002.

17. Ibid.

18. Ibid.

19. Ibid.

20. Smith, "Threats and Responses: The Opposition."

21. Ibid.

22. Statement of the Iraqi Opposition Conference, London, December 17, 2002.

23. Ibid.

24. Ibid.

25. Ibid.

26. Kanan Makiya, "Our Hopes Betrayed," *Observer* (London), February 16, 2003.

27. Craig S. Smith, "Threats and Responses: Hussein's Foes," *New York Times*, December 16, 2002, A14.

28. Smith, "Threats and Responses: The Opposition."

CHAPTER 10

1. George W. Bush, State of the Union Address, January 29, 2002.

2. Javad Zarif, interview by author, August 4, 2004.

3. Najmeh Bozorgmehr, Mark Huband, and James Politi, "Tehran Denies U.S. Claims It Is a Haven for Terrorists," *Financial Times* (London), May 26, 2003, 8.

4. Zarif, interview.

5. Ibid.

6. Edward Wong, "Iran Is in Strong Position to Steer Iraq's Political Future," *New York Times*, July 3, 2004, A6.

7. Ibid.

8. Zarif, interview.

9. Ibid.

10. Craig S. Smith, "Cleric in Iran Says Shiites Must Act," *New York Times*, April 26, 2003, A1.

11. Donald H. Rumsfeld, remarks to Council on Foreign Relations, May 27, 2003.

12. Ibid.

13. Michael Dobbs, "Pressure Builds for President to Declare Strategy on Iran," *Washington Post*, June 15, 2003, A20.

14. Zarif, interview.

15. Nazila Fathi, "Iranian Lawmaker Opens Door to American Talks," *New York Times*, December 16, 2002, A8.

16. Ibid.

17. Thomas L. Friedman, "Dinner with the Sayyids," *New York Times*, August 10, 2003, sec. 4.

18. Neil MacFarquhar, "A Khomeini Breaks with His Lineage to Back U.S.," *New York Times*, August 6, 2003, A9.

19. Najmeh Bozorgmehr, Mark Huband, and James Politi, "Tehran Denies U.S. Claims It Is a Haven for Terrorists," *Financial Times* (London), May 26, 2003, 8.

20. Gal Luft, "The Karine-A Affair: A Strategic Watershed in the Middle East?" *PeaceWatch*, no. 361, *Special Policy Forum Report*, Washington Institute, January 30, 2002.

21. Ibid.

22. Zarif, interview.

23. Ibid.

CHAPTER 11

1. Kurds/Turkmen meeting notes, the Royal Horseguards Hotel, London, January 2003.

2. "Hands Off Kirkuk, U.S. Tells Kurds, Turks," Reuters, February 7, 2003.

3. Ibid.

4. *The Political Scene*, vol. XLVI, no. 9, March 9, 2003.

5. "Hands Off Kirkuk." by Charles Snow, posted March 3, 2003, http://www
.mees.com.

6. Borzou Daraghai, "Iraqi Kurds Oppose Turkish Presence," Associated Press,
February 24, 2003.

7. Borzou Daraghai, "Kurds Will Resist Turkish Troops in Iraq," Associated
Press, February 28, 2003.

8. Jason Burke and Luke Harding, "The Kurdish People Believe Turkey Will
Use War on Iraq to Crush Their Independence Bid," *Observer* (London), March
2, 2003.

9. Statement by the Kurdish National Congress of North America, February
12, 2003.

10. Robin Wright, "Arab-Kurd Compromise Nears," *Washington Post*, January
10, 2004, A14.

11. Ilene R. Prusher, "Kurd-Turk Rivalry Threatens UN Plans for Iraq," *Christian Science Monitor*, March 14, 2003.

12. Louis Meixler, "Turkish, Kurdish Tensions Rise Over Possible Iraq War,"
Associated Press, February 7, 2004.

13. Memorandum from the author to Deputy Assistant Secretary of State for
Near Eastern Affairs Ryan Crocker, February 11, 2003.

14. "U.S., Turks Wrangle Over Command of Troops in Northern Iraq," *Daily
Times*, February 10, 2003. www.dailytimes.com.pk/default.asp?page=story_10-
2-2003_pg4_3.

15. Daniel Williams, "U.S. Cool to Kurdish Call for Uprising," *Washington Post*,
March 29, 2003, A32.

16. Ibid.

17. David Pratt, "Dread Haunts Iraqi Kurdistan," *Sunday Herald*, March 2,
2003.

18. *The Political Scene*, vol. XLVI, no. 9, March 9, 2003.

19. Ibid.

20. Daraghai, "Iraqi Kurds Oppose Turkish Presence."

21. Memorandum from the author to Deputy Assistant Secretary of State for
Near Eastern Affairs Ryan Crocker, February 11, 2003.

22. Louis Meixler, "Turkish, Kurdish Tensions Rise Over Possible Iraq War,"
Associated Press, February 7, 2004.

23. *The Political Scene*, vol. XLVI, no. 9, March 9, 2003.

24. Cameron W. Barr, "U.S. Gives Iraq Opposition Its View of the Future,"
Christian Science Monitor, February 28, 2003.

25. Prusher, "Kurd-Turk Rivalry."

26. Cited by the American Hellenic Institute, Washington, D.C., March 3, 2004.

27. Mark R. Parris, in testimony before the House International Affairs Committee, October 1, 2003.

28. *The Political Scene*, vol. XLVI, no. 9, March 3, 2003.

29. Press Release issued by the American Hellenic Institute, Washington,
D.C., March 3, 2003.

30. Anonymous, March 21, 2003.

31. Iran Press Service, March 2003. www.iran-press-service.com.

CHAPTER 12

1. Undersecretary of State for Political Affairs Marc Grossman, hearing of the Senate Foreign Relations Committee, February 11, 2003.

2. Ibid.

3. Ibid.

4. Undersecretary of Defense Douglas Feith, hearing of the Senate Foreign Relations Committee, February 11, 2003.

5. Senator Joseph Biden, hearing of the Senate Foreign Relations Committee, February 11, 2003.

6. Army General (Ret.) Anthony Zinni, hearing of the Senate Foreign Relations Committee, February 11, 2003.

7. Senator Richard Lugar, hearing of the Senate Foreign Relations Committee, February 11, 2003.

8. Senator Chuck Hagel, hearing of the Senate Foreign Relations Committee, February 11, 2003.

9. Undersecretary of Defense Douglas Feith, hearing of the Senate Foreign Relations Committee, February 11, 2003.

10. Senator Christopher Dodd, hearing of the Senate Foreign Relations Committee, February 11, 2003.

11. Senator Chuck Hagel, hearing of the Senate Foreign Relations Committee, February 11, 2003.

12. Ibid.

13. Undersecretary of Defense Douglas Feith, hearing of the Senate Foreign Relations Committee, February 11, 2003.

14. Ibid.

15. Ibid.

16. Senator Sam Brownback, hearing of the Senate Foreign Relations Committee, February 11, 2003.

17. Undersecretary of State for Political Affairs Marc Grossman, hearing of the Senate Foreign Relations Committee, February 11, 2003.

18. Undersecretary of Defense Douglas Feith, hearing of the Senate Foreign Relations Committee, February 11, 2003.

19. Senator Joseph Biden, hearing of the Senate Foreign Relations Committee, February 11, 2003.

20. Undersecretary of State for Political Affairs Marc Grossman, hearing of the Senate Foreign Relations Committee, February 11, 2003.

21. Senator Lincoln Chaffee, hearing of the Senate Foreign Relations Committee, February 11, 2003.

22. Doug Sample, "White House Agency Discusses Plan for Humanitarian Assistance to Iraq," Armed Forces Information Service, February 24, 2003.

23. Undersecretary of Defense Douglas Feith, hearing of the Senate Foreign Relations Committee, February 11, 2003.

24. Katherine McIntire Peters, "Blind Ambition," www.govexec.com, July 1, 2004.

25. Qubad Talabani, interview by author, September 14, 2004.

26. Joseph L. Galloway, "Thanks to Rumsfeld, Iraq Is Still America's to Lose," www.military.com, December 17, 2003.

27. Eric Schmitt and Joel Brinkley, "State Department Study Foresaw Trouble Now Plaguing Iraq," *New York Times*, October 19, 2003.

28. David Rieff, "How to Plan a Mess," *New York Times Magazine*, November 2, 2003.

29. Ibid.

30. Suzanne Freeman, "Rebuilding Iraq: Who Decides?" *Scholastic News*, http://teacher.scholastic.com/scholasticnews/indepth/war-iraq/new_govt/index .asp?article=who_decides.

31. Gail Martin, "Occupied Iraq," Online NewsHour, http://www.pbs.org/ newshour/bb/middle_east/iraq/postwar/player_garner.html.

32. F. William Engdahl, "The Neo-Cons Now Want to Rebuild Iraq," *Current Concerns*, no. 3, 2003.

33. Adam Curtis, "Iraq's Interim Administrator," BBC News Online, April 7, 2003.

34. Kaleem Omar, "Jay Garner: An Israeli Agent?" *Daily Times* (Pakistan), April 23, 2003.

35. Gail Martin, "Occupied Iraq," Online NewsHour, http://www.pbs.org/ newshour/bb/middle_east/iraq/postwar/player_garner.html.

36. Kathryn Westcott, "The Americans Who Will Run Iraq," BBC News Online, April 10, 2003.

37. Tim Mansel, "The Problems of Post-War Iraq," BBC World News.

38. Judy Dempsey, "Keep Aid Neutral, Urges EU Relief Chief," *Financial Times*, March 31, 2003.

39. Catherine Gordon, "Put Iraq Humanitarian Assistance and Reconstruction Under UN Control," Presbyterian Washington Office, second quarter, 2003.

40. Undersecretary of State for Political Affairs Marc Grossman, hearing of the Senate Foreign Relations Committee, February 11, 2003.

41. Katherine McIntire Peters, "Blind Ambition," www.govexec.com, July 1, 2004.

42. United States Department of Defense news transcript, March 11, 2003.

43. Eric Schmitt and David E. Sanger, "Looting Disrupts Detailed U.S. Plan to Restore Iraq," *New York Times*, May 19, 2003, A10.

CHAPTER 13

1. "Garner Waiting for 'Last Shot' to Rule Baghdad," www.islamonline.net, April 10, 2003.

2. George Packer, "Dreaming of Democracy," *New York Times Magazine,* March 3, 2003.

3. Tim Mansel, "The Problems of Post-War Iraq," BBC World News.

4. U.S. Army Third Infantry Division, After Action Report.

5. Ibid.

6. Katherine McIntire Peters, "Blind Ambition," www.govexec.com, July 1, 2004.

7. Lt. General (Ret.) Jay Garner, testimony before the House Committee on Government Reform, Subcommittee on National Security, May 13, 2003.

8. Ibid.

9. "U.S. Begins Shaping Iraq's Future," BBC News, April 16, 2003.

10. Donald H. Rumsfeld, Defense Department news briefing, April 11, 2003.

11. John Hendren, "A Huge Postwar Force for Iraq," *Los Angeles Times,* February 26, 2003.

12. Deputy Secretary of Defense Paul Wolfowitz, hearing before the House Committee on the Budget, February 28, 2003.

13. Deputy Secretary of Defense Paul Wolfowitz, testimony before the Senate Foreign Relations Committee, May 22, 2003.

14. David Rieff, "How to Plan a Mess," *New York Times Magazine,* November 2, 2003.

15. Ibid.

16. "U.S. Begins Shaping Iraq's Future," BBC News, April 16, 2003.

17. Ibid.

18. Zalmay Khalilzad, "A Free Country Run by Free People," *Wall Street Journal,* April 17, 2003.

19. Peters, "Blind Ambition."

20. Kathryn Westcott, "The Americans Who Will Run Iraq," BBC News Online, April 10, 2003.

21. Tim Carney, "A Marred Follow-Up to a Brilliant Military Campaign," *Dodge City Daily Globe,* June 24, 2003.

22. Ibid.

23. United Nations Security Council Resolution 1441, adopted November 8, 2002.

24. Colin Powell, interview, *New York Times,* March 29, 2003.

25. Suzanne Freeman, "Rebuilding Iraq: Who Decides?" *Scholastic News,* April 2003.

26. Ibid.

CHAPTER 14

1. George W. Bush, remarks designating Ambassador L. Paul Bremer III the Iraqi administrator; transcript issued by the Office of the Press Secretary, the White House, May 6, 2003.

2. F. William Engdahl, "The Neocons Now Want to Rebuild Iraq," *Current Concerns*, no. 3, 2003, http://www.islamonline.net/english/news/2003-04/10/article06.shtml.

3. Jim Hoagland, "Bremer's Legacy," *Washington Post*, May 6, 2004, A35.

4. Ibid.

5. CPA/ORD/16 May 2003/01.

6. Defense Secretary Donald H. Rumsfeld, remarks to the Council on Foreign Relations, May 27, 2003.

7. Juan Cole, interview by Free Europe/Radio Liberty, printed in *Asia Times*, June 18, 2004.

8. Paul Richter and Mary Curtis, "From Ally to Outcast," *Los Angeles Times*, May 21, 2004, A1.

9. Jane Mayer, "The Manipulator," *New Yorker*, June 7, 2004.

10. David Rieff, "How to Plan a Mess," *New York Times Magazine*, November 2, 2003.

11. Zalmay Khalilzad, "A Free Country Run by Free People," *Wall Street Journal*, April 16, 2003.

12. CPA/ORD/23 May 2003/02.

13. Mark Fineman, Warren Vieth, and Robin Wright, "Dissolving Iraqi Army Was Costly Choice," *Los Angeles Times*, August 24, 2003.

14. "Vision Themes" document, prepared by the interagency group on Iraq and presented to Iraqi opposition leaders, December 2002.

15. Political Statement, Iraqi Opposition Conference, December 14–17, 2002.

16. Colonel (Ret.) Scott Feil, testimony to the Senate Foreign Relations Committee, February 11, 2003.

17. Department of Defense Backgrounder on Reconstruction and Humanitarian Assistance in Post-War Iraq, March 11, 2003.

18. Eric Schmitt, "U.S. Generals Fault Ban on Hussein's Party," *New York Times*, April 21, 2004.

19. Jonathan Marcus, "U.S. Game Plan in Iraq Questioned," BBC News, April 21, 2004.

20. Mark Fineman, Warren Vieth, and Robin Wright, "Dissolving Iraqi Army Was Costly Choice," *Los Angeles Times*, August 24, 2003.

21. Ibid.

22. Qubad Talabani interview by the author, September 29, 2004.

23. Interview with L. Paul Bremer III on Radio Free Europe/Radio Liberty, November 13, 2003.

CHAPTER 15

1. Scott Wilson, "Bremer Adopts Firmer Tone," *Washington Post*, May 26, 2003, A13.

2. David Rieff, "How to Plan a Mess," *New York Times Magazine*, November 2, 2003.

3. Mark Fineman, Warren Vieth, and Robin Wright, "Dissolving Iraqi Army Was Costly Choice," *Los Angeles Times*, August 24, 2003.

4. Secretary of Defense Donald H. Rumsfeld, remarks to the Council on Foreign Relations, May 27, 2003.

5. Cited by Defense Secretary Donald H. Rumsfeld, U.S. Department of Defense, July 24, 2003.

6. Cited by Assistant Secretary of Defense for Public Affairs Lawrence DiRita, U.S. Department of Defense, August 7, 2003.

7. Ambassador L. Paul Bremer, interview, Department of Defense, July 24, 2003.

8. Briefing by Defense Secretary Donald H. Rumsfeld, U.S. Department of Defense, September 5, 2003.

9. Briefing by Defense Secretary Donald H. Rumsfeld, U.S. Department of Defense, July 13, 2003.

10. Briefing by Air Force Lieutenant General Norton A. Schwartz, U.S. Department of Defense, August 7, 2003.

11. Briefing with Assistant Secretary of Defense Lawrence DiRita, U.S. Department of Defense, July 16, 2003.

12. Cited in a briefing by Defense Secretary Donald H. Rumsfeld, U.S. Defense Department of Defense, August 21, 2003.

13. Deputy Secretary of Defense Paul Wolfowitz to the Senate Foreign Relations Committee, May 22, 2003.

14. Deputy Secretary of Defense Paul Wolfowitz to the Senate Foreign Relations Committee, July 29, 2003.

15. Briefing with Defense Secretary Donald H. Rumsfeld, U.S. Department of Defense, July 24, 2003.

16. General John Abizaid, interview, U.S. Department of Defense, July 16, 2003.

17. Deputy Secretary of Defense Paul Wolfowitz to the Senate Foreign Relations Committee, July 29, 2003.

18. Briefing by General John Abizaid, U.S. Department of Defense, August 21, 2003.

19. Cited in Briefing with General John Abizaid, U.S. Department of Defense, July 16, 2003.

20. Senator Susan Collins at a hearing of the Senate Armed Services Committee, July 9, 2003.

21. Briefing by General John Abizaid, U.S. Department of Defense, August 21, 2003.

22. Deputy Secretary of Defense Paul Wolfowitz to the Senate Foreign Relations Committee, July 29, 2003.

23. Ibid.

24. Donald H. Rumsfeld, interview by George Stephanopoulos, ABC, July 13, 2003.

25. Senator Carl Levin to the Senate Armed Services Committee, July 9, 2003.

26. Deputy Secretary of Defense Paul Wolfowitz to the Senate Foreign Relations Committee, July 29, 2003.

27. Defense Secretary Donald H. Rumsfeld, interview by George Stephanopoulos, ABC, July 13, 2003.

28. Defense Secretary Donald H. Rumsfeld to the Senate Armed Services Committee, July 9, 2003.

29. Senator Carl Levin to the Senate Armed Services Committee, July 9, 2003.

30. Deputy Secretary of Defense Paul Wolfowitz to the Senate Foreign Relations Committee, July 29, 2003.

31. MASNET and News Agencies, www.masnet.org, October 14, 2003.

32. Deputy Secretary of Defense Paul Wolfowitz to the Senate Foreign Relations Committee, July 29, 2003.

33. Anonymous interview with the author on August 5, 2004.

34. Evan Thomas and Mark Hosenball, "The Rise and Fall of Chalabi: Bush's Mr. Wrong," *Newsweek*, May 31, 2004, 22.

35. Craig S. Smith, "Cleric in Iran Says Shiites Must Act," *New York Times*, April 26, 2003, A1.

36. Yigal Schleifer, "U.S. Now Seeks Turkish Troops for North Iraq," *Pittsburgh Post Gazette*, July 22, 2003.

37. Senator Joseph Biden, hearing of the Senate Foreign Relations Committee, February 11, 2003.

38. Memorandum to Zalmay Khalilzad from the author, March 24, 2003.

39. Ibid.

40. U.S. Committee on Refugees, *World Refugee Survey 2002 Country Report* (Iraq), available online at http://www.refugees.org/world/countryrpt/mideast/2002/iraq.cfm.

41. Jeffrey Fleishman, "Iraqi Melting Pot Nears Boiling Point; in Oil-Rich Kirkuk, Kurds, Arabs and Turkmens Compete for a Place in the New Order," *Los Angeles Times*, January 26, 2004, A1.

42. David Rhode, "In a City Claimed by Kurds and Arabs, U.S. Troops Try to Keep Peace," *New York Times*, April 26, 2003, A11.

43. Radio Free Europe/Radio Liberty, November 13, 2003.

44. MASNET and News Agencies, www.masnet.org, October 14, 2003.

45. Scott Wilson, "Bremer Adopts Firmer Tone," *Washington Post*, May 26, 2003, A13.

CHAPTER 16

1. Ghassan Atiyyah interview with author, Athens, Greece, July 31 2003.

2. Pratap Chatterjee, "Iraq: Selections Not Elections," *CorpWatch*, July 1, 2004.

3. William Booth and Rajiv Chandrasekaran, "Occupation Forces Halt Elections Throughout Iraq," *Washington Post*, June 28, 2003, A20.

4. United Nations Security Council Resolution 1500, adopted August 14, 2003.

5. John Daniszewski, "Iraqis OK Plan for Temporary Governing Council," *Los Angeles Times*, July 8, 2003.

6. Vernon Loeb in "U.S. to Appoint Council to Represent Iraqis," *Washington Post*, July 9, 2003, A20.

7. John Daniszewski, "Iraqis OK Plan for Temporary Governing Council," *Los Angeles Times*, July 8, 2003.

8. Jonathan S. Landay, "The Bush Administration Split Over How to Restore Iraqi Self-Rule," Knight Ridder/Tribune News Service, January 27, 2004.

9. *Question Time* with Foreign Minister Jack Straw, House of Commons, July 15, 2003.

10. L. Paul Bremer III, "Iraq's Path to Sovereignty," *Washington Post*, September 8, 2003.

11. William Douglas and John Walcott, "Bush, Bremer Discuss Speeding Return of Political Authority to Iraqis," Knight Ridder/Tribune News Service, November 13, 2003.

12. Jonathan S. Landay, "Officials Expected to Push for Faster Self-Rule in Iraq," Knight Ridder/Tribune News Service, October 25, 2003.

13. Warren P. Stroble, "U.S. Turnaround in Iraq May Be Too Little Too Late," Knight Ridder/Tribune New Service, November 14, 2004.

14. Joseph Curl, "White House Mulls New Iraq Plan," *Washington Times*, November 14, 2003.

15. Decree issued by Grand Ayatollah Ali al-Sistani, Najaf, June 28, 2003.

16. "UN: Iraq Elections Not Possible in 2004," Al-Jazeera.net, February 23, 2004.

17. Rajiv Chandrasekaran, "How Cleric Trumped U.S.'s Iraq Plan: Religious Edict Forced a Rewrite of Transition Strategy," Agence France Presse, November 23, 2003.

18. Erich Marquardt, "Al-Sistani's Call for Democratic Elections," *Power and Interest News Report*, December 10, 2003.

19. Rajiv Chandrasekaran, "How Cleric Trumped U.S.'s Iraq Plan."

20. Steven R. Weisman and John H. Cushman Jr., "U.S. Joins Iraqis to Seek UN Role in Interim Rule," *New York Times*, January 16, 2004, A1.

21. Ibid.

22. Joel Brinkley, "Some Members Propose Keeping Iraqi Council After Transition," *New York Times*, November 25, 2003.

23. Ibid.

24. Steven Komarow, "Iraqi Governing Council in 'a Serious Crisis,'" *USA Today*, December 4, 2003.

25. Brinkley, "Some Members Propose Keeping Iraqi Council After Transition."

26. Jonathan S. Landay, "U.S. Says It Will Stick with Plan on Transfer of Power in Iraq," Knight Ridder/Tribune News Service, January 17, 2004.

27. Private meeting between UN Secretary General Kofi Annan and the author, March 16, 2004.

28. "UN Envoy Backs al-Sistani on Poll," Al-Jazeera.net, February 2, 2004.

29. Ibid.

30. Rajiv Chandrasekaran, "UN Envoy Backs Iraqi Vote," *Washington Post*, February 13, 2004, A1.

31. Secretary General's report to the UK Security Council, February 21, 2004.

32. Dexter Filkins, "Iraqi Ayatollah Insists on Vote by End of the Year," *New York Times*, February 27, 2004, A1.

CHAPTER 17

1. Charles Recknagel, "IGC Member Discusses Role of Shari'a Law in Interim Constitution," Radio Free Europa/Radio Liberty, February 17, 2004.

2. *Law of Administration for the State of Iraq for the Transitional Period*, Article 52.

3. Ibid., Article 9.

4. Ibid., Article 54.

5. Jane Arraf, *CNN Newsnight*, February 29, 2004.

6. Dexter Filkins, "Iraqi Council, with Reluctant Shiites, Signs Charter," *New York Times*, March 9, 2004, A1.

7. Ibid.

8. Jane Arraf, *CNN Newsnight*, February 29, 2004.

9. Ibid.

10. Alec Russell, "U.S. Army Chiefs Plan 'Strategic Exit' from Iraq," *Daily Telegraph* (London), October 20, 2003.

11. Warren P. Stroble and Ron Hutcheson, "Bush Changes Course in Iraq," Knight Ridder/Tribune News Service, November 16, 2003.

12. Richard W. Stevenson and Thom Shanker, "Bush Says Pentagon's Plan to Reduce Forces in Iraq Next Year Could Be Reconsidered," *New York Times*, November 21, 2003.

13. Jim Mannion, "U.S. Unveils Plan for Smaller Iraq Force," Agence France Presse, November 6, 2003.

14. Warren P. Stroble, "U.S. Turnaround in Iraq May Be Too Little Too Late," Knight Ridder/Tribune New Service, November 14, 2004.

15. Andrea Dudikova, "NATO Secretary General Speaks Out Against Withdrawal of Troops from Iraq," Associated Press, March 19, 2004.

16. Ibid.

17. Ibid.

18. Richard W. Stevenson and Thom Shanker, "Bush Says Pentagon's Plan to Reduce Forces in Iraq Next Year Could Be Reconsidered," *New York Times*, November 21, 2003.

19. Rowan Scarborough, "U.S. Troop Levels for '05 Unknown; in Iraq, It's 'Month By Month,'" *Washington Times*, May 19, 2004.

20. Will Dunham, "Iraq War Woes Deepen Internal Pentagon Tensions," Reuters, May 30, 2004.

CHAPTER 18

1. John F. Burns, "The Long Shadow of a Mob," *New York Times*, April 4, 2004, Week in Review section.

2. "Privatizing Warfare," *New York Times*, April 21, 2004, A22.

3. Jeffrey Gettleman, "Mix of Pride and Shame Follows Killings of Mutilation by Iraqis," *New York Times*, April 2, 2004, A1.

4. Jeffrey Gettleman, "Falluja's Religious Leaders Condemn Mutilation, but not Killing of Americans," *New York Times*, April 1, 2004, A6.

5. Joseph Curl, "White House Mulls New Iraq Plan," *Washington Times*, November 14, 2003.

6. Thom Shanker, "U.S. Prepares a Prolonged Drive to Suppress the Uprisings in Iraq," *New York Times*, April 11, 2004, A1.

7. Nicolas Pelham, "U.S. Fights to Keep Its Iraqi Allies on Board," *Financial Times* (London), April 10, 2004, 5.

8. Ian Fisher and Steven R. Weisman, "Americans Issue a Blunt Warning to Rebels in Iraq," *New York Times*, April 24, 2004, A1.

9. David E. Sanger and Thom Shanker, "Decision on Possible Attack on Iraqi Town Seems Near," *New York Times*, April 25, 2004, A1.

10. Ian Fisher and Steven R. Weisman, "Americans Issue a Blunt Warning to Rebels in Iraq."

11. Edward Wong, "Policy Barring Ex-Ba'athists from Key Iraq Posts Is Eased," *New York Times*, April 23, 2004, A10.

12. Fisher and Weisman, "Americans Issue a Blunt Warning to Rebels in Iraq."

13. Wong, "Policy Barring Ex-Ba'athists from Key Iraq Posts Is Eased."

14. Burns, "The Long Shadow of a Mob."

15. Craig S. Smith, "Cleric in Iran Says Shiites Must Act," *New York Times*, April 26, 2003, A1.

16. Jeffrey Gettleman, "Ex-Rivals Uniting," *New York Times*, April 9, 2004, A1.

17. "Defiant al-Sadr Vows Uprising Will Continue," Al-Jazeera.net, April 6, 2004.

18. John F. Burns, "Leading Shiites and Rebel Meet on Iraq Standoff," *New York Times*, April 13, 2004, A1.

19. John F. Burns, "U.S. Seeks Arrest of Shiite Cleric," *New York Times*, April 6, 2004.

20. Nicolas Pelham, "Imam Flees to Shrine Amid Third Day of Iraq Clashes," *Financial Times* (London), April 7, 2004, 9.

21. Ian Fisher and Steven R. Weisman, "Americans Issue a Blunt Warning to Rebels in Iraq."

22. Nicolas Pelham in "Ayatollah Struggles to Regain Initiative from Young Firebrand," *Financial Times* (London), April 6, 2004, 7.

23. Edward Wong, "Cleric's Militia Upends Shiite Power Balance," *New York Times*, April 21, 2004, A10.

24. John F. Burns, "Cleric, Surrounded by U.S., Hints at Easing His Resistance," *New York Times*, April 14, 2004, A10.

25. John F. Burns, "Iranians in Iraq to Help with Talks on Rebel Cleric," *New York Times*, April 15, 2004, A1.

26. Gareth Smyth, "Tehran Supports Sistani Calls for Calm," *Financial Times* (London), April 10, 2004, 5.

27. John F. Burns and Christine Hauser, "Bremer Raising Pressure to End Iraqi Uprisings," *New York Times*, April 19, 2004, A1.

28. Release by Office of the Press Secretary; transcript of remarks made by President George W. Bush at the White House, April 14, 2004.

29. James Risen, "Account of Broad Shiite Revolt Contradicts White House Stand," *New York Times*, April 8, 2004, A1.

30. Christine Hauser, "Iraqi Uprising Spreads," *New York Times*, April 8, 2004, A1.

31. Alan Cowell, "Turmoil in Iraq Jangles Nerves in Allied Capitals, and Bush Works to Shore Up Support," *New York Times*, April 10, 2004, A7.

32. James Drummond and Peter Spiegel, "U.S. Commander in Iraq Says He Needs More Troops," *Financial Times* (London), April 13, 2004.

33. Guy Dinmore and James Harding, "Bush Attacks Spanish Troops' Pull-Out of Iraq," *Financial Times* (London), April 20, 2004.

34. Christopher Adams and Joshua Chaffin, "Britain and U.S. Spell Out Determination to Defeat Sadr," *Financial Times* (London), April 7, 2004, 9.

35. Christine Hauser, "Iraqi Claims U.S. and Falluja Foes Agree to a Deal," *New York Times*, April 11, 2004, A1.

36. Briefing by Secretary of Defense Donald H. Rumsfeld, U.S. Department of Defense, September 5, 2003.

37. Neela Banerjee, "In an Oil-Rich Land, Power Shortages Defy Solution," *New York Times*, January 8, 2004, A14.

38. Craig Gordon, "Price Tag Problems: Congress Faults Bush on Iraq Planning," *Newsday*, September 10, 2003.

39. Demetri Sevastopulo, "Bremer Seeks to Speed Iraq's Reconstruction," *Financial Times* (London), April 23, 2004, 1.

40. Dexter Filkins, "Bremer Pushes Iraq on Difficult Path to Self-Rule," *New York Times*, March 21, 2004, A1.

41. Transcript of remarks made by President George W. Bush at the White House, April 14, 2004.

CHAPTER 19

1. John F. Burns, "Cleric, Surrounded by U.S., Hints at Easing his Resistance," *New York Times*, April 14, 2004, A10.

2. "The Brahimi Plan," *Council on Foreign Relations*, April 16, 2004, http://www.cfr.org.

3. Christine Hauser, "Politicians React to Plan from the UN for Iraqi Rule," *New York Times*, April 17, 2004, A7.

4. Secretary General Kofi Annan, United Nations press conference, April 28, 2004.

5. William Safire, "Brahimi's Two Mistakes," *New York Times*, April 26, 2004, A19.

6. Warren P. Strobel, "Negroponte: Cooperating with the UN in 'Strategic Interest' of U.S," Knight Ridder/Tribune News Service, April 28, 2004.

7. Richard W. Stevenson and Douglas Jehl, "Must Asserts 'We Must Not Waver on Terror in Iraq,'" *New York Times*, April 14, 2004, A1.

8. Secretary of State Colin Powell, interview by Katie Couric, *Today*, NBC, May 25, 2004.

9. Fred Eckhard, UN spokesman, CNN, May 26, 2004.

10. Massoud Barzani and Jalal Talabani, letter to President Bush, June 1, 2004.

11. Colin Powell, interview by Jeff Greenfield, CNN, May 26, 2004.

12. Secretary General Kofi Annan, United Nations press conference, April 28, 2004.

13. Ibid.

14. Iraqi Foreign Minister Hoshyar Zebari, discussion with author, June 6, 2004.

15. Jane Mayer, "The Manipulator," *New Yorker*, June 7, 2004.

16. Dexter Filkins and Ian Fisher, "Iraqis and GIs Raid the Offices of an Ex-Favorite," *New York Times*, May 21, 2004, A1.

17. David E. Sanger, "A Seat of Honor Lost to Open Political Warfare," *New York Times*, May 21, 2004, A1.

18. Warren P. Strobel, "Negroponte: Cooperating with the UN in 'Strategic Interest' of U.S.," Knight Ridder/Tribune News Service, April 28, 2004.

19. Dexter Filkins, "Extent of Government's Control Unclear As It Formally Steps In," *New York Times*, June 28, 2004.

20. "Iraq Handover Completed—Ahead of Schedule," Al-Jazeera News Network, http://www.allied-media.com/aljazeera, June 28, 2004.

21. Dexter Filkins, "Extent of Government's Control Unclear As It Formally Steps In."

22. "Iraq Handover Completed," Al-Jazeera News Network.

23. Ibid.

24. Ayad Allawi, "A New Beginning," *Washington Post*, June 27, 2004.

Epilogue

1. Senate Foreign Relations Committee. January 18, 2005.

2. Edward Wong, "Top Shiite Cleric Opposes Delay in the Iraqi Election." *New York Times*, November 28, 2004, A1.

3. John F. Burns, "Tape in Name of Leading Insurgent Declares 'All-Out War on Iraq Elections and Democracy," *New York Times*. January 24, 2005, A10.

4. Ibid.

5. Interview with Kofi Annan by Owen Bennett-Jones, BBC World Service, September 16, 2004, http://news.bbc.co.uk/1/hi/world/middle_east/3661134.stm.

6. Cited by Todd S. Purdum in "Grumbling Swells on Rumsfeld' Right Flank," *New York Times*, December 16, 2004, A26.

7. CNN.com, January 31, 2005.

8. Ibid.

INDEX